BLASPHEMY

BLASPHEMY

David Lawton

University of Pennsylvania Press
Philadelphia

First published 1993 by Harvester Wheatsheaf

First published in the United States 1993 by
the University of Pennsylvania Press

U.S. Library of Congress Cataloging-in-Publication Data

Lawton, David A., 1948-
Blasphemy / David Lawton
p.   cm.
''First published 1993 by Harvester Wheatsheaf''—T.p. verso.
Includes bibliographical references and index.
ISBN 0-8122-3219-4. — ISBN 0-8122-1503-6 (pbk.)
1. Blasphemy—History.   2. Blasphemy—Social aspects.   I. Title.
K5305.L39   1993
394—dc20
93–19145
CIP

ISBN 0-8122-3219-4 (cloth)
ISBN 0-8122-1503-6 (pbk)

Printed in Great Britain

For all my friends and students at the University of Sydney
from 1975 to 1992

CONTENTS

LIST OF PLATES

ACKNOWLEDGEMENTS

In preparing this study, I was assisted by a University of Sydney Research Grant in 1991 and by the opportunity to spend the first half of 1991 as Visiting Professor at the University of California, Riverside, where I met with great kindness. I owe a special debt to the Rivera Library at UCR, especially to its inter-library loan staff, who worked very hard to provide me with everything I requested. The Center for Medieval and Renaissance Studies at UCLA kindly invited me to give a seminar on blasphemy, which contributed much to my thinking. I was greatly assisted by staff at the Huntingdon Library, the Clark Library (UCLA), Cambridge University Library, the Bodleian Library, the British Library and, not least, Fisher Library, University of Sydney.

My thanks to colleagues and students both in Sydney and at UCR for their interest and enthusiasm, and to my future colleagues at the University of Tasmania for their worthwhile comments in somewhat stressful circumstances!

I owe a particular debt to Louise D'Arcens and Kirsten Dunlop, and, above all, to Annette Krausmann, without whom I should have finished, if at all, months later. Amanda Beresford has given me professional help and excellent advice. She has also supported me as her partner throughout the writing, and I owe her. Our child Dominick is more patient than he realises, having lived with blasphemy all his life.

I am grateful to the Tate Gallery for permission to reproduce *The Blasphemer*, by William Blake; to the Germanisches Nationalmuseum, Nürnberg for permission to reproduce *Die Judensau*; to the British Museum for permission to reproduce *Enthusiasm Delineated* (first state of *Superstition, Fanaticism and Credulity*) by William Hogarth.

I am grateful to Exact Change for permission to quote from Guillaume Apollinaire, *The Heresiarch and Co.* (1991); to Beacon Press for permission to quote from *Hunted Heretic: The life and death of Michael Servetus 1511–1553*, by Roland H. Bainton, Copyright © 1953, reprinted by permission of Beacon Press; to HarperCollins Publishers for permission to quote from Roland Barthes, *Mythologies* (1973); to City Lights for permission to quote from George Bataille, *Erotism: Death & sensuality* (1962); to Routledge for permission to quote from Homi K. Bhabha, *Nation and Narration* (1990), from Simon During, *Foucault and Literature: Towards a genealogy of writing* (1992), from Sander L. Gilman, *The Jew's Body* (1991), and from Jim Obelkevich, Lindal Roper and Raphael Samuel (eds), *Disciplines of Faith: Studies in religion, politics and patriarchy* (1987); to Newman Press for permission to quote from Josef Blinzler, *The Trial of Jesus: The Jewish and Roman proceedings against Jesus Christ described and assessed from the oldest accounts*

(1959); to University of Minnesota Press for permission to quote from Gilles Deleuze and Felix Guattari, *A Thousand Plateaus* (1987), Copyright © 1987 by University of Minnesota Press, and from Jean-Luc Nancy, *The Inoperative Community* (1991), Copyright © 1991 by University of Minnesota Press; to the Clarendon Press for permission to quote from Jonathan Dollimore, *Sexual Dissidence: Augustine to Wilde; Freud to Foucault* (1991), and Douglas Gray (ed.), *The Oxford Book of Late Medieval Verse and Prose* (1985), by permission of Oxford University Press; to Martin Secker & Warburg Ltd for permission to quote from Umberto Eco, *The Name of the Rose* (1983), and from Norman Lewis, *The Missionaries: God against the Indians* (1988); to Macmillan for permission to quote from Sigmund Freud, *Psychoanalytical Notes upon an Autobiographical Account of a Case of Paranoia* and *From the History of an Infantile Neurosis* in *Three Case Histories* (1963); to Penguin for permission to quote from Sigmund Freud, *Moses and Monotheism: Three essays* and *Totem and Taboo* in *The Origins of Religion* (1985), and from Carlo Ginzburg, *The Cheese and the Worms: The cosmos of a sixteenth-century miller* (1976); to Basic for permission to quote from *The Wolf-Man by the Wolf-Man* (1971), ed. Muriel Gardiner; to Collins Harvill, an imprint of HarperCollins, for permission to quote from Eugenia Ginzburg, *Into the Whirlwind* (1967); to G. Bell and Sons Ltd for permission to quote from *The Diary of Samuel Pepys* (1970); to Cornell University Press for permission to quote from Luce Irigaray, *Speculum of the Other Woman* (1985), from Peter Stallybrass and Allon White, *Politics and Poetics of Transgression* (1986), from Mary B. Campbell, *The Witness and the Other World: Exotic European travel writing 400–1600* (1988), from Jeremy Cohen, *The Friars and the Jews: The evolution of medieval anti-Judaism* (1982); to Oxford University Press for permission to quote from Anthony Kenny, *Wyclif in his Times* (1986), by permission of Oxford University Press; to Leonard Williams Levy for permission to quote from *Treason against God: A history of the offence of blasphemy* (1981); to Schocken Books and Norman Lewis for permission to quote from *The Missionaries: God against the Indians* (1988); to Blackwell for permission to quote from R. I. Moore, *The Origins of European Dissent* (1985); to Viking Penguin for permission to quote from Salman Rushdie, *The Satanic Verses* (1988); to Methuen London for permission to quote from Nawal el Saadawi, *The Fall of the Imam* (1990); to the C. W. Daniel Company Ltd for permission to quote from de Sade, *Justine*, trans. Alan Hull Walton (1965); to the Warburg Institute for permission to quote from Isaiah Schachar, *The 'Judensau': A medieval anti-Jewish motif and its history* (1974); to E. J. Brill, for permission to quote from E. Mary Smallwood, *The Jews under Roman Rule: From Pompey to Diocletian* (1976); to New York Contemporary Press for permission to quote from Sarah Brown Weitzman, *Eve and Other Blasphemy* (1983); and to Walter de Gruyter & Co. for permission to quote from Paul Winter, *On the Trial of Jesus* (1974).

Now gentlemen, what is blasphemy? Of course nobody knows what it is, unless he takes into consideration where he is. What is blasphemy in one country would be a religious exhortation in another. It is owing to where you are and who is in authority. And let me call your attention to the impudence and bigotry of the American Christians. We sent missionaries to other countries. What for? To tell them that their religion is false, that their Gods are myths and monsters, that their Saviours and apostles were imposters, and that our religion is true. You send a man from Morristown – a Presbyterian, over to Turkey. He goes there, and he tells the Mohammedans – and he has it in a pamphlet and he distributes it – that the Koran is a lie, that Mohammed was not a prophet of God, that the angel Gabriel is not so large that it is four hundred leagues between his eyes – that is all a mistake – that there never was an angel as large as that. Then what would the Turks do? Suppose the Turks had a law like this statute in New Jersey. They would put the Morristown missionary in jail, and he would send home word, and then what would the people of Morristown say? Honestly – what do you think they would say? They would say, 'Why look at those poor, heathen wretches. We sent a man over there armed with the truth, and yet they were so blinded by their idolatrous religion, so steeped in superstition, that they have actually put that man in prison.' Gentlemen, does not that show the need of more missionaries? I would say, yes.

Now let us turn the tables. A gentleman comes from Turkey to Morristown. He has got a pamphlet. He says, 'The Koran is the inspired book, Mohammed is the real prophet, your bible is false and your Saviour simply a myth.' Thereupon the Morristown people put him in jail. Then what would the Turks say? They would say, 'Morristown needs more missionaries,' and I would agree with them.

In other words, what we want is intellectual hospitality. Let the world talk.

R. G. INGERSOLL, *Trial of C. B. Reynolds for Blasphemy at Morristown, N.J., May 19th and 20th, 1887: Defence; stenographically reported by I. N. Baker and revised by the author*.
New York City: C. P. Farrell, 1888, pp. 13–14.

Chapter 1

NAMING BLASPHEMY

Much Madness is divinest Sense—
To a discerning Eye—
Much Sense—the starkest Madness—
'Tis the Majority
In this, as All, prevail—
Assent—and you are sane—
Demur—you're straightway dangerous—
And handled with a Chain—

Emily Dickinson

ON NOT DEFINING BLASPHEMY

'Jesus Christ – Wanted for sedition, criminal anarchy, vagrancy, and conspiracy to overthrow the established government. Dressed poorly; said to be a carpenter by trade; ill-nourished; associates with common working people, unemployed and bums. Alien; said to be a Jew.'[1] Two Pennsylvania shopkeepers faced prosecution in 1971 after placing these words on a sign in their shop window. The prosecution, dropped after the intervention of the American Civil Liberties Union, was to have been on a charge of blasphemy. In what was the blasphemy held to lie? First and foremost, presumably, in the offence the sign gave to those who therefore sought to prosecute. In the absence of detailed knowledge of who they were and what they objected to, one can only guess that the grounds of the offence were political. In previous ages, people have been punished as blasphemers for suggesting that Jesus was a man, not the son of God, that he was a separate god from the Father, or that he was crucified because he lacked the power to prevent it. Each of these could possibly be inferred in the words exhibited, but hardly so as to sustain a legal burden of proof. In modern America, none may give as widespread offence as the more obvious suggestion that Jesus was a socialist, and a foreign one at that. Such a reception of the sign cannot be judged false: the objectors are a party in a dialogue. The two shopkeepers who wrote it could even be pleased at finding such attentive readers. The language of their sign is highly emotive, and sets out to elicit a response. To put it simply, this is an instance of negative communication: either the sign is misunderstood and disliked, or it is disliked because it is understood. So far as the authors are concerned, the difference is immaterial.

What we read here is the evidence of a community rift; objection is registered on behalf of a group, either of orthodox Christians, who do not enjoy the implication that they misrepresent Christ, or conservative citizens, who do not enjoy the use of Christ as a standard of rebellion against government. It might help to know the background of the shopkeepers, especially their religious background. If they were Jewish, a reader could be sure that the final phrase, 'said to be a Jew', is distinctly different in tone and intention from the same ideas uttered at other times and in other places: 'Take time to calmly think it over: Was a Jewish girl the mother of God, the mother of your God?';[2] 'This God of you Christians is a Jewish God, not an Aussie God, not a fair-dinkum Aussie God, just a Jewish God with his money bags around his neck.'[3] (All these have in common is that each was accused of blasphemy.) But to seek to know the background is an academic response, irrelevant to the giving of offence that has already taken place. It is confirmation that the words of the sign are unstable; its signification is not quite under the control of those who write it or those who read it. The rift at the community level is replicated in the semantics of the exchange. Indeed, one suspects that both sides could find common ground in opposition, for example, to an atheist who denies any truth, exemplary value or indeed interest in the figure of Jesus Christ. The discourses of belief and political conformity swamp accusers and accused alike.

Blasphemy is always something else – intellectually, a by-product of heresy or sedition or plain free thinking, and emotionally a sign of social dislocation or mental disturbance. It is also, more often than not, someone else's. There have been those who set out deliberately to blaspheme and to be caught blaspheming, a fair number of them simply by cursing God or Jesus, or by casting doubt on the divinity or legitimacy of Jesus, or by otherwise transparent means; but most who have been accused or convicted of blasphemy fall into more complex patterns of behaviour or belief. They set out to argue a system of belief or to commend a way of life, and what is taken to be blasphemy is often, in their view, incidental to their aims or a misrepresentation of them. They tend to feel and say that their words have been taken out of context; but even where this defence is not evidently disingenuous, it fails, for in such cases there is no agreed frontier between text and context, any more than there is between blasphemy and belief. That this or any other defence should be offered at all is a further misunderstanding, another index of negative communication. The accused also feel that the term 'blasphemy' is made meaningless by virtue of its extension to them. John Wright, a Unitarian minister charged with blasphemy in 1817, responded: 'Blasphemy is a word of such terrible sound that it frightens men of weak minds and weak nerves. It has been applied so variously, that all who make use of it attach their own signification.'[4] Wright is entirely correct. Blasphemy is essentially rhetorical; the other form of the word that has entered the English language is 'blame', the opposite of praise.

Blasphemy stands for whatever a society most abhors and has the power to prosecute. It is a form of religious vituperation against those who have transgressed the timeless truths that a society cherishes. That is why its nature, along with the timeless truths, changes over time.

Wright tried to document such change in his defence:

> In those periods of the Christian Church when Priestly domination triumphed over the rights of conscience, and the Scriptures were kept from the people, the promulgation of knowledge was *Blasphemy*. The attempt to expose priestcraft was Blasphemy. To say the doctrine of transubstantiation was an absurdity, was Blasphemy. To deny that a woman was the mother of the Infinite and Eternal Jehovah, was Blasphemy. To say the worship of images is unscriptural, was Blasphemy. To refuse to pay homage to the Sainthood of being canonized by the Church, was Blasphemy.
>
> In the days of William and Mary it was blasphemy to oppugn the doctrines of the Trinity, and the proper deity of Jesus Christ, who was born a babe, grew to manhood, and was put to a cruel and ignominious death at Jerusalem.

Stirring as this is, it is also special pleading. Wright's appeal for religious tolerance is an appeal for the opportunity to continue attacking the orthodoxies of his day and the established Church that upholds them. Blasphemers are expert at anti-clericalism, and at simultaneously appropriating the clerical mantle with the suggestion that they know better. In order for his defence to succeed, Wright understands that he must make his political motives explicit, and be prepared to fight for the right to represent his community. He therefore attacks power, and appeals to his fellow-citizens over the heads of 'Priests or Magistrates':

> Whatever may be the disposition of those who possess power in the present day; however ardently some may wish for the revival of writs *de haeretico comburendo,* while others lament the abolition of penal statutes against Unitarians, it is happy for us that the spirit of the times will not permit the fires of Smithfield to be rekindled. Englishmen will never suffer a court of inquisition to be established in this country, by either Priests or Magistrates. The Demon of Persecution is in fetters, and, like John Bunyan's giant, he can only gnash his teeth and bite his own chains. . . .

Moreover, Wright keeps a reserve power: if he is not allowed to represent his fellow-Englishmen, he fully represents the God that they should all serve. Those who do not support him are by inference themselves blasphemers:

> To earthly rulers who would attempt to interfere with us in matters of religion, this is our reply: 'Whether it be right in the sight of God to hearken unto you more than unto God, judge ye.'[5]

Wright's final defence against the charge of blasphemy is therefore to appeal to shared communal values. In this respect, his speech typifies a frustrated circularity in the transaction of blasphemy. As was the case with the Pennsylvania shopkeepers, accusers and accused in cases of blasphemy occupy a good deal of common ground: they are often culturally identical, and they are almost always proximate. This by no means soothes the conflicts between them, and may indeed be a further irritant: community divisions tend to be especially bitter. One might care to argue that such disputes are intractable precisely *because* they are community disputes. This means, however, that the study of blasphemy needs to weigh what is shared against what is contested, to assess forces making for community as well as for separatism; the contest is staged, often ritually, for control of a shared discourse. It may even be that orthodoxy needs blasphemies, not in order to formulate its ideas but to test, maintain and exercise its social cohesion. The field of blasphemy occupies the sites – local and national, metropolitan and rural – that compose a social ecology.

Blasphemy, then, is culturally relative even as it indignantly refutes cultural relativism: this is not a truism of theoretical writing but a fundamental of definition. It depends upon the truths that a community most values, and in the West these change more over time than most orthodoxies like to think. It functions at the levels of community, discursive positions and semantics. Its nature is rhetorical, more verbal than intellectual: blasphemy is form or sound or interference, where heresy is pure content. Whether it takes oral or written shape, the words count for everything, not their speaker or writer. The personality of the blasphemer is of little importance. Attempts to extenuate legal charges of blasphemy in terms of personal troubles, or personal philosophy, or even intention, rarely succeed. If a defendant on a blasphemy charge can actually establish an individuality, he may be some way towards breaking through the charge. George Holyoake manages this in his memoir of his trial for blasphemy in 1851, after he has made an impromptu comment at a meeting: 'For myself, I flee the Bible as a viper, and revolt at the touch of a Christian.' His subsequent imprisonment for six months has dire effects on his family, but Holyoake's account is well-written (it begins: 'That day is chilled in my memory when I first set out for Cheltenham') and moderate: 'As I very much dislike being an object of pity, those will much mistake me who suppose that this narrative has been written to excite it.'[6] Holyoake's articulate courage here begins to reinstate the social bond that an allegation of blasphemy severs and withdraws. Mostly, however, the offence is constituted in and given by words that might as well be disembodied.

In spite of this, orthodoxy is often prepared to repeat the blasphemies at which it takes umbrage, or to give examples of possible blasphemies. Parliamentary acts against the Ranters in the Commonwealth period, especially the statute of 1650, list in full the Ranter blasphemies they condemn. The *Catholic Encyclopedia* entry on blasphemy helpfully provides several examples, of heretical blasphemy ('God is cruel', or 'The noblest work of man is God') or of imprecatory blasphemy (the admittedly tame 'Away with God'). It follows that the words need to be activated by a speaker before they have the power to offend, and that the denial of the speaker or writer is tactical, part of a larger strategy of repudiation. There is no effort to understand because the words always exist before they are published, as the Other of orthodoxy, waiting to be uttered, the mirror-image that confirms identity. When orthodoxy finds blasphemy, it is not failing to read: it is reading and simultaneously refusing. Both reading and refusal, like the identity they publish, are collective.

Blasphemy, then, is impersonally received; and, however personally it is conceived, however passionately meant by an individual, it is framed in terms of the orthodox discourses that construct it and the institutions that produce it. It may well project ideas but, unlike heresy, it is not philosophical; indeed, blasphemy is brought as a charge against heretics in order to minimise their philosophical impact. While it is a real event in a material world, it does not need material objects as the objects of its articulation, unlike sacrilege. Blasphemy is textual. That is the reason for my interest in it, and it defines the nature of this book, which is not a religious or legal history but a selective historical study of blasphemy as text.

I do not seek so much to define blasphemy as to characterise it, one of its major characteristics being that it is beyond general definition. No one group consistently controls it, either over time, because values change and transcendent values change more than most in our culture (and hardly at all in others), or at any given moment, though at many such moments it is possible to describe what blasphemy means. Blasphemy is an exchange – a conversation gone wrong, or a carnivalised travesty of a public conversation. Though the weight is always heavily on the side of power, the offence exists between the sides involved, in the gap between them, in the exchange itself, an exchange without reciprocity. It is a poisoned form of the hermeneutic circle. Sometimes a dispute about where power actually lies forms part of that exchange, for both sides feel victimised – as in the Rushdie affair, as in some of the controversies in sixteenth-century Europe or seventeenth-century England.

The fact that blasphemy is an unpredictable exchange within and across cultures has made overt restriction of the scope of this book unworkable, though no effort is made to be comprehensive. Blasphemy is a concept distinctive to Jewish and Christian traditions, and Islamic law on religious offences is markedly different. That said, much of the exchange between them has to do with, or has been conducted in terms of, blasphemy. It is important to see their relations as part of a wider global contest between secularist and fundamentalist ideals of law and power.

What is distinctive in Judaism and Christianity is their insistence on blasphemy as an act of language, spoken or written. It is not that far removed from the classical Greek offence of impiety, for which Socrates died, except that Greek impiety may also incorporate behaviour, material damage (as in the sacking of the temple, which becomes in canon law a major form of sacrilege), and actual political treason; or visual inscription, as in the case of Phidias, whose impiety was desecration of the divine image of Athena by representing Pericles and the artist himself on her shield (again, a form of sacrilege). In the Christian tradition, in response to the influence of Judaism, the one offence is split into several, and linguistic profanation is regarded as the worst of all transgressions. The notion that the sin against the Holy Ghost is a form of blasphemy is amply documented; and in the twentieth century, the *Catholic Encyclopedia* defines blasphemy as 'a mortal sin, the gravest that may be committed against religion'. Conversely, protestations on behalf of other religions that blasphemy is unknown within them often mean less than they say: in Buddhist Tibet under the Lamas, for example, the mere presence of a stranger was a profanation, and therefore a capital offence – it is merely that the stranger was not first required to say something shocking, as occurs in Leviticus 24, before being held to have committed a crime. Modern Hinduism has thrown up a somewhat surprising form of fundamentalism, in which transgression takes concrete more often than verbal forms, as in the dispute over the site of the Ayodha mosque; and it would probably be an error to conflate blasphemy with the rumour of profanation, as in the greased rifles of the Indian Mutiny, though the connection between blasphemy and other forms of profanation is indeed an interesting one.

In sum, it seems to be stretching the point to claim, as Leonard W. Levy does, that 'Blasphemy is taboo wherever organised religion exists, and monotheistic systems hold no monopoly on the concept of blasphemy.'[7] It is probably true to say that all religions prohibit the greatest profanation they can imagine. The Jewish and Christian traditions are uniquely logocentric in imagining that the worst form of profanation exists in language; and the Christian concept of blasphemy is the first to be truly wide-ranging and hegemonic. Where God is Word, the Devil is anti-Word – not merely, *pace* Augustine, the absence of Word, but its perversion. The status of blasphemy follows on the importance of Scripture. Islam is therefore the religion most closely allied to Christian notions of blasphemy, but with a significant difference. While Christianity inherits from Judaism ambitious, far-reaching and relatively free modes of exegesis, the interpretation of the Qu'ran is strictly and invariably limited. This difference goes to explain much of the related difference between Islamic notions of verbal transgression and Christian blasphemy. I look at the cross-cultural issues raised by the Rushdie affair in Chapter 6, and at Christian meetings with other religions and cultures throughout this book – for it transpires all too often that these are constituted as, or turned into, extensions of Christian discourses of blasphemy. The very notion of cultural relativism, however ironically, is judged blasphemous. As an instrument of communal attack, blasphemy is not necessarily monotheism rejecting pantheism; but it is commonly monoculturalism rejecting multiculturalism.

In common with many others, I found my interest in blasphemy re-awakened by the Rushdie affair, and was forced to rethink a number of my opinions as the affair progressed. I went through the affair as I now approach this study, as an admirer of Rushdie's work in general, and *The Satanic Verses* in particular. Indeed, my re-reading of that book in the light of the controversy convinces me of its moral complexity and its human and intellectual worth. If I had read in the way that some Muslim critics have assumed its admirers read it, I should not admire it – and I suspect Rushdie would not have written it. I do not address this book to anyone who supports killing writers, as is sanctioned by the perverted and already transcultured monoculturalism of Yusuf Islam and Doctor Siddiqui. But I see it as a misfortune for Muslims in general that writers in several Muslim countries are not just under sentence of death but are actually being murdered in the name of Islam. The fact remains that many Muslims who deplore the *fatwa* dislike the book, or the reputation of the book, and I feel that there is space for dialogue with such readers. But this is not a book, another book, on the Rushdie affair; it is merely a book that arose out of it because as an academic specialising in medieval fiction and the study of religion I find most of the polemical writing on all sides of the issue to be ill-informed, shallowly based and illogical. I aim here to offer a fuller and contextualised study of the history of blasphemy as text in the Western world. This is the nearest I can come to providing the book I should like to have been able to read when the Rushdie affair broke, if only anyone had been prescient enough to write it. For that very reason, I shall not deal fully with *The Satanic Verses* until the final chapter. The key importance of the Rushdie affair for professional students like myself is that it demonstrates, once and for all, the inadequacy of the model of reading we have maintained for too long: the individual reader, the supposedly 'private' reader, reading the individual text. A study of blasphemy is therefore relevant to finding a better model, one that engages with communities, sometimes rival collectivities, and diverse cultural and cross-cultural positioning.

Having stated one position, I should probably deal briefly with another: my position on an issue I nevertheless regard as relatively minor and parochial, the manifestly anomalous status of blasphemy in common law. The current situation, in which legal protection against blasphemy is available to Christianity alone and only to orthodox beliefs of the Church of England, has few defenders. The alternatives are abolition, supported by liberal humanists and friends of Salman Rushdie, or recasting of the law in

order to extend it to other religions. This is the option strongly advocated
by Muslim communities, many Anglicans (including the former Archbishop
of Canterbury, Dr Runcie) and is the polemical purpose of at least half of
Richard Webster's *A Brief History of Blasphemy*. Its definitive articulation
came from a law lord, Lord Scarman, in a context that is worth recalling: the
unsuccessful appeal by the publishers of *Gay News* and the poet James
Kirkup following their conviction for criminal blasphemy in 1977. The
blasphemy was held to have occurred when Kirkup's poem, 'The love that
dares to speak its name', was published in *Gay News* and prosecuted
privately by Mrs Mary Whitehouse. It is a monologue written for a Roman
centurion at the Crucifixion, and is explicitly homoerotic, both in the
feelings for Jesus that were expressed and the acts with his deposed body
that were imagined. In spite of the fact that Kirkup was a distinguished poet
– his respectability occasioned some surprise, as if blasphemers normally
look like a stereotype of bomb-throwing anarchists – and *Gay News* could
hardly be represented as a mass general publication, a conviction was
secured and upheld on appeal to the House of Lords. In the original trial,
the judge chosen by the Lord Chancellor's Office, presumably on the
ground that he would not be seen as prejudiced in favour of the Anglican
Communion, was Judge King-Hamilton, once president of the West
London Synagogue; he congratulated the jury on its verdict and expressed
support for a more widely ranging statute. In the House of Lords, where
the verdict was upheld by three votes to two, Lord Scarman produced what
Robert Post called 'a compelling vision of blasphemy law transformed by
statute into an instrument of pluralism'.[8] Scarman urged that, 'in an
increasingly plural society such as that of modern Britain' (p. 313), there is
a case for legislation extending the common law offence of blasphemous
libel 'to protect the religious beliefs and feelings of non-Christians': he was
thinking not of Kirkup or of the editors of *Gay News* but 'the differing
religious beliefs, feelings and practices of all' that have to be 'protected from
scurrility, vilification, ridicule and contempt'. Far from seeing blasphemy as
a dead letter, Scarman continued: 'My criticism of the common law of
blasphemy is not that it exists but that it is not sufficiently comprehensive.
It is shackled by the chains of history' (pp. 312–13).

   Scarman's urging of a pluralist statute had absolutely nothing to do with
the case that he was voting on, where the issue was and remained Kirkup's
offence to the Christianity of the Church of England. Since Scarman upheld
the conviction, his remarks at best express a preference for a different kind
of statute to justify his upholding it. Moreover, Post argues acutely that for
all the 'purity of Scarman's pluralist intentions, his effort paradoxically rests
on a quintessentially assimilationist value' (pp. 312–13). But the compelling
objection is a logical one, made at regular intervals in American writing on
the issue, by Thomas Jefferson, by the jurist and twentieth-century historian

of offences against religion Theodore Schroeder, and by Robert Ingersoll in his speech defending C. B. Reynolds. Why does English common law only defend the orthodoxy of the Church of England? Because, of course, that is the established Church; but also because other varieties of Christianity conflict with it and do so potentially blasphemously:

> the Church has not been satisfied with calling infidels and unbelievers blasphemers. Each Church has accused nearly every other Church of being a blasphemer.

> I want to say right here – many a man has cursed the god of another man. Catholics have cursed the god of the Protestants. The Presbyterians have cursed the god of the Catholics – charged them with idolatry – cursed their images, laughed at their ceremonies. And these compliments have been interchanged between all the religions of the world.[9]

Muslims respect Jesus as a prophet but deny his divinity; Jews deny both Christian and Muslim revelation. If religions find each other's beliefs blasphemous and blaspheme each other, how can a statute of blasphemy be framed that will protect all religions equally? This is a logical objection that seems to me insuperable, and I have not seen it answered.

If one cannot support the extension of the English law, there seems no alternative to its abolition. I support this – as, indeed, now does Lord Scarman[10] – except that it may prove hard to unpick the tangle of common law, and the attempt may yet prove counter-productive: there are pressure groups in favour of the law as well as against it, and any re-drawing that attempts to conciliate both may prove worse than the present situation. If a review is to take place, it should be concurrent with the review of all other forms of libel – blasphemy is at present the main exception to the legal principle that one cannot libel the dead – and with an attempt to introduce a crime of inciting racial or religious hatred. Mere availability of such a charge might have provided a fair forum for controversy about *The Satanic Verses*. In the meantime, all that is really required is that the blasphemy laws join a good deal of other law that has never been formally repealed in a state of total disuse. It was well on the way there when Mrs Whitehouse brought her charge against James Kirkup and the publishers of *Gay News*. For immediate practical purposes, the end of abolitionists would be easily and economically served by something that should happen in any case, the issuing of a pardon to Kirkup and his publishers, in whose condemnation judicial dreams of religious tolerance made common cause with homophobia.

In English law, blasphemy is one of the four heads of criminal libel, the others being obscenity, defamation and sedition. Blasphemy is always seen as a form of defamation, what Leonard Levy calls 'treason against God', and as close to obscenity, a charge often preferred in the twentieth century when the target is really blasphemy – as with *Ulysses*, or James Branch Cabell's *Jurgen*. The key relationship, however, is that with sedition. Frequently, blasphemy is identified as an active threat to the body politic. Oliver Cromwell is reported to have replied to a parliamentarian urging the release of the blasphemer Biddle: 'You curl-pate boy, you, do you think I'll show any favour to a man who denies his Saviour and disturbs the government?'[11] The legal index of the offence given by blasphemy is held to be a breach of the peace: hence the frequent efforts from the late eighteenth century onwards by organised groups such as the Society for the Suppression of Vice, the Salvation Army and the Festival of Light to create such breaches, in order to prosecute someone for blasphemy. The relation between blasphemy and sedition is one structural reason why the law is slow to give up the offence of blasphemy, and seeks rather to redefine it. There is another. From the early Church onwards, blasphemy is regarded as a threat to legal process itself. The threat manifests itself in the one area in which one can find an easy, constant and relatively immutable definition of blasphemy, but one which is only in a subset of the offence: swearing.

In the Holyoake trial, Mr Justice Erskine ruled out the idea that God was in need of earthly legal defence: 'The arm of the law is not stretched out to protect the character of the Almighty; we do not presume to be protective of our God, but to protect the people from such indecent language.'[12] Redress against blasphemy is for the protection of believers, whose beliefs are susceptible to injury. Traditionally, however, Christianity has been equivocal about the harm done by profane swearing: a conventional representation is that swearers injure and rend the body of Christ himself in what is tantamount to a ritual re-crucifixion, an anti-Mass. In Chapter 3 I argue that what is at stake is a question of representation itself: much medieval blasphemy (by God's arms, by God's bones) insists on the corporeal body of the divine, and thus functions as a dangerous travesty of the doctrine of the incarnation. Some Spanish inquisitors compiled lists of God's body parts in order to condemn and catch such swearing.[13] As well as the issue of representation, there is that of public order. Profane swearing is a sign of unacceptable laxity in the body politic. An American moralist laments:

> If use could make a wrong harmless, that which is about to be noticed would be no evil at all, since it is hardly possible to travel the public roads, or to pass an hour in the streets of our cities or towns, without being painful witnesses of the sinful practice of taking the holy name of God in vain. It is the custom of many on very slight occasions, to use such expressions as these: in the name of God! for God's sake! good God! Lord have mercy! Lord bless me! and the like. Now all this is wrong. That holy name should never be mentioned but on serious subjects, deliberately, with fear and reverence.[14]

A treatise against 'prophane Swearing and cursing' in 1706 calls itself

A Help to National Reformation . . . and a 'Specimen of an Agreement for the forming of a Society for Reformation of Manners'. The aim is to have all men gainfully employed, 'to have the Lords-Day and other publick Fast-Days observed in a solemn and due Manner, to have Stews rooted out, and the streets cleansed from lewd and impudent Women, and detestable *Sodomites* that infect them; to have Men restrained from broaching horrid *Blasphemies,* from *prophane Swearing and cursing'*; to stop drunkenness and to have suppressed 'the execrable impieties of our scandalous *Play-Houses,* those nurseries of Vices and prophaneness (whither our nobility and gentry are unhappily sent to learn the Accomplishments of their younger years)'.[15] The whole programme is applicable to a case like Sir Charles Sedley's.[16] In it a concern for public decency is again connected with an issue of representa-tion: in this case, theatrical representation in general. English blasphemy laws kept company with theatrical censorship in the office of Lord Chamberlain, which interpreted blasphemy as swearing in the most literal sense, for centuries forbidding both the representation of God and the speaking of the divine name on stage.

Exemplary histories of blasphemous swearers and the punishments meted out to them form an extensive and accessible sub-literature from medieval to modern times, the chapbook equivalent of courtesy manuals or etiquette books. Chaucer's Friar's Tale is one such version of the common medieval type, in which a lay ecclesiastical official, a summoner, is carried away by the Devil to hell after he curses by giving himself to the Devil. *The Swearer Silenc'd* (1614) tells of a serving man in Lincolnshire who 'in the very pains' swore

> *God's Wounds! The bell tolls for me; but he shall not have me yet:* Whereupon the blood issued out in the most fearful manner from all the joynts of his body, from Mouth, Nose, Wrists, Knees, Heels, and Toes, and other parts of his Body, and so he died.[17]

In this example, blasphemy becomes the figure of impenitence in the face of death, which we are told in authorities on blasphemy is the sin against the Holy Ghost.[18] We may compare the broadside case of *The Strange Punishment and Judgement of GOD, upon a Cursed blasphemer,* Anthony Painter, 'The Blaspheming Carryer who sunke into ground up to the neck and there stood two days and two nights, and not to bee drawne out by the strength of Horses or digged out by the help of man; and there dyed the 3 of November 1613.' Painter's offence had been 'swearing by the Name of the Most High', daring to 'blaspheme our Saviour Christ', and so crucify him anew. An etching shows Painter in the ground, crying 'I am Damn'd', and the Devil gloating, 'Thou art mine.'[19]

Such literature associates swearing with diabolic possession, and consigns the swearer to the devil. Lapses of language therefore portend lapses of faith. So in a more complex version we find the chapbook publication in 1797 of:

> The Blasphemers Punishment or the Cries of the Son of God to the Whole World; Being a true and faithful Account of one Eliz. Dover a Kt. and Baronets Daughter, Twenty-one Years of Age, who never would believe that there was either God or Devil, Heaven or Hell, or any future state after this Life was ended; till last SUNDAY was 3 Weeks, as she was walking in the Fields with some of her wicked Companions swearing, If there is a Devil, let me see him, that I may know him another Time.

The young woman's foolish invocation of hell-fire has the effect of conjuring up the Devil himself:

> This young woman, taking more notice of the temptations of the Devil than all the advice her parents gave her, she betook herself to all manner of ill courses such as drinking, whoring, and blaspheming the sabbath day, insomuch that in a short time she broke her mother's heart with grief; and going one day to her father's house, with a blasphemous oath in her mouth, she cry'd Give me some money to fulfil my youthful desires, for I will not lose the pleasures of this world, if my soul goes to Hell flames for ever, flying in a violent fashion, and swearing that, that very day she would be revenged on the rogue her father, so going out of her father's house she walked directly into Saint James's park, swearing she would have money to fulfil her youthful desires, she was met in the park by a young gentleman dressed in a suit of black, and as we find this gentleman was no other person than the Deceiver and Tempter of all Mankind.

Satan offers a Faustian contract: 'Madam, if you will resign yourself to me at the expiration of 3 years, and sign this roll with your own blood, you shall not want for any pleasures this world can afford you.' Warned off the proposal by a little bird – so is the Holy Ghost literalised – she swoons and falls into a trance for the statutory three days and three nights. On waking she sends for Dr Bone, the minister of Saint James's Church, his fellow minister and churchwardens, and relates her vision of hell. The threat is dispelled by holy language which overcomes the unholy: at Dr Bone's instruction, she says the Lord's Prayer and asks pardon of Jesus. Two angels then explicate her vision, en route to recording the names of all sinners at the Judgment.[20] Words and names are given a supernatural power; and it is this power that blasphemous swearing is taken to invert. In this popularising sense such swearing is seen as the sin against the Holy Ghost, the worst sin of all. As the Painter moralist thunders:

> Doe you think then you wretched and accursed blasphemers of the Name of the most High (at his terrible looks the earth doth tremble . . . the heaven fadeth away, and the sea flieth out) doe you thinke (say I to you) doe yee thinke to shunne the furie of his face, and the heauines of his arm that cannot

be auoided; O accursed blasphemers, the ffirst and cheefest, more wicked and abhominable than all other sinners, doe you not see that as many times as you open your stincking mouths to blaspheme the Name of the Almighty, as many time the Diuels and frightful fiends doe enter within yourselues through euery blasphemie?

The provenance of such a sub-literature, from the medieval *Summa* onwards, serves to distinguish between false and true swearing; that is, it serves to uphold the validity of the true (legal) oath as opposed to blasphemy, and thus evades, sometimes by glossing it out of existence, the apparent prohibition of James 5: 12: 'But above all things, my brethren, swear not, neither by heaven, neither by the earth, neither by any other oath: but let your yea be yea; and your nay, nay; lest ye fall into condemnation.' As John Downame hastens to explain in 'A Treatise on Swearing' (1609) Christ 'onely forbiddeth rash, vaine and vsuall swearing', not that for public purposes.[21] Similarly, the author of *A Discourse against prophane Swearing and Cursing* (1698) begins by defining 'the nature of an *Oath* in general', which is '*A Religious Affirmation, or Calling the Deity to witness in a controverted matter*'; 'Thus as when men swear by God they pawn his Being and perfections of the truth of what they declare.'[22] To swear in vain is therefore to transgress against the entire system of morality and truth. More sensationally, *The Swearer Silenc'd* shows that it is to pervert law. It tells of 'One hearing Perjury condemned in a Pulpit by a learned Preacher', who laughs:

'I have often forsworn myself and yet my right hand is not a whit shorter than my left'. Which words he had scarce uttered when such an Inflammation arose in that hand, that he was Constrained to go to the chyrurgeon and cut it off, lest it should infect his whole Body.[23]

When blasphemy substitutes for legal truth, the body politic itself is at risk of infection.

Such an emphasis on the religious basis of the legal oath says much about ways in which legal process itself is an extension and justification of orthodoxy. Modern proponents of new blasphemy laws might be better served reviewing the future of evidence given under oath in a society where the distinction between false and true swearing remains meaningful only to a minority of the population. Blasphemy is socially a far more crucial transgression than heresy, which may remain in an exclusively religious domain, whereas blasphemy always spills over into implications for subjects' response to law and government. If authority needs to claim for itself the sanction of the divine, it does not do so silently; and the subjects' relation to authority is made into a ritual speech-act where the words are invested with a magical, or transcendent, power. False swearing undoes the power of the words that authority has taken, or questions the truthfulness of their appropriation. It must be punished because it implies the fateful proposition that words are only words, and all are equally suspect to the religious user.

Distrust of language itself is part of the etymological development of the word 'blasphemy'. The words 'blasphemy' and 'blaspheme' are late Greek and remain largely inactive until they are used in the Septuagint to translate the Hebrew verbs '*nakob*' and '*qillel*', 'to pronounce aloud' and 'to curse' in the classic formulation of the Mosaic law of blasphemy in Leviticus 24. The word 'blasphemy' combines two roots – 'to hurt' and 'to speak' (-*pheme* as in 'fame', so 'defame') hence 'to harm by speaking' as in Leviticus 24 (a hurt sometimes conceptualised in highly physical terms). In Greek it functions as the opposite of the more common religious word '*euphemein*', to use words of good omen, to avoid unlucky words during religious rites, 'hence' – I am citing Liddell and Scott's *Greek Lexicon* – 'as the surest way of avoiding them, keep a religious silence'. So 'euphemy', the root of 'euphemism', is the opposite of blasphemy: its etymological meaning is 'speaking well' but its actual religious meaning is 'not speaking'. Blasphemy is therefore defined by its opposite not only as harmful speaking but, in the religious context, as speaking at all. All speech is risky when confronting the sacred. This node of attitudes goes far to explaining how Christianity went on its way for nearly one and a half millennia without placing its Bible into the hands of those who were unable to read Latin, and how strong the resistance to democratic enfranchisement – giving people a voice – in such a tradition must be, when the 'voice' is just what is most discouraged.

The most regularly cited authority is James 1: 26: 'If any man among you seem to be religious, and bridleth not his tongue, but deceiveth his own heart, this man's religion is vain.' A typical distillation of religious advice on such topics is Henry Hooton's aptly titled *A bridle for the Tongue*, where the contents page itself links related sins of the tongue:

Of Blasphemy	Of Brawling, Quarrelling, or Wrangling
Of Rash Vain Swearing	Of Dissimulation, or Deceit
Of False-accusing, or bearing False-Witness	Of Flattery
Of Calumny, or Slander	Of Lying, Equivocation, Promise-breaking and Discovering Secrets
Of Detraction, or Backbiting, and of Tale-bearing, and Reproof	Of Talkativeness, Garrulity, or Vain Babbling
Of Censoriousness, or Rash Judging	Of Ostentation, or Boasting
Of Scoffing, Derision, or Mocking	Of Querulousness, or Murmuring
Of Contumely, or Reproach	Of Foolish Jesting
Of Imprecation, or Cursing	Of Obscene, and Immodest Talk[24]

In a work like this, all language is seen as a danger zone, full of extraordinary and innumerable hazards. And blasphemy itself is defined as 'speaking any evil Thing of God, making War with Heaven itself, and flying as it were in the Face of the Almighty; or scoffing at Religion, and speaking reproachfully of God's Ordinances . . .' (p. 9). Hooton's net of authorities extends widely through Scripture to Aquinas, who 'makes Blasphemy to consist, either in denying God what justly belongs unto him, or ascribing unto him what is unbefitting his excellent Majesty; To which also some add, ascribing unto Man's self, what is only due to God', and lamenting that 'in these days, by reason of the decay of Religion', governments no longer always enforce old penalties – such as death, or the cutting out of the tongue, even though these are no more than blasphemers 'seem justly to deserve, since Blasphemy is, as it were, Treason against the Glorious Majesty of Heaven'. Hooton compares the 'religious Reverence' of the 'trembling Hebrews' before 'the Name of God, the great Tetragrammaton', with the characteristic blasphemies of our age, mirth and scurrility:

> To this Head may be reduced the ill practice of such as set their Mouths against Heaven, by prophanely making Holy Writ the subject of their Mirth, and Drollery, ridiculing Vertue and Religion, and (in as much as in them lies) laughing all Piety, out of Countenance, without which, Cicero tells us, No Faith could be secured, no Society amongst Men could be preserved, nor that most excellent Vertue of Justice itself subsists; And therefore, to speak loosely, and wantonly about holy Things, or Persons; to make any thing nearly relating to God and Religion, the Matter of Sport and Mockery; or to turn the Sentences and Phrases of the Holy Scripture into Jest, and Ridicule, is (notwithstanding the commonness thereof) a very great Sin. (Section vi, p. 12)

Hooton's insistence on the manner of reference to divine matters, matters of tone as well as content, persists, for example, in Lord Scarman's comment that there could have been no question of convicting Kirkup's poem had it argued its case in a more seemly manner. Here too we must expect judgments to be culturally relative: Thomas Paine was accused of such levity for his attacks on Christianity in *The Age of Reason*, where surely the accusation represents no more than a displacement of anger at its content. At any rate, Hooton's treatment is as typical as any I have found, and reads as a compendium of elements that recur from the early fathers of the Church through to Peraldus, Aquinas, canon law and Luther. As the sermons of a country parson, his work is valuable testimony to which of the abstractions of canon law were actually disseminated on the ground: judging from this, a good many. This is not merely a function of Hooton's late date: the discourse of blasphemy has tended to be the place where orthodoxy wordily justifies the reticence and silences it prescribes.

In many ways, dictionaries tell us less than this. The *Oxford English Dictionary* restricts the meaning of 'blasphemy' to speech-acts, which is etymologically correct and correct in canon law, but does not adequately reflect some medieval uses, and makes almost too neat a contrast with 'heresy', the primary meaning of which is to do with a 'school of thought'.

Canon law divides blasphemy into two main categories, the simple and the heretical, so there is bound to be overlap between the terms. While 'sacrilege' always has the primary meaning, from classical Latin onwards, of 'temple-violation', some of its secondary meanings based on Latin *sacrilegus* are more abstract, and so close to blasphemy; and secondary meanings of apostasy, or extensions of its primary meaning, bring it into close contact with the notion of treason to God. The cultural reason for these overlaps of meaning is developed more fully in Chapter 2. I argue that in early Christianity blasphemy is more important than heresy until the development of an orthodoxy that is strong enough to exclude its opposition as heretical or schismatic. Then, in the medieval period, blasphemy becomes ancillary to accusations of heresy, with the exception (as I show) of attitudes towards Jews and Muslims; it is the Reformation, then, as Levy notes, that re-awakens blasphemy as a major discourse, and blasphemy is the ground on which Protestantism prefers to attack the Catholic Church.

Blasphemy in vernacular languages is therefore revitalised by Protestantism; and in England such revitalisation occurs over a century earlier than elsewhere, given the unique challenge posed by the Wycliffites. Certainly Middle English presents a unique use, range and abundance of examples for 'blasphemy', but the word is not stably differentiated from heresy, apostasy and sacrilege. Sacrilege, though rare, covers linguistic profanation as well as material destruction, as in Trevisa's use of the term for the pagan days of the week, and general impiety. If 'sacrilege . . . is brekyng of the sacrament of holy cherche',[25] it is likely to be linked with blasphemy and heresy. 'Apostasy' covers all infidelity, paganism as well as leaving holy orders; it also incorporates, for Wycliffites, the making of miracle plays ('and so myricalis pleyinge is verre apostacie fro Crist'), fictions and other worldly 'vanytees', all taken as signs of people out of order. It also incorporates sexual deviance: according to *The Ayenbite of Inwit*, a man is called a recreant and false Christian in three ways, because he does not believe as he should, 'as doth the bugger and the heretike and the apostate' – a connection to which Chapter 3 returns. 'Heresy' is rarer as a term than 'blasphemy', but is a general term of abuse for false belief, denial of orthodox belief, and 'conduct inimical to Christianity', including by pagans, Jews, Muslims and (to the orthodox) Lollards. 'Blasphemy' comprises swearing, gambling, drinking, impiety, slander, sexual deviance, heresy, preaching against the Gospel, sacrilege, and any hypocrisy, defamation or rebellion against God. As shown in the *Middle English Dictionary*, to 'blaspheme' is to be someone's enemy: for the friars it is to be a Lollard; and the Lollards use it against the friars and others. We return to the definition with which I started, that of general vituperation in a rhetoric for which orthodoxy is the central and contested site. Beyond this, a meaning is context-specific and must be read as it occurs textually.

The point is that blasphemy is not really an offence at all, certainly not one like robbery and murder where the circumstances of time and place are unproblematic, and only a little more like other forms of defamation, where the job of the court is to determine the possible meaning of the given text. Like all rhetoric, blasphemy exists in the air, between two or more parties, and only at the very end of the exchange, when one side has prevailed over and punished the other, does a form of it fall as an object to earth – an object that is often repudiated and disowned by its authors even as they are condemned for it, and that is problematised by the multiplicity and duration of the exchange. Even in the simple case of the Pennsylvania sign with which this chapter opened, the sign is not the sole object of debate: each debate is its own object, for the questions are everywhere about reading and social reinscription. In what follows I look at examples of blasphemy and the debates they occasion. My purpose is no longer to define blasphemy but to place the particular instances in social networks of identity and difference, of conformity and transgression, and to begin to compile, at least, a map of the cultural sites in which blasphemy affects collective aspects of meaning.

Why is this a field for a literary scholar? Because blasphemy is a linguistic act, and a place where one sees whole societies theorising language. By theory I mean here the frames that we all construct around what we do, frames that are the ideological containers of such collective acts of meaning. Blasphemy is the place for theorising the rhetoric of social institutions. Moreover, the historical documents relating to blasphemy are prejudiced and mostly framed by orthodox meaning systems. These sources should be treated as if they were fiction, or, rather, sharp distinction between fact and fiction is inappropriate to the study of blasphemy. Literature is as important to their making as history or law. Blasphemy almost always involves representation, through texts, languages and performances.

What follows is the first of three documentary sources, in this case drawn from the close of the seventeenth century in England. It is an unequivocal case: blasphemy, not heresy; and its late date guarantees a depth of documentation greater than we normally find for the later medieval period.

SUSANNAH FOWLES (1698)

The Trial of Susannah Fowles of Hammersmith: That was Try'd at London for Blaspheming JESUS CHRIST. And Cursing the LORDS PRAYER. And who also pretended to be possest with a Devil.

On Saturnday the 7th of May 1698 Susannah Fowles of the Parish of Hammersmith in the County of Middlesex, was Indicted at the Sessions house in the Old Baily, for uttering blasphemous Words against Jesus Christ, and Cursing and Damning the Lords Prayer. The Account of her Trial is as follows.

The first Evidence depos'd that the Prisoner's Husband came to him, and told him that his Wife was possest with a Devil: upon which he ask'd him if she had been guilty of any heinous Sin? and was answered, That upon some Discontent she wished several unlawful wishes, such as That the Devil might fetch her, cursed her self if she would live such a Life &c, And upon her being visited she said, she saw an Apparition in the shape of a Man; and afterward seem'd to be possest with a Devil, and had seemingly dreadful Fits, and made a great noise at Prayers; and when she was out of her Fits, she told the Spectators that she saw the Apparition sometimes in one shape, and sometimes in another; and at one time said it was one Mr Thomas, and then making a great squeek, said, Now he is gone out of me; That she used to make a squeek at the end of every Fit, sometimes two Squeeks, and sometimes three; and of the Ministers who visited her, being jealous of her being a Cheat, said at the end of the next Fit she would make four Squeeks, which she did. It was also observ'd, that as soon as Prayers begun she took her Fits and pretended to be altogether senseless; at another time that she said, She saw a short Man with a long Beard, which her Handkerchief was a foot to for length: and it was taken notice of that she never alter'd her Countenance in the time of her Fits; which together with divers Methods which were use'd to make her believe they were at Prayers when they were not, increased the belief that she was a Cheat: And being questioned if she dissembled, she said if she did, it were just with God to Strick her dead: and upon its being declared to her she was a Cheat: she and all her Family spoke not one word. Afterwards at another visiting she seem'd to be in a great Fit; lifting up her hands as if she would have done herself some mischief; but upon speaking the words, Tie her, she let them rest. It was likewise observ'd, that when she was in her Fits, she never cursed nor blasphemed, as those who are possest with the Devil do untill she heard some of the Ministers take notice of it; and then she did.

At another time the Visiters read and prayed with her from morn to night, when she seem'd to be in an Agony; and being forc'd on her knees at Prayer, she swore she would go with him on Friday, naming the Devil frequently; and on the Friday following she said, One of the Windows above-stairs was open, and the Devil was come to fetch her, making a great noise, and lighting a great many Candles and search being made for the open window, it could not be found.

On the 3d of January last, upon one of the Visiters repeating the words, Lord save us, she said, I'll save you; and frequently upon repeating the Lord's prayer to her she said, Curse it, damn it, sink it, and upon repeating the words I believe in God the Father Almighty, she said that's me; & at repeating the words, And in Jesus Christ his only Son, She said, that's my Son. At another time when the words Lord save us were again peated to her, she said, I'll save you, I came to save you all, for which I shed my Blood. And at other times, on repeating the Lords Prayer, she inverted the Expressions; and instead of the words Lead us not into temptation, she said, lead us into temptation; and at the words, Deliver us from evil, she said, bring evil unto us. And upon repeating the words, Glory be to the Father and to the Son, she said that's to me and my Son. And always at the Naming the Name of Jesus, she would say, Curse him, curse him. It was observed that a little before her Marriage she wish't that the Devil might fetch her away if ever she went to live at Hammersmith; which she did notwithstanding that same day.

The Evidence also deposed: that the Prisoner said, she had a Needle and a Paper in writing given her by the Devil; and that she had a Spell given to her to put about her Neck by one Jordan a Papist, some of which Profession she said had sent to her several times, and told her she would never be cured till the Men with hair Coats and bare Legs came from Portugal Embassadors: Which some of the Ministers, who were Visiters and Evidence against the Prisoner, declared, encreased their belief that it was a trick of them to obtain the Credite of having done that which Protestant could not, viz cast out the Devil. Another time one of the Visiters said she could not spit in his Face; but she deceiv'd him, and did it, and another of the Visiters spitting in her face, she return'd it and call'd him Q. in the corner. It was also observ'd that at repeating the Lord's Prayer in Latin she did not fall into her Fits as usual when 'twas said in English, which was a further Confirmation of the Cheat.

To prove which more fully, one of the Evidence deposed that to try her he heat an Iron; and when the Minister was at Prayer, and she in her Fits as usual, even when she pretended to be insensible, he put it to her Hand, which she drew away from it as soon as it touched her; and filling a Pipe of Tobacco, he blew the Smoak of it into her Face, which was like to have stifled her; And afterwards disguising himself in an ugly dress, entered the house when she was alone; upon which she immediatly run out, saying it was the Devil, and was much frightned; which was a further demonstration she was a Cheat. After which, Evidence threatening to knock her on the head if she would not confess the Cheat, she did it freely; and said 'twas purely to get money, which she also own'd to some others of the Evidence. And it appeared that after her being taken up she pretended to have none of her fits.

The Prisoner in her defence said, that great Troubles had occasioned her to fall into a distracted condition, and that she knew not what she did; that she did verily believe she was either troubled with a Devil, or bewitched: that Jordan the Papist had given her things both inwardly and outwardly; and that what she had confest, was only to avoid her being [taken] to prison: But all this being look'd upon as frivolous and evasion, and the evidence being very full and clear, the Jury brought her in Guilty.

She was sentenced by the Court to pay a Fine of 100 Merks, and to lie in Prison till it be paid: to stand three times on the Pillary, viz. at the May-pole in the Strand at Charing Cross and at Hammersmith, and to find Surety for her good behaviour for a Twelve-month.[26]

It is at once obvious how thoroughly this report disempowers Fowles and blocks any neutral construction of her actions. The evidences against her are anonymous, and freely mix opinion with narrative – though the charges originate with her husband, and his role is equivocal and elided in the report. Unusually, we hear enough to know what we do not know. Who exactly was Mr Thomas? And what explains Fowles's strong aversion to Hammersmith? Her desire is emphasised in several ways, but always out of context. Curiously, the ministers who examine her guard their expertise (of diabolic possession, of Latin, and so on) by setting out to establish that she is a cheat. She is laughable, like the twelfth-century Breton blasphemer Eon:

> Eon was a Breton, probably a knight, since he was both *illiteratus* and of good family, who heard himself referred to at Mass one day, in the words *per eundem Dominum nostrum*. Thus assured of his divinity he gathered a following among whom he lived like a king, surrounding himself with 'the magnificence, the trappings and the haughtiness of royalty', terrorising churches and monasteries for two years or more before he was captured and brought before the Council of Rheims in 1148. There he showed Eugenius III and the other dignitaries present a forked stick which he always carried, and explained how when he held it with the fork pointed upwards God ruled two-thirds of the universe and left the remaining third to him, and when he reversed it 'I keep two parts of the world for myself and relinquish one to God'.
>
> The Council dissolved in laughter and concluded that Eon was plainly demented, and must be imprisoned to bring an end to his attacks on the faithful, but subjected to no other punishment.[27]

The historian Ian Moore records this as the one occasion, from many hundreds on which heresy is called madness, on which the heresiarch is treated as a madman. That is the report: yet Eon's followers are ruthlessly put to death, and his very name suggests more Manicheanism than the report allows. Fowles's jury for its part refuses a plea of dementia: they accept the charge that she is a conscious confidence trickster who uses blasphemy to give herself an untoward importance. The suggestions of blasphemy come from her examiners, who tricked her into impersonating God ('That's me') and showing her self-hatred ('Curse him') at one and the same time, like Freud's psychotic Dr Schreber (see Chapter 5): the ideas indeed seem to be put into her mind by the ministers, who operate like skilful psychoanalysts. (Carlo Ginzburg quotes Freud's confession that he would have made a good inquisitor.)[28]

This is a discourse which converts signs into their opposites: Fowles's pillory is to be a maypole, her (post-partum?) depression is a frivolity, and duress is freedom: 'Evidence threatening to knock her on the head if she would not confess the Cheat, *she did it freely.*' Not only are the tests deliberately unfair (a red-hot iron, tobacco smoke in her face); they also involve the ministers themselves in blasphemy. As Fowles impersonates God, one of them successfully impersonates the Devil. Protestant ministers, for whom the entire Latin Mass was 'a kind of sorcery', 'a meer Medley of Blasphemy, Non-sense and Irreligion',[29] none the less turn the Lord's Prayer into such nonsense by speaking it aloud, according to their own standards blasphemously, in Latin. They blaspheme in order to catch a blasphemer. There is an unacknowledged reciprocity in their belief systems, a core of belief, here in diabolic possession, shared by accusers and accused.

It is like a game in which the blasphemer serves and orthodoxy volleys, but in deadly earnest; and it is as unequal as it is unstable, like playing tennis with the referee. I accuse you of blasphemy; you accuse me; and in the end the exercise of power determines the outcome.

This is to say that blasphemy is an exchange transaction, and what is at stake is community and identity formation. In the words of Stallybrass and White in *The Politics and Poetics of Transgression*, such points of antagonism, of specific cultural dissonance, discursive sites 'where ideology and fantasy conjoin', 'are the core items in an exchange-network, an economy of signs, in which individuals, writers and authors are sometimes but perplexed agencies'.[30] I use 'exchange' here, as do Stallybrass and White, conscious of modern Marxist and post-Marxist elaborations of Volume I of *Capital* (e.g. Rossi-Landi's *Linguistics and Economics*, Jean-Joseph Goux's *Symbolic Economies*), all of which argue that it is more than a metaphor, that there is a homology rather than a mere analogy between linguistic exchange and economic exchange. Fowles and her keepers, after all, are joined together not merely by blasphemy, but by debt: her accusers are also her creditors. But it is important to insist that if there is a connection, it is unconscious, and that an orthodox position would deny the very possibility of an exchange. It is unacknowledged.

But how can we be sure that this is the whole truth about Susannah Fowles, who is punished for being a pseudo-blasphemer, a cheat? The date, 1698, may be significant: it is a long time after the massive suppression and oppression of the Restoration, in which many types of Puritan and non-conformist enthusiasm were put down or driven underground, in forms that might surface in just this sort of form, deliberately and strategically unrecognised for what they were. We have to reckon for the effect of what Foucault calls 'the logic of censorship', simultaneously 'affirming that such a thing is not permitted, preventing it from being said, denying that it exists', linking, in a logical paradox, 'the inexistent, the illicit and the inexpressible'.[31] The mid-seventeenth century is the great period of what Anne Laurence calls

> a priesthood of she-believers, . . . a counter-culture of women as opposed to a female attempt to storm the bastions of male ecclesiastical power; that is to say, a culture of women who could not find the religion they wanted in any of the more conventional churches

– both women prophets like Agnes Beaumont and women followers of male prophets such as James Nayler (see Chapter 2).[32] The Quakers particularly among non-conformist sects produced a large number of such prominent but unorthodox religious women. The very name Quaker represents a bodily symptom of religious belief that is marked in its gender, and that stems from 'the bodily quality of female spirituality in the later Middle

Ages',[33] women in England of orthodox views such as Margery Kempe, or of heterodox Lollard sympathies such as Margery Baxter or Hawisia Moone.[34] Though the ground of belief had shifted between them and what I suspect may underlie the case of Susannah Fowles, the behavioural manifestations in the discourse about them are almost identical. It may not have been to Susannah Fowles's personal advantage that she comes at the end of a period in which it was public knowledge, as Christopher Hill notes, that God could 'speak direct to private individuals . . . it was entirely *natural* for perfectly normal people to hear God speaking to them: it was not, as it would be today, *prima facie* evidence of insanity'.[35]

It turns out that, in order to understand the account of Fowles's blasphemy, we need knowledge of late medieval antecedents – though what that knowledge provides is an enhanced understanding of the discourses involved, not the 'truth' of the individual 'cases'. Moreover, such a relatively detailed account from the seventeenth century underlines how little we have to go on to gain such knowledge, and how short we will normally fall. We are not just, or even primarily, looking at historical incidents; we are also looking, inescapably, at *textuality* – and at orality too, at how orally and textually based subcultures meet, and fail to engage. The only constant is the exchange transaction as I have described it, and, supporting it, the implied or overt connection that is almost universal in such accounts between blasphemy and illicit material gain.

There are two historical points that need to be clarified. First, the evidence against Fowles is given anonymously, so that she is unsure who her accusers are. This is the standard procedure. As the writer of *A Discourse against Profane Swearing* (1698) put it the year of Fowles's arrest,

> If the Informers Name be constantly discover'd, he is thereby needlessly expos'd to the Malice and Revenge of the Offender, to whom he intends thereby a real service. . . . And these Inconveniences to the Informer are attended with no real considerable advantage to the Accused Party.[36]

The system is that of the Inquisition or Stalinist purge, in which it is impossible to fight a charge against oneself. Eugenia Ginzburg, a victim of Stalin's purges, records her office typist urging her, at the very outset of her troubles, to plead guilty: 'by not saying you're sorry, you'll make it worse'; and when her long imprisonment in Stalin's labour camps is punctuated by the news of her father's death, her anger turns to the language of blasphemy accusations:

> Bare feet on the icy stone I stand,
> Condemned under the Holy Inquisition's rule,
> Accused of communing with the devil,
> Of opposing the Party line.
> In this refurbished cell
> The centuries close up.[37]

In this account too, the centuries close up: Eugenia Ginzburg, another accused of communing with the Devil, shares her cell with Susannah Fowles.

Secondly, when Fowles is found to be a cheat, she is convicted of a specific and serious offence, the seventh category of offences against religion in Blackstone's Commentaries:

> Seventh species of offenders in this class are religious imposters, such as *falsely pretend an extraordinary commission from heaven*; or terrify and abuse the people with false denunciations or judgments. All these as tending to subvert all religion, by bringing it into ridicule and contempt, are punishable by the temporal courts with fine and imprisonment and infamous corporal punishment.[38]

Fowles's punishment conforms to that specified. Nevertheless she was lucky: the alternative in such a case would be to have been accused of either Blackstone's fifth or his sixth species of offence, witchcraft or sorcery. Many of the details of her case could be taken to indicate magic, and she had her master in the mysterious Mr Thomas. Had Fowles been accused or convicted of witchcraft, she could still in 1698 have lost her life. Her case occurs towards the very end of the great witch hunts of the sixteenth and seventeenth centuries. As Norman Cohn shows in *Europe's Inner Demons*, these were built on slight and stereotyped foundations, where frequency of occurrence was taken to bear the force of proof. The stereotypes are both learned and popular, and are simple constructions of blasphemous discourses developed in the early days of Christianity.[39] Behind the apparent eccentricity of Fowles's case, therefore, stand more than one potent and well-exercised type of blasphemy. They are also literary types. Readers of this book will meet them again.

SIR CHARLES SEDLEY (1663)

In the month of June 1663 this our author sir Ch. Sedley, Charles lord Buckhurst (afterwards earl of Middlesex) sir Tho. Ogle, &c. were at a cook's house at the sign of the Cock in Bow-street near Covent-garden, within the liberty of Westm. and being inflam'd with strong liquors, they went into the balcony belonging to that house, and putting down their breeches they excrementiz'd in the street: which being done, Sedley stripped himself naked, and with eloquence preached blasphemy to the people: whereupon a riot being raised, the people became very clamorous, and would have forced the door next to the street open; but being hindred, the preacher and his company were pelted into their room, and the windows belonging thereunto were broken. This frolick being soon spread abroad, especially by the fanatical party, who aggravated it to the utmost, by making it the most scandalous thing in nature, and nothing more reproachful to religion than that; the said company were summoned to the court of justice in Westminster-hall, where being indicted of a riot before sir Rob. Hyde, lord chief justice of the common pleas, were all fined, and sir Charles being fined 500*l.* he made answer, that he thought he was the first man that paid for shiting. Sir Rob. Hyde asked him whether ever he read the book called *The Compleat Gentleman,* &c. to which sir Charles made answer, that set aside his lordship, he had read more books than himself, &c.[40]

Thence by water with Sir W. Batten to T[r]inity-house, there to dine with him, which we did; and after dinner we fell in talking, Sir J. Mennes and Mr. Batten and I – Mr. Batten telling us of a late triall of Sir Charles Sydly the other day, before my Lord Chief Justice Foster and the whole Bench – for his debauchery a little while since at Oxford Kates; coming in open day into the Balcone and showed his nakedness – acting all the postures of lust and buggery that could be imagined, and abusing of scripture and, as it were, from thence preaching a Mountebanke sermon from that pulpitt, saying that there he hath to sell such a pouder as should make all the cunts in town run after him – a thousand people standing underneath to see and hear him.

And that being done, he took a glass of wine and washed his prick in it and then drank it off; and then took another and drank the King's health.

It seems my Lord and the rest of the Judges did all of them round give him a most high reproofe – my Lord Chief Justice saying that it was for him and such wicked wretches as he was that God's anger and judgments hung over us – calling him 'Sirrah' many times. It's said they have bound him to his good behaviour (there being no law against him for it) in 5000*l.* . . .

Upon this discourse, Sir J. Mennes and Mr. Batten both say that buggery is now almost grown as common among our gallants as in Italy, and that the very pages of the town begin to complain of their masters for it. But blessed be God, I do not to this day know what is the meaning of this sin, nor which is the agent nor which the patient. (Samuel Pepys's Diary, 1 July 1663).[41]

At first sight, the contrast between Sedley's case and that of Susannah Fowles seems to reveal the hypocritical gulf based on gender and class; it brings to mind Sydney Smith's remark that the Society for the Suppression of Vice, founded by William Wilberforce in 1802, was a society for suppressing the vices of those whose incomes did not exceed £500 a year. Fowles is reported by anonymous informants in the privacy of her own household, and has to be entrapped by her inquisitors. Sedley shouts blasphemies in a public place before a large crowd. Fowles's punishment probably ensured that, like thousands incarcerated after the Restoration, she never left prison: not only was the fine itself large, but the bond was probably sufficient to ensure her lifelong imprisonment even had there been a family member willing to pay for her release. Sedley's punishment is a fine with only a week's sentence, and a good behaviour bond in a large sum (Pepys reports £5,000: à Wood's £500 is more likely). That Sedley survived we know from his later career as a poet, dramatist and parliamentarian – as well as father to the mistress of the future King James II.

There is, of course, a massive social difference between the cases of Sedley and Fowles. However, it should not be overstated: Sedley was tried before the Lord Chief Justice at the Old Bailey, who was riled enough to call him 'Sirrah'. He was in serious trouble. His fine was much larger than Fowles's, and his difficulty in paying it is implied by Anthony à Wood's account of his unsuccessful efforts to have it waived. À Wood's version, emphasising the aggravation of the offence in the outcry of 'the fanatical party', by 'making it the most scandalous thing in nature, and nothing more reproachful than that', tallies with the reports of contemporary argument about whether the case should not have been heard before an ecclesiastical court. This strengthens the impression that blasphemy was a crucial part of the case against Sedley, though the charge might have been nothing more than conduct likely to cause a breach of the peace. The law report records his punishment 'for showing himself naked in a balcony and throwing down bottles (pist in) *vie et armis* among the people in Covent Garden *contra pacem* to the scandal of the government'.[42] In this case, therefore, obscenity, blasphemy and sedition are all present, though scarcely distinguishable from one another. Sedley's defence, a plea of guilty and a remark reported by à Wood 'that he thought he was the first man that paid for shiting', is a wise evasion of any recognition that the words he spoke formed the major part of the offence, though as these are reported by Pepys they could hardly have failed to do so. Pepys and à Wood add a discursive support to the view that the episode was a 'mere frolick', though both clearly relish repeating it. As a carousing poet, Sedley is identified as one of the degenerate sons of Shakespeare, Jonson and Marlowe, a forebear of lifestyles celebrated in *Brideshead Revisited* and of upper-class yahoos everywhere.

We cannot understand how such a 'frolick' could have ended, even for a gay blade, in the Old Bailey, until we realise that less than three years into the Restoration the figure of the libertine has an inescapable religious reference. To understand the naked Sedley, we have to have in mind another male figure who preached naked before the people, the Ranter Abiezer Coppe, whose message was one of spiritual union as sexual excess, and of total inversion: dancing, embracing beggars, and with a mission to rescue Christians from the clergy, who call 'good evil and evil good, light darkness and darkness light, truth blasphemy and blasphemy truth'.[43] One practical consequence of the inversion was sexual freedom: 'I can kiss and hug ladies and love my neighbour's wife as myself, without sin.'[44] Coppe's rival as a spiritual libertine, Laurence Clarkson, continued the attack on the clergy and associated it with an equally absolute repudiation of government in the name of 'the communality', declaring it unjust that 'the communality should have to uphold another man's faith'. The role of the clergy was that of social discipline, to compel 'the communality not only in their bodies but conscience, to execute unjust designs one against another, viz. to worship that for God which to them was no God'. In the coalition of magistrate and of minister, the purposes were taxation and social acquiescence, reached by the denial of civil rights and imprisonment of dissenters. Clarkson's progress through England as a preacher was social, spiritual and, not least, sexual, as he acted out with the faithful the discoveries that he was 'full of lust' and that 'to be pure in all things, yea, all acts were pure'. Truth is beyond words; orthodoxy and law therefore are only language. 'The very title sin is only a name without substance.' But Clarkson does not follow the logic of this, for it would weaken the force of his own discourse. At the same time, he argues that the desire to sin is God-given: 'a swearer, a drunk, an adulterer, a thief, these [have] the power and wisdom of God to swear, drink, whore and steal. . . . O blasphemy of the highest nature! What? make God the author of sin? so, a sinful God.'[45] For Clarkson, God is the God of blasphemers, the patron of drunkards and thieves, the whoremaster.

In spiritual libertinism, then, we find the basis of what in English law is the single most important blasphemy trial, that of a yeoman of Surrey, John Taylor, in 1676. The importance of the case lies less in the substance of Taylor's blasphemies than in being the occasion of Lord Chief Justice Hale's famous judgment incorporating into common law blasphemy against the Christianity of the established Church as a form of sedition, ruling

> that such kind of wicked blasphemous words were not only an offence to God and religion, but a crime against laws, State and Government, and therefore punishable . . . for to say, religion is a cheat, is to dissolve all those obligations whereby the civil societies are preserved, and that Christianity is parcel of the laws of England; and therefore to reproach the Christian religion is to speak in subversion of the law.[46]

Taylor was removed from Bedlam where he had been screened and found sane, in order to answer the charge of blasphemy. This is the statement that Taylor was accused of uttering:

> Christ is a whoremaster, and religion is a cheat, and profession is a cloak; and they are both cheats, and all the earth is mine, I am a King's son; my father sent me hither, and made me neither fear God, Devil, nor Man; and I am a younger brother to Christ, and angel of God; and no man fears God but an hypocrite; Christ is a bastard; God damn and confound all your Gods; Christ is the whore's master.

The trial was one of language, phrase by phrase. After every word had been weighed, this is the form of Taylor's statement that was proved against him:

> Christ is a whoremaster, and religion is a cheat, and profession is a cloak, and all cheats; all are mine; and I am a King's son, and fear neither God, Devil or Man; I am Christ's younger brother [proved by three witnesses] and Christ is

a bastard; and damn all Gods of the Quakers, &c; none fears God but an hypocrite [proved by one].[47]

Exhaustive legal process achieved deletion of Taylor's claim that 'the earth is mine', that 'my father sent me', that Christ is 'an angel of God', and converted his curse on all Gods to a curse on 'all Gods of the Quakers', turning a major blasphemy into a sectarian difference. In fact, however, the claim to be God's son remains, and if Christ has a younger brother and is a bastard, then he may as well be 'an angel of God' – the burden of all these statements is to deny the doctrine of the Trinity. This is the bearing of Taylor's view of Christ as 'a bastard': he is human, yet Joseph is not his father. The legal process therefore betrays a concern for language that makes no actual recognition of discourse, and probably manages to destroy the coherence of Taylor's utterance. A modern reader is almost bound to assume that Taylor belongs in a psychiatric ward; Freud considers God-impersonators, such as Dr Schreber, as a large group among psychotics. Taylor's words, like Susannah Fowles's, do indeed show a fluctuation between identity with the divine and active hostility to it that characterises such psychosis. Yet much of the fluctuation belongs to a tension inherent in Taylor's discourse, a split between religious subjectivity as defined by orthodoxy ('religion', 'profession') and as reconstituted in the experience of the enraptured and unorthodox believer. Taylor's apparent claims to divinity belong to a tradition that runs from Seekers through Ranters to the Quakers, one of the indwelling of the Word in the believer as an inner light. By claiming to be Christ's 'younger' brother, Taylor is associating himself with others of like belief, for all are raised to divinity by virtue of that light: to be Christ's 'younger' brother is to deny any inference that the believer thereby uniquely 'becomes' Christ, or supplants him. Yet Taylor is always portrayed as having claimed to be the 'Son of God' – an orthodox misrepresentation that is probably based on genuine misunderstanding. The very attempt, in the 'proved' version, to differentiate Taylor from Quakerism shows a suspicion of their proximity. But the signature is the first phrase, 'Christ is a whoremaster', which is no more than a restatement of Clarkson's libertinism.

Nothing in the words attributed to Taylor is inconsistent with Ranter provenance. This does not prove Taylor sane: being mad is a matter of being judged to lose control of language, to be more spoken by than speaking. There is an appearance of confusion in both versions of Taylor's sayings, and it is impossible to know whether the source lies in his mental state or in the failure of those who condemned him to understand his place in a subculture that was, in any case, underground. There is an immediate effort to remedy this failure in the propaganda occasioned by the case. *A Full and True Account of the Notorious Wicked Life of that Grand Imposter, John Taylor: one*

of the Sweet-Singers of Israel, printed in London in 1678, associated him with
'this Impious Sect of *The Sweet-Singers* of Israel, *or Famyly of love*',[48] which is
anathematised for all the world as if it were a precursor of modern sects
bearing much the same name. It omits Ranter influence, but concentrates
on a misleading association of Taylor with the Muggletonians, reproducing
'One of his Prophane Songs, Copied Verbatim out of his own Book, which
he sent to Muggleton (whom he calls Brother).' Clarkson became a
Muggletonian, and Muggleton like Taylor was convicted of blasphemy,
but there is nothing much else in common between Taylor's libertine
views and those of Muggleton. The song ('Which with much Affectation as
well as Affection, they sing to an old Ballad Tune') admits the distance
between Taylor and Muggleton, and is a plea that they should make
common cause:

> Come Muggelton, my Brother, why should we live at Ods?
> Muggelton, be not mistaken, full certain we are Gods. (p. 5)

It is almost certainly a forgery: an attempt to exploit Taylor's conviction in
order to attack a slightly more reputable and substantial target, Muggleton,
who was himself convicted of blasphemy the year after Taylor in 1677. What
is of interest in the pamphlet is the association between blasphemy and a
'song'. It is not a good climate for Sedley to claim in his defence that, far
from being a blasphemer, he is a poet.

Yet Sedley is a poet – 'this our author Sir Charles Sedley' – and he stands
in the dock of the Old Bailey jealous of his reputation as a man of letters:
the exchange with Lord Chief Justice Hyde is about both being a gentleman
and reading the text of gentlemanliness, *The Compleat Gentleman*. It is not at
all, of course, that Sedley has Ranter sympathies: what he does to the crowd
is to enact a pointed and exuberant parody of a Ranter sermon. Sedley
'stripped himself naked, and with eloquence preached blasphemy to the
people': part of the blasphemy, according to Pepys, includes a parodic
communion, in which Sedley washes his penis in the wine. This of course
transvalues the sacrament, and places the divine in a context of excrement
(the young wit cleverly uses his penis to refill the empty bottles that he
throws at the people). However, it is not the exhibition of Sedley's penis or
his excrement that inflames the crowd – that is merely Sedley's joke – but
the 'eloquence' with which he 'preached blasphemy'. It is Sedley's language
that offends, not his penis, which is supplementary. From the viewpoint of
an enraged 'fanatical party', all sex is oral sex. Sedley offends through his
language for which his excrement is simply the most readily available
metaphor. He is a debauchee of words, and there is therefore a dangerous
association between his blasphemy and his poetry – a lineage from
Marlowe that is unlikely to figure in his courtroom mitigation. Moreover,
he is unable to justify his performance in terms of the Ranter parody that it

unmistakably is: to mention Ranters would be to invite association with them, and the trouble with all such dialogic play with words is that on a monologic reading, such as is inevitably found in a courtroom, they simply repeat what they seek to problematise. The reason for ridicule is the same as the reason for its being misunderstood, fear of the Other, of the heterodoxy that orthodoxy must imagine in order to discover its limits.

There is more than a hint in à Wood's account that Sedley's libertine language and flashing of his penis are taken to be free signifiers: if the performance is represented by 'the fanatical party' as 'the most scandalous thing in nature', then there may be an imagining of sexual transgressions. This is amply corroborated by Pepys's recounting that Sedley acted out 'all the postures of lust and buggery that could be imagined, and abusing of scripture'. Indeed, the affair becomes for Pepys and his colleagues the opportunity for some excited discussion about the growth of buggery in contemporary England and leads to Pepys's splendid confidence to his diary that he does not know what the word means: 'But blessed be God, I do not to this day know what is the meaning of this sin, nor which is the agent nor which the patient.' He knows merely that not knowing is a matter for blessing. When orthodoxy sees libertinism, it sees both blasphemy and sexual deviance. Sexual deviance as well as sexual excess is therefore a signifier of blasphemy.

This is true of a comparable Spanish case, in which a 60-year-old, José Navarro, concealed a statue of the infant Jesus, and made the sign of the Cross, while claiming – in the *persona* of God the Father – to have fornicated with the mothers of his audience, and parodying the *asperges* of the Mass by exhibiting his penis.[49] But the point applies beyond Christian blasphemy. A book with the title *Scandal: Essays in Islamic heresy* turns out to be a study exclusively in Sufism, in which blasphemy combines with transgression, including drunkenness, and with poetry. The transgression involves transvaluing the Islamic value of wine, which is forbidden now but promised in Paradise hereafter. Thus there is a culture for which Paradise is available in the form of drink and, as Sufi poetry both induces orgasm and seeks to represent it, sexual excess, physical love; and it involves sexual deviance in what Wilson calls 'sacred pedophilia', quoting medieval complaints that 'lumped hashish-eaters in the same damnable category with boy-lovers and sufis. The three tastes appear linked in much Islamic literature.'[50] In orthodox eyes, these then combine to form a complete religious inversion; and the inversion is available for any who care to practise it. The charges brought against a Sufi martyr, Mansur ibn al-Hallaj (executed in Baghdad in 922, cited by Wilson), include 'writing a defence of Satan, as "the perfect Sufi and perfect lover" in his *Kitab al-tawasin*' (p. 7). When Sir Charles Sedley appears drunk and naked, speaking of sexual liberty with blasphemous eloquence, the orthodoxy of the 'fanatical party' fears what some Islamic orthodoxy fears in Sufism: the total inversion of religious values. The Ranter Coppe's visualisation of sacred orgasm little more than a decade before Sedley's trial captures the very core of Sufi ecstasy and the suspicious power of its language:

> I have been hugged, hugged, hugged embraced and kissed with the kisses of his mouth whose loves are better than wine, and have been utterly overcome therewith, beyond expression, beyond admiration.[51]

This may strike orthodoxy as a somewhat over-literal reading of the Song of Songs.

Responding to such language, orthodoxy imagines Ranterism and libertinism in the age-old image of its worst fears and clichés. They imagine orgies, both heterosexual and homosexual, both lust and buggery; drinking and swearing; public nudity and public sex; buttock-kissing and coprophilia; and, above all, dire travesties of the sacraments:

> They affirm that all Women ought to be in common, and when they are assembled together (this is a known truth) they first entertaine one another, the men those of their own sex, and the Women their fellow females: with horrid oaths and execrations, then they fall to bowzing and drink deep healths (O cursed Caitiffes) to their Brother God, and their Brother Devill; then being well heated with Liquor, each brother takes his she Other upon his knee, and the word (spoken in derision of the sacred Wit) being given, viz. *Increase and Multiply*, they fall to their lascivious imbraces. . . .

Worst of all a Ranter meal parodies communion: 'Ranters at dinner – one eating a piece of beef, tearing it asunder, said, "This is the flesh of Christ, take and eat."'[52] These are nothing but rather tame selections from the small but lurid repertoire of charges gathered together and analysed by Norman Cohn in *Europe's Inner Demons*. We meet these charges in more extensive form when considering the representation of Jews in medieval blasphemy. They come into the mainstream of western European culture by being used against the early Christians, and then by being adapted by Christian institutions to condemn Jews, Muslims, witches, sorcerers, libertines and heretics of all kinds. They – whoever they are – practise magic, imagined in whatever form magic is thought to take at a given place and time; they have orgiastic love-feasts, complete with idolatry and fetishism; and they indulge in ritual cannibalism by murdering small children and eating them in some reconstituted consecrated form. It is a discourse that is constant in form for the best part of a thousand years, and protean in its use. All its elements are fervently believed and, when joined together, equally and absolutely untrue.

That, at least, is Cohn's persuasive conclusion. He does not quite deny the existence of witches in the medieval period – that is, women who make spells or curse; he denies the validity of the representations of witchcraft coming from orthodox sources, and above all he rejects the sum that is made from the total of disparate elements. Cohn's examination of sources reveals forgery as well as delusion: the organised existence of witchcraft in the medieval and early modern periods is a contemporary construction of learned sources and prejudices, and also a later invention or imaginative reconstruction of evidence to make historical witch-hunts conform to a basis of historical fact. Cohn's argument is that the allegations made by witch-hunters of the sixteenth and seventeenth centuries have no historical basis. But his work also shows that they had a powerful discursive basis, and he talks of the collusion of those accused and the authorities in setting up the cultural frames that support a deep structure of inversion, the notion that all aberrant or divergent practices combine esoterically in a counter-culture that is the mirror-image of orthodoxy. This is just how exchange transactions work; and Ginzburg (1991) offers a strong re-reading of the discursive connections. The rise of witchcraft stereotypes entails the growing importance of demonology and the Devil, for on such a counter-image of irreligious authority a unified picture of inversion can be made to substitute for myriad and incoherent divergences.

There arise, in early modern charges and modern historiography, the simple notions of the witches' sabbaths and the Black Mass as supposedly linked practices. These are effectively gendered: the agents of evil in the sabbath tend to be women, and in the Black Mass they tend to be men, with women as their victims. Both are offered as signs of antecedent pagan ritual surviving in Christian culture. Cohn is not unduly sceptical about a range of folk practices throughout Europe; again, his concern is to reject the notion, the kind of conspiracy theory, that has them all related and, in macro-structure, homogeneous. In effect, however, the Black Mass cannot be any kind of pagan survival: it depends on a painfully literal inversion of the Christian sacrament, sometimes no more complex than saying words backwards, and Cohn would argue that the witches' sabbath is a similar construction. Cohn therefore alleges that historians have accepted fantasies and fictions as historical fact, and have accepted a burden of evidence that is clearly tainted by untruths.

It is, says Cohn, 'the historian's task to distinguish between fact and fantasy so far as is humanly possible' (p. 124). This is exemplary. Yet, as we have seen, there is a distinction between the historical basis of such charges and their discursive grounding. One of my current interests is in the discursive formations that allow such slander to thrive in different cultures, countries and times. In looking at just two cases – Fowles and Sedley – I have already found different subjects that lead to the two major stereotypes of (women) witches and (male) libertines. In these two figures lie most of the semiotic elements from which discourses of blasphemy are constructed. Certainly, it is discourse that should be under examination; it is no good listing static elements, such as incest and cannibalism, and asking whether they are learned or popular in origin, for what makes them dangerous is their activation within a common culture and discourse that use both popular and learned elements without being greatly concerned where they come from. How they come from a wide range of provenance and combine at different historical moments in over-determined discursive formations is a major concern of this book.

I have called Sedley's performance close to a parody of the discourse it alludes to and draws upon. The parody occurs at a time when such parody, more or less systematic, is becoming more possible at the level of discourse and institution, of writing and social practice. A generation or two later, in the eighteenth century, young Englishmen of Sedley's class and interests are able to live out a pastiche of orgy and devil worship in secret organisations like the Hell-Fire Club, and to do so midway between praxis and play. In late eighteenth-century France, at the time of the spectacular and violent dissolution of an *ancien régime*, the discourse is reinvented in the writings of the Marquis de Sade. One example will suffice: *Justine*, the book Maurice Blanchot calls the most scandalous ever written. A moral dilemma from the early stages of the book is reasonably typical. The heroine has been taken into the services of the Marquis de Bressac, and is given by him the commission to kill his mother. She refuses, and he counters that if she does not help him he will kill his mother in any case and ensure that she gets the blame. After unsuccessful appeals to him to change his mind, Justine offers a staged retreat, in order to convince him that she will do his bidding. No sooner does he outline the details of his plot, than he hears that 'an uncle of whom he never expected to be the heir has died and left him a fortune of 80,000 livres'.[53] Justine is led to exclaim: 'Is it in this manner that celestial justice punishes the plotting of criminals?' – a 'blasphemy' that she immediately kneels to beg God to forgive, hoping that the change in fortune will also change the heart of the Marquis. It does: with a Wildean swagger – 'I have told you twenty times, there is nothing like a preoccupation with crime for attracting good fortune' (pp. 142–3) – he accelerates his plans: his mother must die within two days. Justine of course informs the Comtesse, and so saves her life. Justine none the less expresses compunction at her 'perjury' towards the Marquis (p. 147). All is in vain: the Marquis detects that she has been unfaithful, and poisons his mother next morning. He takes Justine to the woods, where in the 1787 version she is whipped and in the 1797 version she is mauled by dogs, in one of Sade's grotesque and extended passages of prurient melodrama. She is tortured, naked, covered in blood, and denounced by her evil enemy as the murderer of his mother. All her virtue is frustrated, and the outcome is in inverse proportion to it. Yet she accepts it with Christian resignation:

'Oh God,' I cried. 'You have willed it. It was by Your decree that the innocent should once more become the prey of the guilty. Dispose of me as You will, Father, for I am yet far from the evil which You have suffered for us. Grant that those I endure while adoring You may render me worthy, one day, of those recompenses You have promised the weak – the weak who always keep You in mind in their tribulations, and whose glorify You in their anguish!' (pp. 152–3)

It is, I think, unlikely that a reader will read this without sensing irony. The suffering to which Justine has been exposed is the work of the evil Marquis, not God; it offends religion, and thrives; and we are told too that, though the Marquis is homosexual and was first seen buggering a servant in the woods (as if cruelty were not enough of a witness to his unnaturalness), Justine has fallen in love with him, so that her love for the Marquis and his treatment of her unsubtly shadows and travesties her moment of devotion.

The text frequently confronts religion, not least by allowing its evil characters to launch a sustained rhetorical attack on the very idea of God. Our sense of identity is formed in early childhood, and is not God-given, writes Sade in striking anticipation of Freud (p. 195):

If nature was offended by various tastes, she would avoid planting them in our breasts. (p. 197)

What will become . . . of your laws, ethics, religion, gibbets, paradise, God, and hell – when it is proved that a particular organisation of the nerves, a particular reaction in the body, a certain degree of acridity in the blood, makes man what he is, for better or for worse? (p. 195)

This is just what Clarkson the Ranter taught: that 'the very title sin is only a name without substance' (p. 117); 'I judged it was all a lie and that there was no devil at all, nor indeed no God, but only nature.'[54]

What Cohn calls the unconscious revolt against religion in the discourse of witch-hunting is made conscious and explicit in Sade; it is what holds Sade's text together. Towards the end of the book, Justine meets an old acquaintance, La Dubois, who repeats the lesson taught by the Marquis: 'For thirty years, a perpetual indulgence in vice and crime has led me step by step towards fortune' (p. 254). Aren't you afraid of the next world, counters Justine, and of the justice of God? She elicits the classic Sadean *credo*:

I believe that if there were a God there would be less evil on this earth. I also believe that if evil exists in our world, then its disorders are necessitated by this God, or it is beyond his power to prevent them. I can't be at all frightened of a God who is either weak or wicked.

Justine of course condemns these 'execrable sophisms' and 'odious blasphemies'. But the reader cannot doubt where wisdom lies, in spite of

Justine's adopted name of Sophie: in a text written and plotted by Sade, it lies, grotesquely and exaggeratedly, with the triumphs of evil. Still apologising for her blasphemy, Justine is led away to execution (p. 271); then at last she is recognised by her older sister Juliette, reprieved and apparently redeemed. Sade's contempt for such conventions of the novel is evident in the manner of her death soon after: killed as she closes a window by a thoroughly unscientific bolt of lightning that enters her mouth and leaves by her vagina. The righteous can never be saved, say the Ranters, inverting everything: 'the Godly shall go to hell, the wicked to Heaven'.[55]

In the 1797 version of *La nouvelle Justine et Juliette* the sorrowful reaction of Justine's sister is replaced by a scene of necrophiliac libertinism: Justine's body becomes the scene of Sade's most inventive version of a Black Mass. He recapitulates, and brings to a new level of blasphemous ingenuity, the type of orgy displayed by the religious order of the convent of Sainte Marie-des-Bois, whose brothers, intent on the service of the Virgin, seduce young girls at confession, maintain large numbers of them as prisoners for use in their numerous orgies (by giving them Father Antonin's magic contraceptive potion), and eventually kill them. The brothers practise the Black Mass: they dress one of their young girls in the vestments of the Virgin, 'and each of them inflamed his odious desires by submitting her to the irregularity of his caprice while she was thus clothed' (p. 214); they then stretch her naked on her belly on a large table, with candles and the image of Our Saviour at her head, and 'dare to consummate upon the loins of this unhappy creature, the most fearful of our mysteries'. Justine, watching, is so overwhelmed that she faints; this does not save her from becoming the table at another such feast. A note in Alan Hull Walton's unexpurgated English edition of 1965 insists: 'such masses were actually performed' (p. 214). For, as the anti-Ranter propaganda says, 'this is a known truth'.

We have not come as far as it may seem from Sedley, for Sade's work reconstructs the discourse of libertinism that Sedley's case implies, but goes much further in exploring the possibilities of a seriously irreligious subject position within it. Interest in Sade's work is historically close to interest in witchcraft. Montague Summers, for example, wrote with gaudy prurience on both. Georges Bataille, writing on orgiastic behaviour and ritual orgy in *Erotism*, insists on the historicity of the Black Mass and the Witches' Sabbath just as he introduces Sade as blasphemer: 'De Sade denied Evil and Sin. He even had frequent recourse to blasphemy. He sensed the silliness of profanation if the blasphemer denied the sacred nature of the Good that Blasphemy was intended to despoil, yet he went on blaspheming.'[56] Why, with such insight into the determining power of discourse, should Bataille have been so emphatic about the historical actuality of other elements in that discourse? We are back with Cohn's argument against Michelet, demonstrating that Michelet invents the 'black mass' in 1862 in his portrayal of witchcraft as 'a justified, if hopeless, protest by medieval serfs against the social order that was crushing them'.[57] Cohn is able to show that Michelet's invention, in a book written hastily over two months, does not come from historical sources. It is simply a re-imagining of the discourse of irreligious libertinism; and I do not doubt that one stimulus to Michelet's re-imagining was in fact his reading of Sade.

Cohn is right to show the unreliability of the so-called historical sources, and the fictitious nature of the construction of witchcraft from late medieval to modern times; but the discourse exists in history too, and it appears to be a strange function of this discourse itself that those who speak it should so often insist on its truth. There is now an interesting parallel in Ranter studies. J. C. Davis, in *Fear, Myth and History: The Ranters and the historians*, has argued strongly a thesis similar to Cohn's about witchcraft: 'the Ranters were not really a movement or even a collection of individuals known to each other with broadly similar ideas', but 'a creation of a sensation press in the early 1650s'.[58] Davis denies the Ranter identity except in the writing of their enemies. His book has been received in some circles as a form of blasphemy in its own right, drawing a heated response, for example, from E. P. Thompson. Nigel Smith argues that the issue is one of the relation between Ranters and other spiritual enthusiasts; 'if the Ranters were a fiction, they were one of their own as well as of others' making'.[59] Moreover, it is a truism that life imitates art; the very existence of a literary type will inspire imitation in actual practice, as in early twentieth-century suburban Black Masses.

Sedley's performance is therefore a product, an afterlife, of others' fiction. It is both a real event and a theatrical impersonation. It functions as a form of cultural transmission, drawing on discursive generality (the fear of libertinism) and historical specificity (the fear and practice of Ranterism). I do not think that I have over-read the possible significance of the Sedley case; one of the reasons that blasphemy is taken so seriously is that what is visible on the surface is always held to portend treacherous depths. What saved Sedley is indeed the ambiguous status of his performance, dangerous as this is: compared with Taylor's determined scraps of dogma, it looks unmotivated and otiose, suspended between language and event in a somewhat unreal area of the carnivalesque that we can call, in shorthand, play or game. It is unsettling, because blasphemy goes to show the constructed, discursive nature of fact and fiction, truth and falsehood. We read a similar type of disturbance and unreality in the texts of the Marquis de Sade, and it marks a conjunction between blasphemy and literature. But literature of this kind has the power of historical agency. What are its social and cultural implications?

In the subtexts of the two cases given detailed analysis so far, I have found most of the stereotypes that underlie the discourses of blasphemy: the allegations brought against the Templars in 1307, for instance, could have been compiled by the Marquis de Sade by way of a particularly censorious reading of Sedley with elements of overt sorcery and witchcraft added for good measure. That both examples came from the late seventeenth century is a fair indication of the significance I place on that period for key changes in the way blasphemy is regarded and treated (these are developed in Chapters 2 and 3); that both come from England is also not accidental – in view of the unique circumstances of Commonwealth and Restoration, which unleashed and then sharply restrained public sectarian divergences of behaviour and opinion. However, even in a schematic introduction such as this, there is need for an illustration of a different type of blasphemy: this time of blasphemy, unlike Sedley's or Fowles's, that is read as overtly heretical. Since before the Reformation accusations of blasphemy within the Church are commonly subordinate to those of heresy, I again take a case from after the Reformation, this time from Italy.

Menocchio (1532–1600)

To begin with, not only did he blaspheme 'beyond measure' but he also insisted that to blaspheme is not a sin (according to another witness, he had said that to blaspheme against the saints wasn't sinful, but to blaspheme against God was). He added sarcastically, 'Everybody has his calling, some to plow, some to hoe, and I have mine, which is to blaspheme.' He also said strange things, which the villagers reported in a more or less fragmentary and disconnected way to the vicar general: 'The air is God – the earth is our mother'; 'Who do you imagine God to be? God is nothing but a little breath, and whatever else man imagines him to be'; 'Everything that we see is God, and we are gods'; 'The sky, earth, sea, air, abyss, and hell, all is God'; 'What did you think, that Jesus Christ was born of the Virgin Mary? It's impossible that she gave birth to him and remained a virgin. It might very well have been this, that he was a good man or the son of a good man.' Finally, it was said that Menocchio possessed prohibited books, particularly the Bible in the vernacular: 'He is always arguing with one person or another, and he has the vernacular Bible and imagines that he bases his reasoning on it, and he remains obstinate in these arguments of his.'[60]

Carlo Ginzburg's book, *The Cheese and the Worms: The cosmos of a sixteenth-century miller* (1982) is one of the classics of modern historiography. It reconstructs from the extensive archives the trials before the Holy Office in 1584 and 1599 of Domenico Scandella known as Menocchio, the miller of Friuli. After his second trial, in either 1599 or 1600, Menocchio was put to death for 'having denied the virginity of the forever blessed Virgin Mary, the divinity of Christ Our Lord, and the providence of God' (p. 128). His condemnation occurs at almost exactly the same time as that of Giordano

Bruno: 'a coincidence that seems to symbolise the two-fold battle being fought against both high and low in this period by the Catholic hierarchy in an order to impose doctrines promulgated by the Council of Trent' (pp. 127–8). Both Menocchio and Bruno are victims of the Counter-Reformation and so of the revitalisation of discourses of blasphemy as a result of the Reformation.

In Menocchio's case, blasphemy – and his exculpatory attitude towards it – turn out to be keys to a personal system that is esoteric, obscure and eclectic. Ginzburg enthrallingly reconstructs it from the hints and mis-understandings of the trials. In the first place, Menocchio denies the Trinity, and adheres fully to the humanity of Christ. This is what he has in common with Bruno, who confesses that he is unable to understand or accept the doctrine of the Trinity, and both the arguments with which they support their views probably derive from Michael Servetus, the Spanish Catholic heretic burned in Calvin's Geneva (Chapter 2). Ginzburg claims that Menocchio's characterisation of the Holy Spirit as 'breath' accords well with Servetus's work, however 'feeble and disfigured' the echo of it may be. Ginzburg surmises that Menocchio had access to the (now lost) Italian translation of Servetus made in 1550; but in his judgement this does not support a case for Menocchio as a learned dissenter. In the reports of his fellow-villagers, Menocchio's opinions sound more atheistic than his presentation of them at his trials or Ginzburg's reconstruction would imply. And this has to do with that 'vocation to blaspheme' that Menocchio jokingly claims in the passage quoted.

There is the almost inevitable profane version of Christ's humanity that calls the Virgin Mary a whore: 'Oh how can you believe that Christ or God Almighty was the son of the Virgin Mary if the Virgin Mary was a whore?'; 'How can it be that Christ was conceived by the Spirit if he was borne by a whore?' (p. 102). This is just like Taylor's opinion discussed above. From a man who argues that blasphemy is not a sin because it hurts nobody, such provocation reveals a similar paradox of blasphemy to the one Bataille detects in the Marquis de Sade: if it really caused no offence, there would be no point in doing it. Ginzburg shows, for instance, that while many of Menocchio's opinions are held in common with Radical Anabaptists, others, such as his favourable view of sacraments and indulgences, are in sharp conflict with any known foreign model. Menocchio's ownership of the vernacular scriptures is significant, but so is his attitude to them: confuting the normal clerical fear of their availability to the laity, which is of a fundamentalism attacking the Church's teaching, Menocchio repudiates the doctrine and scriptural writings together, stating that 'Holy Scripture has been invented to deceive men' (p. 11). While this is highly individual, his anti-clericalism is a constant in almost all blasphemers, who contest authority against those who regard it as their monopoly. Wright's attack on the collusion of magistrate and minister in 1817 is, *mutatis mutandis*, entirely in keeping with Menocchio. Thus Menocchio's blasphemies are made up in part of his reading – his preparedness to be a free-thinker is itself a tribute to the dissemination of ideas that stemmed from the printing-press and its role in and against the Reformation; but the other part, such as his bizarre cosmogeny as signalled in his favourite image for the primal substance of creation, the cheese and the worms of Ginzburg's title, is oral in nature and testifies, according to Ginzburg, to 'the tenacious resistance of a peasant religion intolerant of dogma and ritual, tied to the cycles of nature, and fundamentally pre-Christian' (p. 25).

Ginzburg here counters one religion with another. There is no need to follow him in this. He is surely right to insist on the importance of oral tradition as a means of cultural transmission and several recent studies have added substance to accounts of non-dogmatic peasant beliefs in various parts of Europe. But there is no logical reason to see these as uncontamin-ated by or wholly alternative to Christianity, or to set them in a European common market of popular pantheism and make them add up into one 'peasant religion'. Menocchio's pantheism, as Ginzburg says, is a mixture of high and low, popular and learned, orthodox and heretical: 'it was not the book as such but the encounter between the printed page and the oral culture that formed an explosive mixture in Menocchio's head' (p. 51). I should argue that its very mixed quality is what makes it typical, and a useful example for this study: in Menocchio's case we find general characteristics of blasphemy mixed with highly context-specific ones in a way that usefully suggests how often we must work at the borders of oral and textual, learned and popular, religious and cultural, local and translocal. What Menocchio's case demonstrates are the limits of universality. These limits are geographi-cal as well as intellectual. One of Ginzburg's most surprising findings is that Menocchio may have read an Italian translation of the Qu'ran. If so, he may have turned to it, as did Servetus, with an interest fuelled by his rejecting the doctrine of the Trinity. In the case of Menocchio, we know from his account what book would have triggered his interest: *Mandeville's Travels*, the classic of armchair travel that became a favourite book throughout Europe after its composition in the mid-fourteenth century. The book divides into two parts, the first of which describes a pilgrimage to the Holy Land, with a good deal of geographical knowledge and encyclopaedic authority, the second of which describes the lands that lie outside and beyond Christendom. It is his awareness of such lands that turns Menocchio into an advocate of religious tolerance: God will save Jews and Muslims as well as Christians, and there is no need for them to be converted to effect their salvation. This is a recognition of cultural as well as religious differ-ence, and its inspiration lies in Mandeville's long accounts of Muhammad and Islamic beliefs, and the many other marvels that lie beyond the

Christian pale. In his written recantation of 1584 Menocchio gives as one of his reasons for error the fact that 'I read that book of Mandeville about many kinds of races and different laws, which sorely troubled me' (p. 88). The text of cultural difference lies at the root of blasphemy.

Mandeville's Travels visualises a world with Jerusalem as its geographical and spiritual centre, and on its margins many types of monstrous races derived from Pliny's *Historia Naturalis*, such as pygmies, giants, sciapods (people with a single huge foot with which they protect themselves from the sun), cynocephali (dog-headed people), blemyae (people without heads and with eyes in their chests). It is the world of late medieval maps, such as the Hereford map; and it is a cultural text, with its fantastic and sometimes disturbing edges, that forms a wider type or pattern.[61] The same text produces the later medieval psalters, books of hours and other manuscripts with extraordinary, free and carnivalesque designs in their margins. These marginal illustrations or *drolleries* have been described at length by Eco in *The Name of the Rose*, where they are taken to be a text of transgression that the blind monk Jorge kills to punish:

> This was a psalter in whose margins was delineated a world reversed with respect to the one to which our senses have accustomed us. As if at the border of a discourse that is by definition the discourse of truth, there proceeded, closely linked to it, through wondrous allusions in aenigmate, a discourse of falsehood on a topsy-turvy universe, in which dogs flee before the hare, and deer hunt the lion. . . . The entire margins of the book were invaded by minuscule forms that generated one another, as if by natural expansion, from the terminal scrolls of the splendidly drawn letters: sea sirens, stags in flight, chimeras, armless human torsos that emerged like slugs from the very body of the verses. At one point, as if to continue the triple 'Sanctus, Sanctus, Sanctus' repeated on three different lines, you saw three ferocious figures with human heads, two of which were bent, one downward and one upward, to join in a kiss you would not have hesitated to call immodest if you were not persuaded that a profound, even if not evident, spiritual meaning must surely have justified that illustration at that point.[62]

Around the sacred text, invading it and interacting with it, these marginal designs speak of another world of inversion or parody, or simply of difference. They are not to be appraised by modern concepts such as 'grotesque', 'surreal', or 'fantastic', as Michael Camille argues in his book *Images on the Edge: The margins of medieval art*; in what he calls their 'garbage-world' they test the limits and conventions of representation. But they are fundamentally the same text as the world maps, with a sacred centre and monstrous margins. Camille argues that the margins 'problematize authority while never totally undermining it', and that the centre is 'dependent upon the margins for its continued existence'.[63] That is why Eco uses such marginalia in *The Name of the Rose*: their possible meanings (humorous or blasphemous) become the visual equivalent of the heresy-hunting that occupies the historical centre of the novel, and the debate over both types of meanings extends into murder.

If *Mandeville's Travels* is one such text that has an open and tolerant attitude to its own and the world's margins, it does so only in one sort of reading, of which Menocchio's is representative. There is another type of reading altogether, and it is represented by those who put *Mandeville's Travels* to a use at once unexpected and predictable: explorers and colonisers. The book went with Columbus on all four voyages, and he refers to it frequently in his journals. The attempt to interpret what he saw in its light is all-consuming. There is much modern debate about what Columbus thought he was doing, and this is no place to add to it. There is a private religious dimension in his writing that supports and sometimes transcends the apocalypticism of his public progress. What is certain is that the world view of *Mandeville's Travels* helps dictate Columbus's choice of names: 'turkey' for an indigenous bird, 'West Indies' for islands off the coast of the mainland, 'Indians' for native peoples, and so on. As late as the seventeenth century de Bry's maps of the Amazon are still illustrated with one-breasted women and blemyae. They must be there because Mandeville says they are. *Mandeville's Travels*, and the tradition of monsters and marvels to which it gave new life, helped formulate the European response to the New World; what we now take to be fiction constituted its reality. The Spanish in Mexico called Aztec temples 'mosques' and treated the Mexican Indians as if they were Muslims. This is a different kind of reading of Mandeville's type of geography, one that sets off a process of stealing and missionary work, complementary yet often in conflict with each other, that leads in a generation to millions of deaths and the laments of Las Casas about the genocide wrought by his countrymen. It is a different reading of margins and of centres, as Mary Campbell argues acutely: 'Christianity is in fact the first western religion in which the sacred territory is located emphatically Elsewhere. So the notion of the Other is already exhausted: alien people are irrelevant or demonic.'[64]

The discourse evoked by such a reading is that of the Crusades. It is based on a strong desire to reclaim and recuperate the margins, and Defoe presents it well, if ironically, in *The Political History of the Devil*:

> nor has the Devil lost his hold in some parts of the world, nay, not in most parts of the world to this day; he holds still all the eastern parts of Asia, and the southern parts of Africa, and the northern parts of Europe, and in them the vast countries of China and Tartary, Persia and India, Guinea, Ethiopia, Zanquebar, Congo, Angola, Monomotapa &c, in all which, except Ethiopia, we find no vestiges of any other worship but that of idols, monsters and even the devil himself; till after the very coming of our Saviour, and even then, if it be true that the Gospel was preached in the Indies and China by

St Thomas, and in other remote countries by other of the apostles; we see that whatever ground Satan lost, he seems to have recovered it again; and all Asia and Africa is at present overrun with Paganism or Mahometanism, which I think of the two is rather the worst; besides all America, a part of the world, as some say, equal in bigness to all the other, in which the devil's kingdom was never interrupted from its first being inhabited, whenever it was, to the first discovery of it by the European nations in the sixteenth century.[65]

For Menocchio, then, *Mandeville's Travels* and the reports of the New World occasioned a growing sense of cultural relativism and become arguments for tolerance. That is the response of Montaigne too, in his essay 'On Cannibals'. It is not that of the colonisers and the religious orthodoxy with which they march. But there is common cultural ground in both camps, the culturally tolerant and the Crusaders: a fascination with cannibalism. For religious orthodoxy, it is the worst fear: the hellish horror of the New World, and later, as Captain Cook will report, of the South Seas, is its cannibals. The cannibalism discovered by the colonisers was real and their attempts to suppress it often unsuccessful. Friars in Mexico tried to teach the Lord's Prayer, Pater Noster, by using words of equivalent sound in the local language, '*pantli*' and '*nochli*'; words which, unknown to the friars, described the joys of eating the fruit of human flesh, and so unknowingly represented Christianity as itself a ritual of cannibalism.[66] Stephen Greenblatt would argue that it is: cannibalism was actually feared as a travesty of the Mass, and is the hidden agenda of the colonisers themselves, who cannibalised all cultures. A prurient horror of cannibalism goes hand in hand in the early explorers with a conviction that the natives idolised them: Columbus smugly keeps recording that he was taken to be a god. Captain Cook, who was fascinated and repelled by cannibalism and human sacrifice in the South Seas, nevertheless encouraged Hawaiians to regard him as a god – with the direct consequence that he was killed and almost certainly then cannibalised by them. The poet William Cowper regarded this as divine retribution on Cook, punishment for his blasphemous pretensions. What is important is that Cowper could recognise the discourse of blasphemy when he saw it in action. The fear of cannibalism did not require the discovery of actual cannibals to feed it. It existed in Chapter 148 of *Mandeville's Travels*, the reading of which led Menocchio to leap to the conclusion that 'when the body dies, the soul dies too, since out of many different nations, some believe in one way, some in another' (p. 47).

Cannibalism exists in Mandeville, as it exists in much medieval art, because it is a fear that existed in the European psyche long before Europeans met cannibals in any new world. It is a fear hidden at the heart of the old world. De Bry closed his collection of plates from the New World with two depictions of ancient Britons and a text that brought out their savagery and cannibalism.[67] When the writer of *Mandeville's Travels* wanted a climactic description of the most fearful savages imaginable he borrowed from the Roman historian Tacitus a description of his own ancestors, the ancient Germanic tribes. If the centre depends upon the margins, it is also a model for them.

Cannibalism, which Montaigne and Menocchio read as the open sign of cultural relativity, is the strongest of all stereotypes of blasphemy: Jews, for example, eat Christian children ground up into Passover matzos (Chapter 3). The discourse of blasphemy and that of colonialism are therefore related: practically, it is a conviction that native cultures are blasphemous *per se* that silently licenses their destruction. The biblical *locus classicus* of blasphemy is Leviticus 24, where the offender is a stranger to the Jewish rules he has transgressed. Moses rules that he must nevertheless die in the Jewish way, by stoning. There is no sense of cultural relativity in the discourse of blasphemy. So both blasphemy and colonialism have to do with the treatment of strangers. If the care of strangers is a test of civilisation, blasphemy and colonialism are discourses implacably uncivilised, pushing back the point of amicable co-existence into utopia, the apocalyptic nowhere where lions lie down with lambs. If, as Michael Ignatieff argues in *The Needs of Strangers*, the care of strangers 'gives us whatever fragile basis we have for saying that we live in a moral community', then the business of blasphemy and colonialism is to construct amoral communities.[68] They are discourses for constructing alterity, discourses of the centre for conferring marginality. Menocchio, like Montaigne, resists them with a single tool: reading, but a different kind of reading from theirs – reading from the margin. He is right to connect two positions: if cultures and religions are relative, then blasphemy is no sin.

Chapter 2

CARNIVALISING BLASPHEMY
Christians and Their Enemies

Those who would spare heretics and blasphemers are themselves blasphemers.

JOHN CALVIN in Bainton (1953): 170

The body believes in what it plays at: it weeps if it mimes grief. It does not represent what it performs, it does not memorize the past, it enacts the past, bringing it back to life. What is 'learned by the body' is not something that one has, like knowledge that can be brandished, but something that one is.

PIERRE BOURDIEU (1990): 73

BLASPHEMY TO HERESY AND BACK

I have argued that blasphemy exists as an interchange, an exchange transaction, and as a discourse of alterity that is not fully controlled by its users. One might say that the users of the discourse are on one side of an exchange transaction with the discourse itself. The alleged blasphemer may be quite innocent of an intention to blaspheme, or may have set out to do just that; in the first case the response that registers blasphemy will appear as a misreading of one sort of discourse in the light of another; in the second case, the way that the blasphemy is received is likely to differ from the way that it is intended. The more complex the discourse, the more possibility for a multiple and even exponential sequence of misreadings and mutual misunderstandings. The history of blasphemy is one of increasing complexity: from being a single and well-defined act, as in the Jewish Bible, to being a multiplicity of acts, or even no act at all but a state of being. In the Christian tradition blasphemies do not come singly; and, as the case studies of Chapter 1 show, one sort of blasphemy is taken to imply others, so that the issue becomes no longer a criminal act but a moral degeneracy that occasions such acts. This chapter explores the broadening and diffusion of blasphemy in Christian culture, and its distinctive importance. It does so by counterpointing shifts in the Bible and doctrinal controversies in early

Christianity with their discursive repetition and reshaping as a result of the Reformation.

I have written in the previous chapter of monoculturalism and multiculturalism. I should insist that these terms are never absolute. Cultural relativism is itself relative. Monoculturalism may well be constructed out of the meeting of several cultures or languages, as is the Trinitarianism of the early Church, and multiculturalism hardly ever signifies harmonious existence or inter-relation, if only because it keeps running into various questions of blasphemy. Institutions may be one or other at different stages of their historical development: the history of the early Christian Church, for example, passes from an apparently multicultural desire for religious tolerance in the Roman Empire through a mixed phase in which the Church redefines itself more sharply by way of creed and doctrine, into a monocultural phase of control within the Empire marked by an intolerance of opposition. What this progress traces is a shift of subject position within the discourse of blasphemy, from defending oneself against others' charges to being an accuser in one's own right – same discourse, different position. Multiculturalism, then, may be only a sign of relative weakness. In this guise, it may conceal a form of fundamentalism that, in strength, will seek to inhibit its rivals. The wish to compete against a monopoly may well contain the wish to become a new monopoly rather than any real desire for dialogue.

When Sebastian Castellio responds to the burning of Michael Servetus in 1553 by compiling and publishing his work *Concerning Heresies* and arguing for a religious tolerance grounded in an authentic pluralism, he is the author of a decisive cultural innovation. The multiculturalism he propounds is obviously different from that defensively upheld by the early Church, though both are a response to religious persecution. Even here, Castellio stops short of commending total tolerance.

> But heretics hurt others. I know it, and I shall be glad to see all real heretics and enemies of the truth dead, if they do not amend. But what shall we do? The tares hurt the wheat, but to pull them up before the harvest is to pull also the harvest.

Castellio realises that the formulation of blasphemy differs from one time to the next, and this leads to his wonderful anticipation of Dostoevsky's story of the Grand Inquisitor in *The Brothers Karamazov*:

> If the churches do have Scribes and Pharisees, then let Christ come when He will and they will say again as of yore, 'He has blasphemed'. They will always have power and be approved of the people as they formerly were. Thus the truth will be repudiated until the light of the Lord discloses them. If we pass a law to put false prophets to death, certainly Christ Himself will be killed with His followers. They will be done to death before they are recognised. But they ought to be known before they are killed.[1]

This position is probably more like Ernest Gellner's 'rational fundamental-ism' than what Gellner dismissively calls 'cultural relativism':[2] Castellio does not want to abandon the notion of absolute truth, but he accepts that it is often unknown, or that it is not known in time. Nevertheless, his acceptance is based on a realisation of cultural difference and historical change. Castellio's militant championing of religious tolerance as a positive value is itself such a change – it is unlike anything in the Christian tradition before him. It is an attack on the discourse of blasphemy itself, a refusal to engage with any subject positions it offers. Whereas the Reformation revives and revitalises the discourse, its aftermath, as seen in Castellio's work, breaks with it. Since the tolerance is grounded in the idea that persecutors mistake transient cultural standards for eternal truths, Castellio offers an identifiably new form of cultural relativism.

The doctrinal breaking point is the doctrine of the Trinity – that is, the doctrine that in orthodox terms sets out the nature of God. Dissent from it is a prime occasion of blasphemy. In Judaism, the nature of God is concealed in the name of God, which it is blasphemy to utter. In Christianity, the name and the nature are fixed in words, in doctrine and in creed. But the question remains one of verbal propriety, what it is orthodox to utter about God. Blasphemy extends not only to the name and nature of God but to the representation of the divine. One might say, therefore, Castellio opens God up to cultural change. That is why he denies the usefulness of blasphemy, knowing that it will be found by some readers in his work.

Blasphemy is always in process, and the terms used to describe it are in a state of constant movement – moving, that is, as often and unpredictably as belief itself moves. Another key term should be seen as equally contingent: marginality. For there are times when the 'margins' are either metaphorical or ideological, marking the notion of an invisible limit, say, that the blasphemer oversteps. At other times they are more literal: Christendom is always a geographically limited universal, and the concern for its frontiers, especially against Islam, is strong. There is still ideological determination here – Christianity remains at the centre after the fall of the Crusader kingdom of Jerusalem, but the sense of the margins' impingement becomes more pressing. Indeed, the possibility that the margins may exert influence is real for both orthodox and heterodox. We need the notion of the 'anomalous' from Deleuze and Guattari to supplement that of the marginal: the anomalous are those who are on the margins because they are in the vanguard, and they succeed in changing the direction of the centre. Most heretics, for example, set out to be anomalous, and it is orthodoxy's concern to keep them merely marginal. The New Testament represents itself as the triumph of the anomalous, and the history of the early Church is a complex and volatile contest between anomaly and marginality.

If one of the major sites of blasphemy is the nature and representation of

God, another is the institution that regulates belief: in a word, law. The discourse of blasphemy functions in opposition to fundamentalism or monoculturalism among those who would be anomalous, and in alignment with them among those others who would keep the first group marginal. For the latter, those who would confirm marginality by assigning blasphemy, the discourse of blasphemy is one that would do something Castellio states he cannot, it would give its reading the force of law. In Latin, there is a close etymological relationship that exposes the semantic link in other languages: the reader (*lector*) is the reflex of law (*lex*). Law is taught by doctors, whose views become doctrines, ideas turned into law. Law is by nature territorial. Blasphemy is therefore a means of marking territory, as in the Jewish geographical space, or of claiming it, as the early Christians did, or of fighting to keep it, as in the Reformation.

The following chapters do not offer an account of a stable discourse in historically changing circumstances. They do indeed testify to the limited repertory of types and stereotypes that make up the discourse, but that only serves to sharpen the contrast with the unpredictability of their employment, and the way in which different uses change not only their nature but that of the entire discourse in the various permutations of law, representation, subjectivity and alterity. In the account of discursive generalities and historical specificities, both are in mutual flux. I try to characterise determinations and determinisms, both major innovations and grand repetitions. This chapter looks at the Christian development of blasphemy and its revival in the Reformation, and reopens the still uncomfortable issue of Jewish guilt. Chapter 3 deals with later medieval blasphemy in terms of community and representation, and Chapter 4 with attempts from the seventeenth century to modern times to use blasphemy as a legal means for attacking cultural and religious difference and regulating subjectivity. Chapter 5 then gives a long textual account of a creatively modern blasphemy, deregulating subjectivity, and Chapter 6 explores the limits of such creativity and returns to the politics of reading at the level of community and culture. I recognise that my account contributes to the rhetoric it describes. That is why I view it primarily as a textual study rather than a history, and why I have emphasised the provisionality of its terms. I argue in later chapters that my difficulties of description are primarily to do with the state of the discourse in the light of modern uncertainty about terms such as community and culture.

There is no such uncertainty in the Jewish Bible. Blasphemy is a transgression of the third commandment, against profanation of the name of God. The commandment is not merely a proscription of cursing, though this is what the Talmud emphasises; it applies to irreverence, at times even to the use of the divine name. The Christian distinction between 'proper' and 'loose' swearing has no Jewish counterpart. ('You shall not revile God, nor curse the ruler of your people', Exodus 22: 28.) The offence of blasphemy encompasses idolatry (as in Ezekiel 20: 27, where in whoring after their strange gods and serving 'wood and stone . . . your fathers have blasphemed me'), sacrilege (as in the destruction of temples in Psalm 74:10), and treason, though this is a dubious connection, in that Jezebel's charge of blasphemy against Naboth is a trumped up one: 'Now didst blaspheme God and the King' (ɪ Kings 21: 10). In the Jewish Bible, unlike the New Testament or the Christian tradition, no blasphemy is repeated in the text of the Scripture. We are told of stoning, and of the rending of garments with which blasphemy is correctly greeted, but never of the substance of the blasphemy, as if to repeat it is to do further damage and to transgress equally. Blasphemy is an offence and threat to an entire community. That is why those present at a blasphemer's trial must help carry out the sentence, stoning to death as a means of communal atonement. Any injury to the dignity, law and observance of the one true God may be blasphemous, as in Ezekiel 20: 27 and in ɪɪ Samuel 12: 14, where Nathan reproaches David for stealing the wife of Uriah the Hittite and arranging Uriah's death: 'by this deed thou hast given great occasion to the enemies of the LORD to blaspheme'. But the Talmud insists that the name of God must be spoken for blasphemy to occur. The connection between the name of God and the act of language is primary: 'my name continually every day is blasphemed. Therefore shall my people know my name: therefore they shall know in that day I am he that doth speak: behold, it is I. . . .' (Isaiah 52: 5–6).

'I am he that doth speak.' As Elaine Scarry asserts so cogently, the God of the Jewish Bible is voice not body; the Christian Bible takes that voice, eventually Hellenises it as the *Logos* of John 1, and turns God into Body.[3] Blasphemy in Christianity passes from being a cognate human challenge to the nature of God, voice raised against voice, to a form of invective that openly or tacitly disputes the unity of body and the divine in Christian revelation. In John 10, Jesus is accused by Jews of blasphemy: 'for a good work we stone thee not, but for blasphemy, and because thou, being a man, maketh thyself God'. Jesus replies with the strategic articulation of the blasphemy with which he is accused: 'Say ye of him, whom the father hath sanctified, and sent into the world, Thou blasphemest; because I said, I am the Son of God?' (John 10: 33–6). The Scribes and the Pharisees are presented in all four gospels as assembling a case against Jesus based on their conviction that he is a blasphemer. 'This man blasphemeth' (Matthew 9: 3); 'why doth this man thus speak blasphemies? who can forgive sins but God only?' (Mark 2: 7); 'Who is this which speaketh blasphemies?' (Luke 5: 21). Their determination to put him to death is presented as the outcome of this conviction: 'Ye have heard the blasphemy: what think ye?' (Mark 14: 64); 'then the high priest rent his clothes, saying, He hath spoken blasphemy:

1. William Blake, *The Blasphemer*, water-colour, Tate Gallery.

what further need have we of witnesses? behold, now ye have heard his blasphemy' (Matthew 26: 65).

The gospels serve to reverse the relation of accusers and accused: those who invoke blasphemy are to be convicted of it. In case this is not clear from the reading of the gospels, it is reprised in the death of Stephen in Acts (a relation acknowledged by the early Church's placement of St Stephen's Day immediately after Christmas): Stephen is accused of speaking 'blasphemous words' against Moses and against God, 'against this holy place and the law' (Acts 6: 13). Stephen is given a speech in his defence that sums up a Christian reading of the entire Jewish Bible and makes of it the preamble to Christ's appearance as God in human body; he is then stoned – 'and Saul was consenting unto his death' (Acts 8: 1). The subsequent conversion of Saul, and his name change to Paul, mark the decisive victory for Christianity in the fight for textual control of blasphemy. Paul, 'who was before a blasphemer and a persecutor, and injurious' (1 Timothy 1: 13) publicly confesses his old persecutions of Christians: 'And I punished them oft in every synagogue, and compelled them to blaspheme' (Acts 26: 11). Blasphemy is now redefined as insistence on the letter of the Jewish law, the letter that slays as opposed to the spirit that liberates: the Romans who insist on circumcision (Romans 2: 24) are blasphemers. This is consistent with the teaching of Jesus in Matthew 15: 18–20: it is language, coming from the perverted heart, that brings the stain of sin, not breaches of rules of bodily practice:

> But those things which proceed out of the mouth come forth from the heart, and they defile the man. For out of the heart proceed evil thoughts, murders, adulteries, fornications, theft, false witness, blasphemies. These are the things which defile a man: that he eat with unwashen hands defileth not a man.

At the very time that the divine enters the human body, it insists on the primacy of the spirit. Jesus introduces a new and inexcusable category of blasphemy that is more serious than blasphemy against himself:

> All manner of sin and blasphemy shall be forgiven unto man; but blasphemy against the Holy Ghost shall not be forgiven unto man. And whosoever speaketh against the Son of Man it shall be forgiven him: but whosoever speaketh against the Holy Ghost, it shall not be forgiven him, neither in this world, neither in the world to come. (Matthew 12: 31–2; cf. Mark 3: 29, Luke 12: 11)

This is the 'sin unto death' of 1 John 5: 16: but what is it? Among other things, it is a test of faith: the need to ask is an index of failure. Instead of a law about the divine name, blasphemy becomes a series of textual cruces about the divine nature: the man/God, God in a body. Writing, the letter and the law, signify the absence of the body; the Spirit affirms its presence.

But one aspect of the letter is denotation. The meaning of words is undermined by the spirit. Definitions tumble into strategic incoherence. The blasphemy against the Holy Ghost is never defined – it is unspeakable, and (without grace) unknowable. However, if blasphemy is rewritten, so is the body. I would argue that this rewriting occurs in one related and protracted process of carnivalisation.

Carnivalisation, in Bakhtin's terms, is demonstrable. First, the definition of blasphemy is blown up to gigantic proportions, to the point that it becomes both all-encompassing and inscrutable. Among the early Christians there were probably many who thought of themselves as Jews, and it took more than one generation for the separation of Jewish and Christian identities to be accepted as necessary and irreversible. The Roman war against the Jews, and the destruction of Jerusalem in 70, was probably crucial. Over time, then, Jews as a group become what the roles of Scribes and Pharisees in the gospel suggest, enemies of the Christians at a communal level. The augmented discourse of blasphemy is turned increasingly against them: Jews are the proto-blasphemers. In the letter to Smyrna at the beginning of Revelation, God is represented as saying: 'I know the blasphemy of them that say they are Jews, and are not, but are the synagogues of Satan' (Revelation 2: 9). It is not a huge step from claiming that some Jews are false Jews who serve Satan to say that all of them are; and the step probably occurs during the course of early Christians' reading of Revelation, whether that was originally a Christian text or not. At any rate, the enemies of true believers – though they are never named – are rejected en masse, as a body, and reconstituted textually in a monstrous carnival body of the beast with 'seven heads and ten horns, and upon his horns ten crowns, and upon his heads the name of blasphemy' (Revelation 13:1). The beast, whose number is 666, has worldly authority and power over all whose names are not written in the Book of Life. His authority is blasphemy, and his is the power to blaspheme:

> and there was given unto him a mouth speaking great things and blasphemies, and power was given unto him to continue forty and two months. And he opened his mouth in blasphemy against God, to blaspheme his name, and his tabernacle, and them that dwell in heaven.

This gigantic and grotesque Body has mouths that emit poisons and evils, mouths that are really venomous orifices.

However, the need to carnivalise one's enemies as a Body, albeit a perverted one, is related to a review of the body in its role in Christianity itself: the grotesque Body of the Beast is a counterpart to and reflex of the ideal body of Christian believers, the Body of Christ. This is an inevitable consequence of the simultaneity with which Jesus is held to be man and God. For his is a body both unlike any other and held to be like everyone else's: the son of God the Father, he nevertheless takes flesh from the Virgin

Mary; he dies like any other mortal on the Cross, but rises again from the dead. In what body is he resurrected? The New Testament insists that he rises in a real flesh-and-blood body, touchable by the doubting Thomas. Yet this is a real body unlike any other, for it is no longer mortal or corruptible. In this new form, Jesus then ascends to heaven. In what sort of form does he enter heaven – in his human body, or some other form? Does he retain his human body, and if not, what happened to it (since it did not die)? If so, how can he remain of the same substance as his Father, who sent him into his human body? Even without these complications, Christianity has already transformed the human body, for it promises that its central characteristics, mortality and corruptibility, will be waived for all Christian believers too: a body that rises from the dead is not the body we know, but a radical rewriting of it. We have arrived at a difficult area of Christian belief, where Stanley Spencer has graves opening all over Cookham churchyard and sprightly suburbanites rising again in their prime and their Sunday best. The apocalyptic Beast is no more transformed in the direction of the grotesque than is the body of believers in that of the ideal, and the carnival representation of the bad thus serves to reflect and stabilise the image of the good. The body of Christ has a threefold significance for believers. First, the nature of that body in and out of history opens up questions of belief that cannot easily be solved: particularly the question of its partaking in the same substance as God the Father. Secondly, the body of Christ is amplified into a Mystical Body, which is the ideal counterpart of the carnivalesque Grotesque Body; it too is drawn to gigantic proportions and becomes full of openings, in order to receive the believers who live in it. If the carnival Body could be other than grotesque, one might want to call this Body carnivalised. Thirdly, the solidarity of that Mystical Body which is the Church is guaranteed by sacramental communion with itself in the form of Bread: the Body of Christ is held together by the body of Christ. There is the closest possible connection in the semiotics of Christianity between debates about Christ's substance and debates about his substantiation: the Trinity and the Eucharist march together from the great Councils, beginning with that of Nicaea in 325, to the Reformation.

The Council of Nicaea begins a new phase in the life of the Church, one of universality and doctrine – it is one that therefore focuses on heresy rather than blasphemy. For the first three hundred years of its life, Christianity was overtly multicultural and multilingual. Thus elements of Hebrew Scripture such as messiahship and the Servant of the book of Isaiah are reworked in Hellenic form into the gospel presentation of Jesus as the son of God, and questions about the nature of God then pass into Greek. But Christianity moves into separate linguistic directions: by the time of the Nicene Council, just over half the bishops could speak Greek and the rest spoke Latin. Early formulations of the godhead's identity by Greek fathers such as Origen become suspect in the Latin West. There are semantic differences between Origen's term *hypostasis* and the closest equivalent Latin term *persona*, which gives the term for the Three Persons of the Trinity. In due course, the entire theology of orthodoxy, including the decisions of the Nicene Council, will have to be reworked by Augustine in his *De Trinitate* into a Latin form culturally palatable to Western orthodoxy. Until Nicaea, too, Christianity has a pronounced *local* character. Individual churches are in communion and correspondence with each other, but they vary both in their ritual and in their doctrine, for each has its own teacher – Origen in Alexandria, Eusebius in Caesarea, and so forth, with the result that orthodoxy varies mildly or wildly from place to place. Moreover, all this goes on in an intellectual climate by no means a stranger to controversy, friendly or otherwise, but in which Pauline teaching on letter and spirit encourages a non-doctrinal identity. These factors all work to establish a common trend. When there are major differences between one local teacher and another, or major differences emerge in different Christians' sense of what being a Christian is about, subsequent dispute will invoke blasphemy as much as, or more than, heresy. Accusations of heresy and blasphemy run together throughout Christian history, and heresy is the more specialised charge. In the early Church, with its pronounced local character, difference is seen as much affectively, as a defamation of Christ or a profanation of the faith, or indeed as apostasy or treason, as it is dogmatically, as heretical doctrine. When the Church begins to work universally, by council, heresy-hunting maps more intellectually the rhetorical and moral high ground formerly occupied by accusations of blasphemy. Being a Christian is now assessed by doctrinal speech-acts, creeds.[4]

The oldest universal creed of the Church, the Apostles' Creed, is little more than a narrative digest and harmony of the gospels, without new doctrine. The Nicene Creed, on the other hand, is a doctrinal reworking of the Christian message. Its current position for public recitation at Mass/Communion was first used in 471 by Peter, bishop of Antioch, and in the West in Toledo in 589. The position does no more than clarify its pre-eminence in the Church. It owes this entirely to an unexpected circumstance: a dream that convinces the Emperor Constantine that he has been given victory in war by the God of the Christians, with the result that he declares Christianity the state religion of the Empire. Constantine is largely uninterested in doctrine; like many politicians, however, he places a premium on consensus and the strength that comes with group solidarity. It is Constantine who calls the Nicene Council, who gives it a deadline, and who requires of it that its decisions, whatever they may be, be unanimous. At that time the major dispute is that between Trinitarians and what in modern times one would call unitarians, of whom the foremost was Arius. For Arius Christ was the Son of God, and with the Holy Spirit was divine, not by his essential nature but by the grace of God. God was pre-eminent, and ground of all being. Jesus was a creature, made by his Creator, though a perfect one; and he had a beginning in his creation. The notion that Jesus was without limits was introduced into the Creed to confute this, in the phrase translated by Cranmer (and omitted from the 1549 prayer-book) as 'whose kingdom shall have no end'. Probably very few modern Christians understand that the Creed they use contains such esoteric references to and refutations of doctrines long ago judged heretical. In the so-called Athanasian Creed of the sixth century, for example, which fully articulates the doctrine of 'one God in Trinity, and Trinity in Unity', one verse answers the heresies of Sabellius and Arius ('Neither confounding the Persons nor dividing the Substances'), and the most difficult part of the Creed doctrinally answers at least six different heresies about the nature of Jesus. The first relevant verse on Jesus as God and man, 'God of the Substance of the Father, begotten before the worlds', answers Arius, as does the third, 'equal to the Father, as touching his Godhead: and inferior to the Father, as touching his Manhood'. The next verse, 'Who although he be God and Man yet he is not two, but the Christ', responds to the Nestorians, and the second verse of the sequence, 'Perfect God, and Perfect Man: of a reasonable soul and flesh subsisting', is meaningless without a knowledge of three early heresies – the Ebeonite (Christ was not perfect God but perfect man), the Docetan (vice versa), and that of Apollinarius, who denied the 'reasonable soul'.

It would be entirely untrue to say that 'Christianity' had remained unmoved by such dissident views before Constantine. On the contrary, all were hotly controverted. It was rather that Constantine brought Christianity as we know it into existence by executive order: the universal Church, overriding local differences and controversies, and progressively monolithic in faith and practice. In order to be any of these things, the institution as a whole could not accept vast differences of the order such issues indicate, especially when relating to the nature of Christ himself, and so to the very core of the faith. What happened at the Nicene Council is instructive. The majority of bishops sought a politic compromise, but Constantine himself was influenced by the enemies of Arius, led by Bishop Alexander, and would accept only Alexandrian-sounding compromises. The Council therefore took refuge in one word, '*homoousios*', which means 'of co-substance', and referred to Jesus as 'Being of one Substance with the Father, By whom all things were made'. This seemed a clever compromise, since it failed to arbitrate on the question of whether Christ was created con-substantial by his Father, who in co-substance made everything. In fact, a century later the ecclesiastical history of Socrates Scholasticus of Constantinople records the further strife caused by the new formula, which seemed not unlike a contest in the dark; for neither party appeared to understand distinctly the grounds on which they calumniated one another. Those who objected to the word *homoousios*, conceived that those who approved it favoured the opinion of Sabellius and Montanus; they therefore call them blasphemers, as subverting the existence of the Son of God. And again the advocates of this term, charging their opponents with polytheism, inveighed against them as introducers of heathen superstitions.

Socrates is struck by the level of misunderstanding involved, and registers that both sides admitted 'that the son of God has a distinct person and existence, and all acknowledged that there is one God and three Persons, yet from what case I am unable to divine, they could not agree among themselves, and therefore could in no way endure to be at peace'.[5] Socrates already has the air of one from a newer generation to whom such controversies seemed mannered and absurd. Presumably that is because the Nicene Creed for Socrates and his generation had fulfilled its purpose: it had become a given. Yet to some at the Council it must have seemed that Christianity itself was freely entering into error, removing any credal reference to Jesus as the Word of John 1 and leaving the Holy Spirit – whose existence was invoked as God's intermediary between time and eternity and, during the lifetime of Jesus, as go-between with his Son – seemingly as a brief afterthought. Presumably, too, opinion varied then as it varies now. The Anglican Church historian M. F. Wiles argues that 'the primary emphasis of the second and third centuries was the demonstration of the distinct existence of the three persons of the godhead'. Another ecclesiastical historian, G. L. Bray, responds: 'on the contrary, it is not difficult to show that the first and fundamental concern of all the patristic writers was to preserve a pure monotheism'.[6] It all depends whether one stresses Trinity in Unity or Unity in Trinity.

Why three? One answer is: in order for there not to be two. To claim Christ is divine necessitates two, and the third agency moving between Heavenly Father and earthly Son, an agency that had already spoken of the Son through the Prophets, makes for a cohesion that is less conducive to any semblance of God as a split subject. Most of the parties engaged in bitter controversy would have concurred not only on the major doctrines listed by Socrates Scholasticus but also on a keen sense of the salvific purpose of Christ's ministry in a successful and hegemonic divine plan. They would have united against the Hellenising Gnostics of the second century, who believed in the dualism of matter and spirit, and believed that only Spirit could become immortal through resurrection. Since God was Spirit, and matter is evil, he was not the author of Creation, and Jesus, though a deity of sorts, was neither his son nor immortal. It is the saviour who moved Adam and Eve to eat the fruit 'of the tree of acquaintance with good and evil, and which is the afterthought of the light', in order that the spirit should not be totally divorced from light. Sexual intercourse is the defilement of life by matter, and its first two fruits, Cain and Abel, are really the two gods of the Old Testament, Elohim the unjust (with 'the face of a bear') and Yahweh the just (with 'the face of a cat').[7] No wonder that Gnosticism gets called blasphemous – Origen, for example, objects to its doctrine of metempsychosis as 'blasphemous tales'. Trinitarianism is itself a response to dualism. The disputants at the Nicene Council or the Council of Constantinople would have agreed in condemning all such Gnostic ideas as absolute blasphemies. The ones who ended up being condemned may well have felt with some justice that Christianity itself had changed not a little around them: certainly, it had never drawn such lines of doctrine around itself as the secular power enabled it to do, and even insisted that it did. So these were people who regarded themselves as orthodox or who set out to be anomalous, intending to take orthodoxy with them, and on whom marginality and exclusion were visited as the sentence of power.

Such factional warfare had begun with allegations and counter-allegations of blasphemy, but the change in political circumstances and the doctrinal tools for their resolution converted the intra-mural discourse of the medieval Church from the fourth century into that of heresy and blasphemy together, the province of the absolutely marginal: non-Christians, such as Jews and Arabs, and those who excluded themselves from basic Christian beliefs as enshrined in the creeds, those who denied the Trinity or that the elements of the Eucharist turned into the body and blood of Christ. That is why Levy reasonably moves quickly from the early Church to the Reformation, and why I feel justified in emulating him with one or two major differences. I find the discourse of blasphemy, even more than that of heresy, in the response to Wycliff's view of the Eucharist, and I shall trace the uses of blasphemy in later medieval persecutions of the Jews.

I hope that I shall not offend some Christian readers of this book by adding that in my view the orthodox doctrines on the Trinity and on the Eucharistic elements are themselves carnivalesque. They are extensions of Tertullian's *Credo quia absurdum*; indeed, their major attraction as doctrine is their palpable absurdity. This seems to me strategic. A body that emerges out of bread and wine is not an ordinary kind of body: it foregrounds not the corporeal nature of the man-God but the transformation of all believers' bodies, and the body of belief, that his death and resurrection signify. The believers' attention is thereby encouraged to shift to mystical reading of the body itself, through questions of figuration to those of transfiguration. Similarly, the very difficulty of three in one and one in three stresses the supplement that is the Godhead of the God-man. The doctrine minimises the risk that God the Father will be visualised as a man like the incarnate Jesus, with a side to be pierced and legs to be broken. There is something uncanny about the resurrected Jesus and his symbols in the upstairs room, breaking the bread that is his body and showing his humanity by eating bread and fish that elsewhere symbolise himself. What kind of God/man is this who returns from the dead in order to consume his own body? The verbal difficulty stretches definition out of the range of normal semantic competence, it turns the divine into a series of monumental, identical yet asymmetrical and unfathomable bodies. I take it that this is a metamorphosis of the carnivalesque that comes from, and is supported by, discourses of blasphemy and their development in the New Testament.

The monolithic Christendom that develops from the conciliar movement of the fourth and fifth centuries works mainly in terms of heresy, though what lies outside the monolith is blasphemy, the blasphemy of the beast. Blasphemy thrives as a discourse in the first three centuries of Christianity when thought is relatively free and Christians are unmistakably not. What succeeds it, with the backing of State power, is a form of ideological control, through doctrine policed by a discourse of heresy, that excludes the blasphemer. The relative freedom of thought in early Christianity follows from the strong Greek influence, as much in Judaism as in Christianity: the allegorising exegesis of Origen is squarely based on the Jewish exegesis of Philo and the schools of Alexandria. The Latin influence on Western Christianity to some extent works against such freedom: in Augustine, and Jerome, there is a desire for discipline and regulation, both of the text of Scripture and of interpretation. Western Christendom, through Jerome, puts the Bible into Latin and out of the reach of ordinary Christians. It is strikingly less liberal than Islam, which is to provide the sacred text of the Qu'ran but tightly restrict its interpretation. In other circumstances, there might have seemed less distance than we normally allow between Christian practice and those Islamic restrictions on interpretation. If Christianity had not inherited a strong Hellenistic tradition of exegetical freedom, would such freedom ever have seemed characteristic of the Western Church?

For the Western Christianity of the Crusades, Eastern Christianity itself sometimes seemed on the other side of the invisible limit: hence the Crusaders' sacking of Constantinople in 1204. Blasphemy ceases to be subordinate to heresy again when the monolith of Christianity itself splits at the Reformation. The grounds that lead to blasphemy being re-invoked are the Eucharistic elements, on which mainstream Protestantism and Catholicism divide, and the Trinity, on which they combine to defeat socinianism or unitarianism, the notion that Jesus was the perfect man but is not God, who is exclusively rather than inclusively one. Giordano Bruno, who questions the Trinity, is censured in Calvin's Geneva in 1584 and burned in Rome in 1600. Historically, perhaps an even more significant victim is Michael Servetus, who 'has the singular distinction of having been burned by the Catholics in effigy and by the Protestants in actuality'.[8]

Servetus was burned in Geneva in 1553, after a trial in which Calvin took over the prosecution. The capital sentence was for spreading heresy, but Calvin's attack on Servetus was as much emotive as intellectual and made full use of the discourse of blasphemy. Servetus was born in 1511 in a Spain nearly purged of Jews, but one that retained a reputation for possible heterodoxy as a result of Jewish contact and the Marrano population. Spaniards had to try harder, and so most developed a particularly fiery and unbending orthodoxy. Servetus went the other way: he made good use of cultural influences to which as a Spaniard he had been exposed, and so had to spend some time in his trial denying that he was Jewish, or that he admired the Qu'ran (which he knew). As his career progresses, Servetus also embraced Anabaptism and Florentine Neoplatonism, and developed academic expertise in a variety of fields: medicine and geography as well as divinity (including the study of the Bible). His first book against the doctrine of the Trinity was written when he was 19 years old, and it poured scorn on the authority of Peter Lombard's *Sentences*, which maintained that the Trinity was on every page of the Bible; Servetus pointedly declared that the doctrine was absolutely absent from Scripture. He rejected everything to do with the Council of Nicaea, to which he attributed the downfall of the Church, and subscribed to the misconception that Constantine had made the Church a 'donation' of temporal sovereignty. All power and authority was to be swept away, together with all Christian ministry: there would be no more need for mediators and advocates. Servetus therefore predicted the apocalypse, and fought his theological battles in the language of Revelation. Late in his career he wrote of the Trinity to the ministers of Geneva: 'Your gospel is without God, without true faith, without good works. Instead of God you have the three-headed Cerberus.' According to Servetus, Word was not Jesus but a mode of God's existence, John 1 meaning that Word indwelled Jesus when he was alive. Jesus was a man, but a perfect one – because of him we are all called children of God, an idea which prefigures the Quaker view that all may be like Jesus because of indwelling Word as inner light. Servetus actually uses the metaphor of light: Christ is to the Father 'as the ray and the sun are one light'. Even more striking is his use of speech, which returns God to his Jewish status of voice: 'Christ is in the Father as a voice from the speaker.'[9] The publication of Servetus's anti-Trinitarian views led to his hasty departure from Spain in 1531. He went to Protestant Basel, assuming that his agreement with the Reformers on the Eucharist would lead to a decent reception, but soon found himself endangered in a city that had ordinances against 'anabaptists, despisers of the sacrament and deniers of the divinity of Jesus'. For the Reformers, indeed, the combination in Servetus of Protestant views on the Eucharist with heretical views of the Trinity was especially unwelcome. Melanchton noted sombrely to a correspondent: 'as for the Trinity, you know I have always feared this would break out some day'. Having broken with established doctrine in one area, the Reformers were all the keener to stand by it in the other. Before he was 21, Servetus found himself hunted by Catholic and Protestant authorities alike. He slipped into France, assumed a new identity as Michel de Villeneuve, and started a new career as a doctor – he seems to have discovered the circulation of the blood – and writer.

In his new life, Servetus was unable to avoid controversy, gaining fresh notoriety for his glosses on an edition of Ptolemy. Servetus wrote that the Holy Land was 'barren, sterile, and without charm, . . . the "promised land" only in the sense that it was promised, not that it had any promise'. Bainton points out the irony: Servetus was here simply translating a gloss from Leonard Fries from a perspective that was anti-Crusader. The Geneva charges finally include blasphemous annotations to the Bible and to the geography of Ptolemy;[10] and as 'Villeneuve' (not known to be Servetus) he had already been before the Inquisition in Lyons to defend his views on astrology. Eventually, Servetus revealed his identity to Calvin, with whom he had entered into correspondence in the hope of finding a sympathetic spirit. The correspondence is characterised on both sides by arrogance and self-righteousness. Servetus sends Calvin corrected versions of his own letters, and returns his copy of Calvin's *Institutes* with copious critical annotation. It is such behaviour that provided the excuse for Coleridge's stunningly unkind remark, demonstrating his own orthodoxy: 'if ever a poor fanatic thrust himself into the fire, it was Michael Servetus. He was a rabid enthusiast, and did everything he could in the way of insult to provoke the feeling of the Christian Church.'[11] In spite of the increasing friction in the correspondence, Servetus nevertheless sends Calvin page proofs of his last book, *Christianismi Restitutio* (*The Restitution of Christianity*), which become proof of Villeneuve's identity as Servetus when Calvin finally betrays him to the Inquisition in Vienne. Calvin's betrayal of Servetus to his own ideological enemies is covert, taking the form of a letter from one of Calvin's followers to a relation in Vienne, protesting against the lack of Catholic zeal in tolerating the presence of Servetus 'unmolested among you, to the extent of even being permitted to print books full of such blasphemies as I must not speak of further'. Servetus is a heretic, the ground of his heresy is the Trinity, and the sentence he deserves is death:

> And when I say a heretic, I refer to a man who deserves to be as summarily condemned by the Papists, as he is by us. For though differing in many things, we agree in believing that in the sole essence of God there be three persons, and that his Son, who is his Eternal Wisdom, was engendered by the Father before all time, and has had [imparted to him] his Eternal virtue, which is the Holy Spirit. But when a man appears who calls the Trinity we all believe in, a Cerberus and Monster of Hell, who disgorges all the villainies it is possible to imagine, against everything Scripture teaches of the Eternal generation of the

Son of God, and mocks besides open-mouthed at all that the ancient doctors of the Church said – I ask you in what regard you would have such a man?[12]

Servetus is arrested and arraigned but escapes. He flies, incredibly, to Geneva, where he attends church on a Sunday, is recognised and apprehended. Calvin then finishes what he had started, prosecuting Servetus on a comprehensive list of charges that include blasphemy against Calvin himself, keeping up a protracted debate with him in Latin (but this was for ease of dissemination of Servetus's criminality throughout Christendom), and gaining a conviction that freely mixes heresy and blasphemy:

The sentence pronounced against Michel Servet de Villeneufve of the Kingdom of Aragon in Spain who some twenty-three or twenty-four years ago printed a book at Hagenau in Germany against the Holy Trinity containing many great blasphemies to the scandal of the said churches of Germany, the which book he freely confesses to have printed in the teeth of the remonstrances made to him by the learned and evangelical doctors of Germany. In consequence he became a fugitive from Germany. Nevertheless he continued in his errors and in order the more to spread the venom of his heresy, he printed secretly a book in Vienne of Dauphiny full of the said heresies and horrible, execrable blasphemies against the Holy Trinity, against the Son of God, against the baptism of infants and the foundations of the Christian religion. He confesses that in this book he calls believers in the Trinity Trinitarians and atheists. He calls this Trinity a diabolical monster with three heads. He blasphemes detestably against the Son of God, saying that Jesus Christ is not the Son of God from eternity. He calls infant baptism an invention of the devil and sorcery. His execrable blasphemies are scandalous against the majesty of God, the Son of God and the Holy Spirit. This entails the murder and ruin of many souls. Moreover he wrote a letter to one of our ministers in which, along with other numerous blasphemies, he declared our holy evangelical religion to be without faith and without God and that in place of God we have a three-headed Cerberus. . . .

For these and other reasons, designed to purge the Church of God of such infection and cut off the rotten member, having taken counsel with our citizens and having invoked the name of God to give just judgment . . . having God and the Holy Scriptures before our eyes, speaking in the name of the Father, Son and Holy Spirit, we now in writing give final sentence and condemn you, Michael Servetus, to be bound and taken to Champel and there attached to a stake and burned with your book to ashes. And so you shall finish your days and give an example to others who would commit the like.[13]

Servetus is burned at the stake, according to pious report screaming for mercy: '*Misericordia! misericordia!*' The wood is picked green, with the leaves still on, and his death is slow. A copy of his book is tied to his thigh. Thus Calvin, who had preached religious toleration, becomes the prime mover in a judicial killing, and makes a virtue of it: 'those who would spare heretics and blasphemers are themselves blasphemers'. The new Protestant Church of Geneva in one generation replicates the progress of the early Church through its first three centuries, raising the rhetoric of blasphemy into a weapon of theological repression. It is a moment of profound significance. For one thing, it provokes Castellio's compilation *Concerning Heresies*: Servetus may have resembled Calvin in the desire to make converts and turn Christendom to his single view, but Castellio has no such desire and speaks from within Christianity for the first time in twelve centuries for real religious tolerance based, as I have argued, in a limited form of cultural relativism, and breaking with discourses of domination and subordination. The death of Servetus indirectly gives voice to the thousands of Anabaptists who had been persecuted a little earlier in the century, with Luther's blessing. From then on, arguments for unitarianism and against the divinity of Christ act as a reproach to a Christendom which, though split, still refuses to tolerate difference. And so, in the end, something new arises out of the major historical repetition. The death of Servetus helps show the extent to which the Reformation reverts to and re-enacts the agonies and mistakes of early Christianity. History repeats itself, in what Vico calls a *ricorso*.[14] For this sort of history is a discourse – in part, a discourse of blasphemy.

Naming the Beast

So far this chapter has moved from the New Testament to the Reformation in order to trace a discourse and its return. Now, to extend the demonstration, I must reverse that movement, starting at a point in the seventeenth century and retracing the discourse that is there acted out to its New Testament source. This study returns to the English seventeenth century, to the Commonwealth period – a time of a revolution's consolidation, in an atmosphere where moral austerity could still be received as the face of a new freedom from royal tyranny. Such periods tend not to be short of victims, and I wish to look at the fate of one: James Nayler, Quaker, who was sentenced by a parliament of zealous Puritans in 1656 for 'horrid blasphemy'. Nayler's case shows an extraordinary range of subject positions from which a single discourse of blasphemy may be used.

Quakerism was itself a product of the English Revolution, and could appear very much more extreme than its increasingly sober form after 1660, as Quaker communities worked hard for the right of social acceptance and tolerance of their religious practice. To characterise the later period first: Richard Crane's pamphlet *Something spoken in Vindication and Clearing of the People of God called Quakers*, published in 1660, protested against the new king's 'Declaration concerning Ecclesiastical Affairs . . . for prohibiting of all unlawful Seditious Meetings and Conventicles, under pretence of the Worship of God', maintaining of the Quakers

> That they have not forfeited their Liberty in the Declaration, nor made ill use of the king's Indulgence, by any Plots, or Murders, or Insurrections in a pretence of Worship and serving of God, the Lord is Witnes, and you have tried us, and found that we are none of those People, the King's Proclamation takes a hold upon, but ought to have our Meetings.[15]

It was the beginning of a new tone in English Quakerism, conciliatory and relatively moderate. Freedom of conscience was legally established for the Quakers in 1689, and even then, in the single sheet 'Letter to the Quakers' (1690), they are accused of hypocrisy and trimming for their supposedly fawning and flattering support of William III when they are really bloodthirsty Cromwellians. The publication of answers to such a text becomes easier and less dangerous after 1689, but one detects in them a spirit of caution, a desire not to imperil the newly granted freedoms. What we find, on the whole, is the publication of works written earlier but circulated only in manuscript, as in George Whitehead's polemic: *Christ's Lambs defended from Satan's rage: in a Just Vindication of the People Called Quakers . . . from the Unjust Attempts of John Pennyman and Abettors in his Malicious Book styled The Quakers Unmasked* – a reply to Pennyman's book of 1676, sent in manuscript in 1677 but not published until 1691. Another example is the collection of works by Roger Haydock, edited in 1700, five years after his death in 1695. Haydock had been a travelling Quaker evangelist from his conversion at the age of 25 in 1667, and served terms of imprisonment in Cheshire and Lancashire in the 1670s and 1680s. In 1676 and 1677, he conducted a dispute with John Cheyney, priest of Arley Hall, which led to two works by Haydock, *The Skirmisher confounded* and 'A Hypocrite unvailed and a Blasphemer made manifest' (in Haydock [1700]), and two by Cheyney which were published at the time, *A Skirmish upon Quakerism* in 1676 and, also directed against Quakers, *A Vindication of Oaths and Swearing* in 1678. There was a similar and even more vitriolic exchange in the 1670s between William Penn and John Faldo.

The relatively moderate tone in vindications written after 1689 can be gauged in Richard Ashby's *The True Light Owned and Vindicated and the Believers in It Defended and Blasphemy and Blasphemers justly detected* (1699), an answer to an attack by Norfolk priests that begins with a Preface to the Reader:

> One Eminent Proof of the *Christian* is, a Peaceable Spirit, and his living, as much as in him lies, at Peace with all Men: Indeed it is a State and Station so desirable by us, that had we met with Reflections in Revilings which were only Personal, we value the Peace and Comfort of *Retirement* so much, that we should have willingly lain down under it, with only speaking to the Persons

that have injured us: But the occasion of our now appearing is Doctrinal, in Defence of the Holy *Light within*, which some *Priests in Norfolk* have Charged with Exposing Us, the Followers of it, to *Blasphemy*, as touch'd by us.[16]

The opening of the pamphlet repeats the point: 'Controversie we love not'. The replies are made necessary by the efforts of Norfolk priests 'to blacken the People called Quakers with most gross Charges of Blasphemy' in order to make them 'obnoxious to the Government, who have granted us the Free Exercise of our Consciences towards God; for which Priviledge we have been and are truly Thankful unto God and the Government'. The response contents itself with reproducing and answering one charge at a time. The purpose is to show that 'instead of Proving the Quakers Blasphemers, they (the aforesaid Priests), have brought the *Guilt of Blasphemy* upon themselves, in all those Particulars, they have charged the Quakers withal, which is plainly Proveable upon them' (p. 6). Haydock, though far less restrained in tone, uses the same technique, arguing of Cheyney in the language of Psalm 7: 15 that 'He made a Pit, and digged it, and is fallen into the Ditch which he made.' Ashby's pamphlet goes as far as it can to indicate doctrinal and scriptural orthodoxy, even using the Trinitarian language of the Nicene Creed in a chastened manner that might have astonished a Quaker of the 1650s. The passage itself imitates the language of a legal affirmation:

> We do Solemnly and in good Conscience, Testifie and Declare, in Behalf of the People called Quakers, That Profess and Teach no other *Light within*, for Man to be led and guided by, than what the Holy Scriptures hold forth . . . concerning the *Eternal God*, and Jesus Christ, the Eternal Son of God, and the Eternal Spirit, proceeding from the Father and the Son, who with the Father and the Son, is one God, blessed for ever. (p. 7)

It is quite clear from the responses themselves that the attacks on Quakers, even at this late stage, are conducted in terms of blasphemy. Haydock's epigraph in 'A Hypocrite unvailed and a Blasphemer made manifest' is from Revelation 13: 6: 'He opened his Mouth in Blasphemy against God, to Blaspheme his Name, his Tabernacle, and them that dwelt in Heaven.' Cheyney's thesis is typical: 'No wise man will entrust his Soul with the Quakers' "religion".' His rhetorical strategy is also representative:

> I shall not here insist that they are guilty of gross Blasphemy and Idolatry, in making the Light within every man God. All that I shall here observe is the confusion and Darkness which these men are in, requiring of all men to Salvation a belief of this Principle, abounding with so much self-contradiction, and being unintelligible.[17]

It is a charter for misrepresentation. Faldo's attack in *A vindication of Quakerism no Christianity* purportedly presents 'the Quakers' Principles, detected out of their Chief Writers; and confuted by Sin and right Reason, with a key to their Terms and Phrases, Discourse of Apostolical Inspirations, and an account of their Foundation laid in POPERY'.[18] Clearly, for Faldo, all errors conjoin, and all roads lead to Rome: the association of 'Quakers' Canons' with Catholicism ('their Symbolizing with Rome therein') is among the more memorable and mindless distortions of religious controversy – especially in view of Faldo's own presentation of Quaker beliefs: 'The Quakers Deny the Scriptures'; 'The Quakers deny all the Ordinances of the Gospel'; 'The Quakers profess no Reward in an upper world'; 'The Quakers deny the Christ of God'; 'They deny a Trinity of distinct Persons to subsist in the Godhead'; 'They deny Original Sin'. For Faldo, Quaker blasphemy seems to lie in their notion of the inner light, which he interprets as a claim to incarnation within the individual Quaker believer: 'that every man hath a *light* in him which is Christ the *Eternal Word* of God', so that 'God is *now* manifested in the flesh as he was in the son of Mary above 1600 year since' (p. 20). Ingeniously but incoherently, Faldo twists this into a denial of Christ's body. Quaker belief, he claims, is that Christ was bodiless, and that he 'was never seen with bodily eyes' (p. 19). This says nothing about Quaker beliefs but everything about the anxieties that accompany Trinitarian discourse.

The most vicious of all later attacks is that by Francis Bugg, *George Whitehead turn'd Topsie-Turvy* in 1700. Bugg, in an attack on the writings of George Whitehead, sought to vindicate liberty of conscience. In the case of the Quakers, however, he makes an exception. The Quakers are new Arians who 'appear like the Pharisees'. They

> tell you they own the Scriptures to be given by Divine Inspiration but in truth they deny the scriptures to be the Written Word of God; For it is (say they) a Rotten Foundation, Dust, Death and Serpents Meat. In like manner they dissemble the Doctrine of the Trinity, when they pretend to own it.[19]

Bugg works skilfully with the disparity between the Quakers' moderate public face and the possibilities of selective quotation from their own books. Faldo's principle of selective and decontextualised quotation thus wins Bugg's joyous assent, and the case it demonstrates is one of 'vile Heresies, Seditions and Blasphemous Principles . . . the like of which was never broached before in England'. The most effective part of Bugg's work is his 'Preface, By Way of Parable', which offers a transparent recasting of the origins of Quakerism in the language of the apocalypse:

> There was an Island, very Populous, and well Situated, the Air good, and the People generally of a sound Constitution, and governed by wholesom Laws, and professed the most Reformed Religion of any Nation round about them: But so it fell out, that in the North Part of this Island, *Anno* 1650, ther arose a great Sea-Monster, of a Luciferian Pride, who pretended, that he, and all that received, embraced, and had the same Spirit that moved him, were equal to God: That he was the Eternal Judge of the World, and knew who were Saints,

who were Devils, and who were Apostates, without speaking ever a Word; and he having betrothed himself to a young Harlot, she conceived, and brought forth her Young; to whom she drew out her Breasts, and gave them Suck, and they multiplied exceedingly, and many of them became fiery flying Serpents, and spread themselves like Locusts, all over the Island; some entering the Churches, where they stung both Men, Women, and Children; others entered into the Market-places, Barns, Orchards, and private Chambers; like the Frogs in *Egypt*, poysoning the Air, and infecting much People. (p. xiv)

Bugg consciously employs what he considers to be the Quakers' own discourse, and he relishes turning it against them. He offers an account of what he calls the 'dreadful thunderbolts' of their language, which are 'fit only for Bedlam'. The Quakers call the orthodox

Baal's Priests, Conjurers, Thieves, Robbers, Blind Guides, Devils, Serpents, the Sir-Symons of the Age, a Viperous and Serpentine Generation, Witches, Bloodhounds, Merchants of Babylon, *Dogs, Sodomites, we* (said this Intoxicated People in their mad Zeal) *have nothing for them but Woes and Plagues, who have made drunk the Nations, and laid them to sleep on downy Beds of Sin-pleasing Principles, whilst they have cut their Purses, and pickt their Pockets;* Tophet's *prepared for them to act their Eternal Tragedy upon; whose Scenes will be renewed, Direful, Anguishing Woes, of an Eternal Irreconcileable Justice,* &c. (p. xvi)

And it is the very derangement of Quaker discourse that Bugg uses to justify rough treatment against them: 'Are these mad People then to be dealt with as a Man would deal with any other well-disposed People? I think not' (p. xvii). It is a clever and effective pastiche of the language of much Quaker controversy, especially before 1660. As Levy writes: 'For all their talk of the love of God, Quakers used Billingsgate, laced with biblical epithets, against other Christians. After spewing jeremiads, Fox would deny that he was railing.'[20] This is the ground of continual linkings of Quakerism and Ranterism, and such ongoing suspicions of the Quakers' new-found sobriety that Baxter could produce the following equation, based on the belief that all heretics are either too lax or too austere or both: 'the Quakers were but the Ranters turned from a horrid profaneness to a life of extreme austerity'.[21] J. C. Davis notes an ongoing exchange transaction: 'the heaviest irony is . . . that the Quakers, tainted by associations with Ranters and desperate to free themselves from such associations, nevertheless accused each other of Ranterism and so kept the term alive well into the late seventeenth century'.[22]

In fact, the exchange transaction operates on every level and across an extraordinary broad surface. What Bugg realises with devastating accuracy is that the Quakers in the 1650s unleash the discourse of blasphemy in its vaguest and most appalling form, straight from the book of Revelation. They are fighting what Fox calls 'the Lambs War' against 'the synagogues of Satan', and their enemies serve the Devil or the Beast. In the 1650s this was hardly a message of love and mutual tolerance, and the Quakers regularly violated the religious worship of other sects. In their return to primitive Christianity, they sought persecution, which itself became a guarantee of their ministry as the Rule of the Saints. They were God's instruments, often arraigned for blasphemy themselves and accusing all others of it (*The Ranters' Monster* of 1652, for example, produces a rollcall of the Grand Blasphemers). One might even argue that they unleashed the discourse of blasphemy in the hope that it would be used against themselves – as it often was: biblically literate crowds would stone Quakers as they passed by. For such treatment increased their certainties that they were servants and followers of Christ, like Stephen in Acts, imitating his suffering and turning death itself into a profession of their beliefs. When they attacked others in such extreme and intemperate language, they were not, to their eyes, engaging in cruel, exaggerated and parochial invective: they were reclaiming the grand language of the Bible for the events of their own lifetimes in which biblical happenings were being again unfolded. Their use of the language of Revelation is cognate with the homely reclamation of the Song of Songs in Sarah Blackbury's homage to the Quaker leader James Nayler: she 'came to him, and took him by the hand, and said, Rise up, my love, my dove, my fair one, and come away: Why sittest thou among the pots?'[23]

Thus we find the extreme fluctuation between love and Billingsgate, Revelation and the Song of Songs, in the discourse of Quaker leaders in the 1650s – not least in the writings of their most effective propagandist, Nayler himself. The Quaker liking of point-by-point refutation is in place in Nayler's work, as in *A Discovery of the Beast Got into the Seat of the False Prophet, who hath Opened his mouth in Blasphemy, to deny the Father, the Son and the Spirit, to guide man out of his Natural state; That so he might establish his beastly kingdome*: in this typically apocalyptic piece, Nayler demolishes the thesis of one Thomas Winterton, who has accused Quakers of blasphemy. Nayler is not content with proving Winterton in error; he has to be the False Prophet in league with the Beast. Similarly in *Satans design discovered*, Nayler's refutation the same year (1655) of 48 lies by one 'Thomas Moor', who 'under pretence of worshipping Christ's Person in Heaven would exclude God and Christ, the Spirit and Light out of the world', Nayler proceeds to the rhetorical point that the end of the world is happening:

> Perilous times are come; now is the earth and the air corrupted and filled with violence and deceit, ungodliness abounds everywhere, Satan is loosed and gone forth to deceive, multitudes of spirits are sent abroad and hath power given to enter all that dwell in the earth, who inhabit in dark places . . . wo to the world . . . (p. 18)

In this work, Nayler's rebuttal of detailed allegations leads to his advancement of twelve propositions about the crucial Quaker doctrine of the inner light: it is the Word of God, indwelling the hearts of believers, but only those who preach perfection, and it is proof against error. It is a manifesto for Quaker ministry: 'no man can be a Minister of Christ, nor preach him truly, but who preacheth perfection', and 'God and his word is now manifest in the bodies of his Saints in the same manner, and as freely as formerly he hath been.' Finally,

> the ground of all Errors, Sects and Opinions, Heresies and blasphemies, that are in the world, is in being led from the guidance of this spirit and all live in error, but who are guided by it, but none ever errs who was guided by it, nor ever shall. (pp. 57–8)

We can add to this view of Nayler's ministry from his angry rejection of the 'lies, Slanders and Deceits of T. Higgenson' in a book entitled, from the sweet side of the discourse, *Love to the Lost* (1656).

> As I deny the person of Christ, the death of Christ, the blood of Christ, the once offering Christ for all etc. That I say the light in every man is God, and Christ, and Redemption is the baptism of Christ, is God's Righteousness, and many such like abominable lyes, never spoken by me.

There is much positive teaching here on the Fall, on Word, worship, error, heresy, faith, hope and love, on perfection, government and obedience, works and election, new birth, baptism and the Lord's Supper, on justification, law, ministry, free will, resurrection and so on: an articulate, intelligible and intelligent set of positions based on the indwelling of Word in the Body of Christ. On the Eucharist, Nayler simply notes: 'This is the Thing the World's Professors are contending about', and comments further 'so far from being made one in the Blood of Christ, that they are shedding one another's Blood about Form'. It is Quaker anti-formalism that enables Nayler to set out a revised doctrine of imitation of Christ: as the word indwells the just believer as inner light, so the believer becomes the truthful agent and instrument of Word, raised not to be a god, but to be a partaker in divinity. Objections that this may seem blasphemous are brushed aside. Those with the inner light understand, and the rest are 'vain janglers, imitatours, and licentious persons, shut out of the Scriptures, who are not guided by the same spirit that gave them force', and who thus echo 'The old Serpent's voice, or Antichrist discovered opposing Christ in his kingdome'.[24] There is no room for tolerance when the saints are fighting to redeem humanity in the last days: one must fight fire with fire, *A Foole answered according to his folly* (1655c), allegations of blasphemy with counter-allegations.

Given the ferocity of Quaker vituperation, their readiness not only to answer but to damn their opponents, their antinomianism and their insistence that true holiness confers perfection, orthodox condemnation of

Quaker blasphemy is widespread and based on what is, for the most part, an understandable misconception: that Quakers believed themselves to be Gods. George Fox was charged more than once with claiming to be the equal of God. His answer was that 'Saints are the temples of the Holy Spirit, and God doth dwell in them', 'he that sanctifieth and he that is sanctified is one':[25] this is not a claim to be Christ but to be united with Christ in the practice of perfection. I do not here claim to understand the difficult point of Quaker theodicy that makes the distinction – only to express my conviction that in Quaker theodicy such a distinction was regularly made, and that modern commentators who sorrowfully would consign seventeenth-century Quakers to a psychiatric ward are probably wrong to extend sympathy rather than thought. In any such distinction, however, the line of demarcation is hazardous. There is evidence that some Quakers, both in Fox's circle and in Nayler's, went beyond the intellectual distinction to an apparent acting out of adoration. George Fox's wife Margaret Fell treated him as the Messiah, and Fox spoke of himself as 'the Sonne of God', but adjusted the written version to read 'a sonne of God' – the difference in article is more than usually significant. Fox and Nayler both believed that the spirit within them, for which they acted as spokesmen, was that of truth: when, therefore, the two Quaker leaders disagreed, they were bound to assume that the other had turned from Christ to the Devil: 'If the seed speake which is in Christ . . . it is not blasphemie but truth, but if the seed of the serpent speake and say he is Christ it is the liar and the blasphemie and the ground of all blasphemie.'[26]

What led Nayler and Fox to disagree was a dispute about leadership. Fox's circle encouraged him to claim it , and Nayler's circle encouraged Nayler. Fox told Nayler that 'thou and thy disciples and the world is joined against the truth'; 'the darkness is entered into thy disciples'. The breach between them culminated in the famous scene in Exeter at which Fox offered Nayler his foot to kiss. Ralph Farmer, writing against the Quakers in 1655, summed up the logic of the situation in a telling phrase: 'James Nayler and George Fox at daggers drawn discovers their cheat of being both led by an infallible Spirit.'[27] The discursive outcome was that Fox and his supporters unleashed the whole force of the discourse of blasphemy against Nayler. A Bristol Quaker wrote to Margaret Fell:

> there is such filthy things acted there in such havoc and spoil and such madness among them as I cannot write, but there is about ten of them in all with him, and they call him 'I am' and 'the Lamb', and they are bringing him to this city. They have made truth stink in those parts, and truly my dear George Fox bore it so long . . . that it's become a mountain, and he sees he suffered it too long now.[28]

Fox and his Bristol supporters were not to suffer it longer. At the trial that followed his entry into Bristol, Nayler just once expressed his opinion of Fox: 'George Fox is a lyar and a firebrand of hell.' The context may hint that Fox supplied information against Nayler. Certainly, Nayler appeared to blame him for his downfall. Fox probably played with Nayler the role that Calvin hoped to play when he betrayed Servetus to the Inquisition: another great religious leader who somehow confused Jesus with Judas, and settled for the Chief Priest.

It seems that when Nayler and his followers entered Bristol in 1656, they acted out Christ's Palm Sunday 'entrance into Jerusalem: one walked bareheaded; another of the women led his horse; others spread their scarves and handkerchiefs before him in the way, crying continually as they went on, "Holy, holy, holy is the Lord God of Hosts, Hosanna in the Highest".' With his followers Nayler was apprehended by the Bristol magistrates, and sent by them to Parliament to be examined by a parliamentary committee on a charge of blasphemy – for allowing himself to be the object of religious worship, and for assuming the titles of Christ, including the name Jesus, 'the fairest among ten thousand, the only begotten Son of God, the Prophet of the most High, the King of Israel, the everlasting Son of Righteousness, the Prince of Peace'.

The Commons proceedings were irregular. There was no obvious law that Nayler had broken, given the rewriting of the blasphemy law in 1650, and the Commons decided to ignore the fact and punish Nayler for what they voted to call 'horrid Blasphemy', here intended not merely as an intensification but as a higher legal level of ordinary blasphemy, and as 'a grand Imposter and Seducer of the People'. The proceedings were also highly prejudicial to Nayler. The Commons had correspondence from his followers, including from Hannah Stranger, who had conferred on him the numerous titles already listed and whose husband had written a postscript urging that Nayler's name 'is no more to be called James but Jesus'. Nor was their testimony less damaging. 'He is the only begotten Son of God,' testified one Dorcas Erbury, unhelpfully: 'I was dead and he raised me.' Asked 'why she pulled off his stockings, she answered, Because he is the Holy One of Israel, and deserves and is worthy of it.' As early as the trial itself developed the rumour that Nayler had confessed; most historians' accounts routinely record that Nayler's recantation was later published. In fact, Nayler's 'recantation' was published in London by Edward Farnham in 1659, recording Nayler's new view that he had been possessed by the Evil One – 'it is the old Spirit of the Ranters, Demonic possession'; and it is a plain forgery. Nayler refuted it in a pamphlet of the same year published by Thomas Simmons: *Having heard that some have wronged my words which I spoke before the Committee of the Parliament concerning Jesus Christ and concerning the Old and New Testaments, some have printed Word which I spoke not: also some have printed a Paper and calls it James Nayler's Recantation: unknown to me.*

The false recantation is the product of the propaganda industry that swung into action even as Nayler's fate was being debated by the Parliament. The earliest is John Deacon's *The Grand Imposter Examined, or, The Life, Tryal and Examination of James Nayler, The Seduced and Seducing Quaker, with the Manner of his Riding into Bristol* (1656). Deacon repeats all he can of Nayler's blasphemy and (he claims) apostasy, and appeals to precedent: blasphemers die.

> I do here give thee an account of what passed betweene James Nayler and his Judges, as thinking it a part of my duty towards God and man, that therby thou mayest see and know there is but onely God, and one onely Jesus, which is the Christ, who was crucified by the Jews at Jerusalem: Which whosoever denies, let him be accursed. (p. 1)

Nayler's defence was made harder by other incidentals: his cryptic but plausibly Messianic habit of signing his works 'one whom the world calls James Nayler'; and a document allegedly found in the possession of one of his women followers that purported to be a translation of a letter by the Roman president of Judea describing the physical appearance of Jesus. Nayler was held, perhaps correctly, to have tried to copy this portrait of the look of Christ in his own physiognomy, beard and haircut.[29]

But this does not make Nayler another deluded Jesus impersonator, like William Hackett in the reign of Elizabeth i. There is no reason to doubt his assertion in his 1659 pamphlet, 'I was never of any faith contrary'. The records of his cross-examination reveal a predictable failure of communication between accusers and accused:

Q. Art thou the only Son of God?
A. I am the son of God but I have many brethren.
Q. Have any called thee by the name of Jesus?
A. Not as unto the visible, but as Jesus, the Christ that is in me.

By these answers Nayler immediately gives notice that he will stand on Quaker theology of the inner light: all who own it have Christ indwelling them, and that indwelling is what is worthy of worship. The various acts of homage he received were directed to that indwelling Christ, not to Nayler himself, and he concluded that it would be wrong to reject them. To the next question, 'Dost thou earn the name of the King of Israel?', he attempts to explain this distinction: 'Not as a creature, but if they give it Christ within, I earn it, and have a kingdom, but not of this world.' If the last clause reminiscing John 18: 36 were not unfortunate enough as an afterthought, Nayler adds, on behalf of the indwelling Word: 'my kingdom is of another world, of which thou wotest not'. The further echo of Christ's words here proves infectious. Soon the committee has caught it, and asks: 'By whom were you sent?', which is no way of giving Nayler a chance to avoid the discourse of Messiahship. By and large, Nayler continues to press his distinction: he was born 'according to the natural birth', but spiritually his mother is 'No carnal creature' (he refuses a request to elaborate, as he refuses when asked: 'Is thy name Jesus?'). His answers are not, by his lights, difficult or dishonest. He tries hard to be candid yet theologically accurate:

> Q. Art thou the everlasting Son of God?
> A. Where God is manifest in the flesh, there is the everlasting Son, and I do witness God in the flesh; I am the son of God, and the son of God is but one.

The trouble is that his best answers count heavily against him. In the following, Nayler would win heavily by any forensic test. His answers are both correct and intelligent, but the questions are put to him in terms that already bear the burden of the imposture with which he is charged, and by the very nature of the discourse his answers therefore echo that imposture:

> Q. Art thou the unspotted Lamb of God, that taketh away the sins of the world?
> A. Were I not a lamb, wolves would not seek to devour me.
> Q. Art thou not guilty of horrid blasphemy, by thy own words?
> A. Who made thee a judge over them?

To refute a charge of pretending to be Christ, Nayler echoes Christ.

We have a sharp sense of what Nayler wanted to say but knew that he could not. We have seen that Sir Charles Sedley could not admit to mimicry of the Ranters, because that would raise the danger of his being convicted of a serious offence; and Sedley's purpose was satiric, not serious. It is all the more impossible for Nayler to confess to what he is clearly doing, *mimicking Christ*. As Levy wrote: 'He was the reluctant Jesus in a Passion Play because he had become convinced by the agony of his spirit that God intended him as a sign.'[30] The relation between Nayler and Jesus is therefore exactly that of impersonation or imposture, and it fluctuates as a relation between actors and their parts always does fluctuate. What Nayler acts out in his praxis is no more than he writes in his discourse: both bring the text of the New Testament to life in contemporary England with the intention of saving souls before the Last Day. Because Nayler and his followers really believe that the Last Day is at hand, they do not seek to make fine distinctions between blasphemy and truth, between fact and fiction – the very fine distinctions by which in their absolute immanence they are to be convicted. If they are actors, they also believe in the inner light; they are the method actors of the spiritual life. The only reason that they did not also emulate different traditions of theatre by getting up the seven-headed monster of Revelation is that such a theatrical construction would have been superfluous: such a monster is what they actually saw when they beheld their enemies. To speak any such irrefutable defence, as so often in blasphemy cases, would immediately have secured Nayler's conviction. He therefore continues with his impersonation: he acts out his answers, and echoes Jesus. The misunderstandings prosper, having reached so decisive a fork in the discourse. As he is led away to punishment, the attending ministers ask Nayler whether he believes in Jesus Christ – so far has legal process come from the offence with which he is charged, impersonating him.

The records of interrogation here are detailed, specific and highly contextualised. Yet reading them is like reading a novel, a novel that does its best not to mention a key fact, that Nayler's fall was altogether in the interest of George Fox, whom Nayler rivalled as Quaker leader, and who had already broken with him. It is also like reading a novel one has already read, and read more than once, in the accounts of medieval heretics such as Aldebert or Henry of Lausanne, whose followers, according to the astonishing account, 'became so excited by the lasciviousness of the man . . . that they testified publicly to his extraordinary virility and said that his eloquence could move a heart of stone to remorse',[31] or Tanchelm in the early twelfth century who, like Nayler, preached that he possessed the Holy Spirit and with his followers constituted the true Church; who was held to have used his sexual appeal to women to enslave his followers, to have made blasphemous confessions, and to have 'distributed his bath water to his followers to be used as a sacrament, and to compare with the consecrated wine that the clergy offered'.[32] To set such disparate accounts side by side, and to see in them similarities of theme, detail and structure, is to be assailed by doubts. Is blasphemy used by orthodoxy as an invention that secures condemnation while distracting attention from heretics' dangerous ideas? Or does the existence of such literary stereotypes simply guarantee their re-emergence, like a virus, in the behaviour of otherwise utterly different dissenters? In other words, is it orthodoxy that constructs the subjectivity of the dissenter?

Nayler's punishment is set by the House of Commons after long and intense debate. The most recent biography of Nayler has done much to show that the pattern of voting on the affair has little to do with factions and much to do with different people's sense of conscience and religious tolerance. Lord President Lawrence: 'this business lies heavy on my heart. If you hang every man that says Christ is in you the hope of glory, you will hang a good many.' Doctor Clairges: 'I shall speak no more, but let us all stop our ears and stone him, for he is guilty of horrid blasphemy.' George Downing: 'We are God's executioners, and ought to be tender in his honour.'[33] Carlyle's depiction misunderstands almost every single issue, yet despite itself remains altogether too just not to quote:

> To Posterity they sit there as the James-Nayler Parliament. Four-hundred Gentlemen of England, and I think a sprinkling of Lords among them, assembled from all the counties and Boroughs of the Three Nations, to sit in solemn debate on this terrific Phenomenon; a Mad Quaker fancying or

seeming to fancy himself, what is not uncommon since, a new Incarnation of Christ, Shall we hang him, shall we whip him, set him to oakum; shall we roast, or boil, or stew him; – shall we put the question whether this question shall be put; debate whether this shall be debated; – in Heaven's name, what shall we do with him, the terrific Phenomenon of Nayler? This is the history of Oliver's Second Parliament for three long months and odd . . .[34]

The judgment was indeed arrived at piecemeal, after Nayler was summoned to the bar of the Parliament but forbidden to speak. The motion that he was guilty of blasphemy was moved on Monday 8 December at 8 p.m., and immediately amended to insert the word 'horrid' before 'Blasphemy'; the question was then resolved in the affirmative, and the matter adjourned. When the House resumed on 9 December, there were two further adjournments, and an adjournment on the 10th. On the 11th, the motion for adjournment was defeated by 84 to 87; but the House then adjourned, and on the 13th, the House adjourned by 65 to 108. On 16 December, it was at last moved that Nayler be put to death: the motion was defeated by 96 to 82. The next motion, that part of his punishment should be to have his hair cut off (clearly someone believed that he cultivated a resemblance to Jesus) was defeated. There followed a weary series of motions and amendments until on 17 December, the following composite punishment was passed in time for Christmas:

Dec. 17. Resolved, that James Nayler be set on the pillory, with his head in the pillory, in the Palace-Yard, Westminster, during the space of two hours, on Thursday next; and shall be whipped by the hangman through the streets from Westminster to the Old Exchange, London; and there likewise be set on the pillory, with his head in the pillory, for the space of two hours, between the hours of eleven and one, on Saturday next; in each place wearing a paper containing an inscription of his crimes; and that at the Old Exchange his tongue be bored through with a hot iron: and that he be there also stigmatized in the forehead with the Letter *B*; and that he be afterwards sent to Bristol, and be conveyed into and through the said city on horseback, bare-ridged, with his face backward, and there also publicly whipped the next market-day after he come thither; and that from thence he be committed to prison in Bridewell, London, and there restrained from the society of all people, and there to labour hard till he shall be released by parliament; and during that time to be debarred the use of pen, ink, and paper, and shall have no relief but what he earns by his daily labours.

Finally, there are accounts of his punishment being carried out on 18 and 27 December, when 'some of his followers licked his wounds, and paid him other honours both ridiculous and superstitious'.[35] This refers to the three women prisoners, Martha Simmonds, Hannah Stranger and Dorcas Erbury, and to Nayler's faithful follower and biographer Robert Rich, who had demonstrated in Westminster Hall itself against the conviction. As Nayler's biographer Brailsford writes, 'the subject is so painful that one is thankful to borrow another man's description':[36] that of the Quaker Tomlinson, who speaks of the size of the red-hot iron that bored into Nayler's tongue, and the smoke he saw rising from his forehead; or even the hostile Deacon:

> After an hour and three quarters, they took him forth of the pillory, and having bound him fast with his back to the same, the executioner pulled off his Cap, and having hoodwinkt his Face, and taken fast hold of his Tongue, with a red hot Iron he bore the Hole quite thorow; which having done, and pulling this Cloth off that covered his Face, he put a Handkerchief over his Eyes, and so putting his left Hand in his Poll he taking the red hot iron Letter in his other Hand, put it to his Forehead, which gave a little Flash of Smoak. Which being done, Rich licked the same, as did the Dogs the Wounds of Lazarus.[37]

Nayler was led off for the little over three years that remained of his life: he was to die at the same age as Servetus, when the Spirit moved him to travel on foot back to the north of England in order to see the wife and family that the Spirit had moved him to abandon, like Bunyan's Christian, at the start of his ministry. Nayler was mugged by thieves on the road; and, as is typical of his sad life, there was no Samaritan at hand. He had spent the intervening period writing fine and moving outpourings on (equally prefabricated) themes of Christian love and discipleship.

My parenthesis in the last sentence is not intended as flippant. The point is that everyone who acts in this affair speaks and acts out an already constructed discourse. I have argued that Nayler's entry into Bristol is the equivalent to his discursive reworking of the themes and language of the book of Revelation. Equally, the effect of Parliament's sentence, anti-climactic as the failure to kill Nayler seemed to some, was to parody Nayler's original entry in its extravagant theatricality: ritually mutilated, he is taken back to Bristol and ridden in backwards on a horse. Parliament literally reverses the discourse that they will use, and by reversing it they normalise it – for Nayler's was the reverse discourse, designed to shock those who witnessed it into reappraisal. Thus a common discourse, derived from the New Testament and redolent of the fissures of early Christianity, is employed by all the actors in the affair. They carnivalise discourse itself (in Nayler's use of the discourse of blasphemy), text (the New Testament, and Nayler's acting out of the Passion) and event (Parliament's theatrical reversal of Nayler's enactment of Palm Sunday). In every case, too, the reverse transaction of blasphemy is to be seen in the vicious way that the discourse kicks back at its user: Nayler, who specialises in accusing others of blasphemy, is convicted of it by those he accuses, just as his mimicry of the entry into Jerusalem is itself travestied in the backwards ride; and those who judge him in the name of an unusually loose and coalescent orthodoxy will soon be judged themselves and imprisoned by their thousands, accusers alongside accused, when a more traditional form of orthodoxy is restored in 1660. All this is enough to confirm the truism that discourses speak us as much as, or more than, we speak them; and when they have done speaking, they write our sentence.

That what happens to the discourse is carnivalesque is shown, I think, in the nature of Parliament's judgment. Asks a new edition of Nayler's life in 1719: 'in the Name and Authority of Christ Jesus, who made them Judges of the Heart?'[38] But it is not the heart that they judge. It is the body. Nayler's body, grotesquely mutilated and literally inscribed with its scarlet letter, is paraded as the Grotesque Body of Blasphemy itself, exaggeratedly broken, playfully destroyed in order to display the scale of its own undoing: not as an act of cruelty, but as a rhetorical and discursive hyperbole. Equally, behind Nayler's original entry into Bristol lies a kind of reverse carnival: the whole point, as he keeps telling an uncomprehending committee of enquiry, is that his physical body is unworthy of the role that it fills and the homage it receives, so that it is gigantised, or rhetorically amplified into a figure of the Spiritual Body of Christ, the inner light. These are the two poles of bodily reconstruction that I have found in reading the New Testament. Nayler's life and the religious controversies of the 1650s are one more site for their rather repetitive history. In some sense, then, we are left with an irreducible image of Nayler both as imposter and as 'the Quakers' Jesus'. The play goes on even in the act which is meant to signal its end. In a later attack on Fox, Robert Rich writes of James Nayler, 'the dear Lamb', 'as I went with him from London to Bristol to receive his Crucifixion there'. For all the parties, there is no getting out of the discourse that invites Rich to put up his sign above Nayler's pillory: 'This is the king of the Jews.'[39]

This study therefore returns to the New Testament and the trial of Jesus. That is not only where the discourse begins historically, but where in the Nayler case it always is discursively.

TRIALS OF JESUS

It is a commonplace that the Servant songs of Isaiah, especially Chapter 53, form much of the typological basis of the New Testament. In that chapter – Handel's popularising use of which for the Passion libretto of the *Messiah* stands at the end of seventeen centuries of exegesis – the Servant 'is despised and rejected of man' (verse 3), an atonement sacrifice who 'hath borne our griefs and our sorrows' (verse 4), being 'wounded for our transgressions' (verse 5), 'oppressed and . . . afflicted, he opened not his mouth' (verse 7), 'and he made his grave with the wicked' (verse 9), in order that 'with his stripes we are healed' (verse 5). The death of the Servant after some sort of quasi-legal condemnation is envisaged here as, in the Christian programme, part of the script for the life of Jesus. Jesus cites Isaiah 53 during the Passion in Luke 22: 37. It is typologically predictable that the Passion of Jesus should contain a trial and condemnation, though the narrative of this varies from one gospel to another.

In general, the Synoptic gospels form one group and John another, though Luke varies significantly from Matthew and Mark and is in some respects closer to John. Matthew's account in Chapters 26 and 27 can stand for itself and in broad outline and for that in Mark Chapters 14 and 15. Chapter 26 begins with Christ's prediction of his Passion, and the Jewish plot hatched by the High Priest Caiaphas to snare Jesus by false witness. Judas is introduced as the traitor in this conspiracy, the man who will betray Jesus to the Jews and whose name is a type name meaning simply 'Jew'. On the certainty of the coming betrayal and death, Jesus constructs the Last Supper. The very basis of the Christian sacrament is therefore bound up with the whole narrative of the plot against him; and at the Last Supper Jesus again predicts his betrayal and singles out Judas as the future traitor. (John's gospel goes further. Here Jesus gives Judas a sop of bread and wine, and it is with the sacramental sop itself that Judas is selected: 'and after the sop, Satan entered into him', 13: 27. It is as if Jesus recruits Judas to betray him.) The desertion of Judas is one aspect of the Jewish failure to stand by Jesus in these accounts: Jesus predicts that Peter will betray him thrice, and in the garden of Gethsemane he finds the disciples sleeping. Judas arrives, and seals his apostasy with a kiss. Jesus forbids violence on the part of his followers, for 'how then shall the scriptures be fulfilled, that thus it must be?' (26: 54); 'all this was done, that the scriptures of the prophets might be fulfilled. Then all the disciples forsook him and fled' (26: 56). Jesus asks why his enemies come with such a show of force: 'Are ye come out against me as a thief with swords and staves for to take me?' asks the King James Bible (26: 55); and in a crucial translation variant, the New International Version has him ask 'Am I leading a rebellion?' Jesus is led back to a night-time meeting of the Sanhedrin at the house of Caiaphas where at last ('to put him to death', 26: 59) two false witnesses are found, who talk of Jesus's boast that he will be able to destroy the Temple of God and rebuild it in three days (26: 62) – which functions in this narrative, of course, as a prolepsis of his death and resurrection. This leads to the High Priest's question: Is Jesus the Messiah? 'I adjure thee by the living God, that thou tell us whether thou be the Christ, the Son of God.' Jesus's answer – 'Thou hast said. Nevertheless I say unto you, Hereafter shall ye see the SON OF MAN SITTING ON THE RIGHT HAND OF POWER, AND COMING IN THE CLOUDS OF HEAVEN' (26: 64) – leads the Chief Priest to rend his garments, proclaiming 'He hath spoken blasphemy' (26: 65), and to the judgment of the Sanhedrin: 'he is guilty of death' (26: 66). They then beat him, he remains silent (as in Isaiah 53), and Peter denies him thrice.

What follows in Chapter 27 appears to be a series of non sequiturs. First,

Jesus is handed to Pilate. Next, the narrative breaks off to conclude the fate Next, the narrative breaks off to conclude the fate of Judas, who in remorse gives back his thirty pieces of silver to the Chief Priests, who in their turn spend it on buying 'the potters' field to bury strangers in' – a narrative detail which operates as an eccentric typological fulfilment of Jeremiah (quoted in verses 9–10). Then the narrative reverts to Pilate, who asks Jesus not whether he is the Son of God but whether he is the King of the Jews: to which he receives the standard non-committal reply, 'Thou sayest'. Urged on by inner promptings and by his wife's dream, Pilate tries to persuade the multitude to release Jesus as his Passover amnesty – but the crowd calls out for 'a notable prisoner', Barabbas. This is another type-name; Barabbas means only 'Son of the father'. The gospels do not give his Christian name, which is Jesus. John identifies Barabbas as a rebel (verse 40) – though the King James Bible translates 'robber', probably the leader of a recent uprising against Roman rule. Luke (23: 15) has Pilate offer the choice three times, and identifies Barabbas as a traitor, who has engaged in murder and sedition. There follows Pilate's hand-washing, the buffeting of Jesus by the Roman soldiers who 'mocked him, saying, Hail, King of the Jews!' (Matthew 27: 29), the drink of vinegar mixed with gall, and the dicing for his garments at the foot of the cross – all in fulfilment of typology, the last explicitly identified (27: 35). Other such details follow, such as the rending of the veil of the Temple. Pilate's inscription over the cross is the prototype of Rich's: 'This is the King of the Jews.' Jesus is crucified between the two thieves (27: 38).

Matthew's account largely follows Mark's in its scenario of a formal trial. Luke, as Levy writes, is significantly different:

> The Sanhedrin met only once, in the morning on the Passover holiday and in Caiaphas's home, but Luke does not mention a charge concerning the Temple, false witnessing, blasphemy, or the tearing of judicial robes. The crucial question was simple and Jewish; 'If you are the Christ, tell us.' It provoked Jesus' Son of Man answer. The Sanhedrin took that as a confession of an unnamed crime and immediately brought Jesus before Pilate on explicit political charges (Luke 22: 66–71, 23: 1–2). Thus, in Luke the Sanhedrin neither tried nor convicted Jesus. It merely conducted an inquiry; on hearing Jesus' messianic claim it turned him over to Pilate for prosecution on political accusations.[40]

Luke also has the Chief Priest's servants buffet Jesus, and uses the motif of their blasphemy ('and many other things blasphemously spake they against him', Luke 22: 65). On Jesus's removal to Pilate in Luke, the Jews are quite clear that Jesus is accused of 'perverting the nation', and the relation between messiahship and kingship is articulated. Jesus is held to forbid 'tribute to Caesar, saying that he himself is Christ a king' (23: 2). In Luke, Pilate sends Jesus to Herod, in whose jurisdiction he is held to fall; but

Herod returns him, for he too is unable to find him guilty. It is Luke, too, who gives us the difference between the two thieves, one of whom insults Jesus and the other of whom shows faith and is promised: 'Today shalt thou be with me in Paradise' (23: 43). John is even more different. The Sanhedrin never meets to try Jesus formally but makes do with Caiaphas's brief private examination of him before he is sent to Pilate. Annas as well as Caiaphas is involved in the Jewish consultations, Barabbas is a political offender and the motive behind their reference to Pilate is the Jewish recognition that 'It is not lawful for us to put any man to death'.

There are major inconsistencies and differences between the Synoptic gospels and John, in some details of which Luke agrees with John. There are also major difficulties presented in the reading of any one account. The key inconsistency is that Matthew and Mark have the Sanhedrin meeting without proper motives, at the wrong time and in the wrong place for the purpose of trying Jesus. The obvious procedural violation is a matter of such clear prejudice that it constitutes a strong argument for a flagrant mistrial. That at least is the conclusion arrived at in 1948 by the American lawyer David C. Breed, who examined the whole case from the viewpoint of one preparing Jesus's appeal and found seventeen reversible errors. They include particular details ('Our feeling is that Caiaphas went too far and that a modern Court would reverse the judgment on this point'), and the whole process: 'The Jewish trial was illegal from start to finish under the then existing Jewish law.'[41] At the same time, Breed realises that 'to a Christian lawyer' the errors served a purpose:

> No one can fully understand the technical legal violations of the Trial of Christ and not be impressed again with the accuracy in which God in his grace has fulfilled such prophecies as that beautiful 53rd chapter of Isaiah with which we close our study. (p. 76)

To the eyes of such a Christian lawyer, therefore, 'the crux of the case' is not procedural flaws but perverted judgment: 'if the Sanhedrin had really heard and honestly weighed the evidence they would have concluded that Christ is the Messiah – is our Redeemer' (p. 60). This is the only conclusion that obviates Breed's problem: namely, that the gospels are not consistent in their presentation of the process itself. If there were such a major and blatant injustice as the night meetings, one would not expect Luke and John to overlook it. Nor, except to the eyes of a Christian lawyer, is the manifest construction of the accounts, especially in Matthew and Mark on typological lines, testimony to their reliability on strictly factual grounds.

The presentation of the details of a Jewish conspiracy in Matthew and Mark is, of course, factually suspect. Conspiracies are commonly what we allege to happen when we suspect collusion but cannot prove it; and this is one possible reading. It accords too with the emphasis on many kinds of

Jewish shortcoming in these two gospels – so much so that according to most textual scholars in its original and authentic ending Mark has no appearances at all of the risen Christ to the disgraced disciples. There is a question of fact – did the Sanhedrin have the power of capital punishment? – which is the subject of learned dispute; but it hardly matters. For the penalty that Jesus suffers is not the penalty for blasphemy, which is stoning, but rather the Roman punishment for political offences, crucifixion. The interweaving of the political and religious in these accounts is manifest in the figure of Barabbas, another Jesus who is Son of the Father: Levy is not the only writer to propose that he is a mere narrative doubling, carrying the burden of rebellion against Rome, and that in reality there may only have been one Jesus in Pilate's prison that Passover.[42] Moreover, the Chief Priest is made to rend his garments at a statement from Jesus that he is the son of God; but this would not have been blasphemy under Jewish law. For the Jews, as for Nayler and the Quakers, all believers are the sons or daughters of God. It is for Christians that the claim would be blasphemous, provided that it were untrue. Jesus does not commit any known kind of Jewish blasphemy. On such a reading the account substitutes blasphemy for a political offence, and makes Jews rather than Romans bear the opprobrium of killing Jesus. Indeed, in medieval drama, it is sometimes not Roman soldiers who actually crucify Jesus, but Jews. The trial as recorded in the New Testament was not illegal, but unhistorical.

That is the conclusion of Leonard Levy, who accurately represents one side in a two-sided twentieth-century debate on the trial of Jesus:

> The most famous and influential blasphemy trial in history was a religiously inspired fiction. The Jewish Sanhedrin, the great council of seventy presided over by the high priest, neither tried Jesus for blasphemy nor convicted him of any crime. The depictions of the formal trial of Jesus by the Sanhedrin in the Gospels of Mark and Matthew really mean to convey with dramatic force the Jewish rejection of Jesus. Theologically, the trial scenes in Mark and Matthew are crucial, because they reveal the identity of Jesus as the Christ. Readers understand that he had not blasphemed God and that the blasphemers were those who found him guilty, for they refused to accept him as Son of God and Messiah. (p. 29)

The point, according to Levy, is to exculpate the Romans from responsibility for the death of Jesus. Pilate is weak, though honourable, but he is not evil – that role belongs to the Chief Priest and Council, who plot Jesus's death. For early Christianity developed away from Judaism, and it hoped for Roman tolerance for its survival, especially after the Romans destroyed Jerusalem in 70. The gospels have a theological purpose – faith rather than historiography – and 'also an apologetic one'.[43]

Levy's position in the controversy conforms closely to the Jewish view; and it is a measure of the issue's importance that one of the major books on the subject is by Haim Cohn, a founding Justice of the Supreme Court of Israel. Cohn introduces his book by addressing what is at stake in Christian belief in the historicity of the gospel accounts:

> It is a belief still so strong and apparently so changeless that the largest concession which the great liberals among the hierarchy of the Catholic Church would nowadays be prepared to make would be to absolve the Jewish people as a whole, and the Jews and later generations, from the guilt which – they hold – attaches irrevocably to the Jews whom the gospels accuse of an active part in the trial.[44]

Cohn's account falls a little short of the position adapted by the Second Vatican Council which passed an act forgiving the Jews for their part in Christ's death – impertinently, perhaps, since Christ had to die and the Jews were the chosen agents of his death, as John's story of the sop Christ gives to Judas illustrates. But for Cohn, as for any Jew in the twentieth century, the backdrop to the issue is not textual study or academic divinity, but the Holocaust. I am reminded of how Jonathan Dollimore insists in *Sexual Dissidence* on the materiality of his subject, and why it matters:

> Reading culture involves trying to read the historical process within the social process, and in a way adequately aware of the complexity and discrimination of both, and with as much sensitivity and intelligence as possible. Lives and freedoms literally depend on it, especially where cultural discrimination is concerned – by which I mean both violent repression (as in racial or sexual discrimination) and that which passes as cultural discernment. I also mean to imply that the first sense is often closer to the second than adherents of the second usually admit. In both senses, and sometimes inseparably, it can be said that discrimination is the essence of culture. Which means that 'barbarities' of the 'civilized' present can never be rationalized as merely the remnants of a superstitious or less enlightened past.[45]

As Dollimore tells it, it transpires that a binary Christian discourse of evil is at the root of the Western cultural demonisation of the homosexual. The same discourse for Cohn and Levy underlies gospel accounts of the trial of Jesus. Through them they have affected more lives more palpably, more tragically and in greater numbers than in any other field of discourse.

Cohn's work is flawed by its lawyer's tricks and his confidence that he can work through a cover-up to what really happened: 'what had really happened was allowed – or caused – to fall into oblivion; what had been inexactly and tendentiously reported as having taken place became the Gospel truth and was made history' (p. 327). It meets bitter objection from proponents of the second major view in the controversy, the Christian. For most Christian commentators, an attack on the historicity of the gospels at this point even more than others is extremely dangerous, for Christian theology is based on Redemption through Passion; if the account of the trial is fictitious, where does that leave other key details of the account such as the Resurrection itself and, indeed, the Eucharist? If there was no trial, was there ever a Last Supper (as a Passover meal, another Jewish reference)? Most studies lack the judicious tone of A. E. Harvey's *Jesus on Trial*. Harvey carefully weighs 'the known conditions of Jewish legal practice',[46] and suggests that the account in John's gospel comes close to describing them fairly. Harvey therefore proposes to shift the weight of the Christian position towards the Johannine version and away from the Synoptic gospels, which offer 'an unsatisfactory piece of reporting. Many of the details are implausible, and many important questions remain unanswered' (p. 127). This is seconded in David R. Catchpole's study of *The Trial of Jesus* (1971), but Catchpole far more stridently objects to what he calls 'the "political Jesus" theory': 'the "political Jesus" theory is a failure' (p. 270). This notion of Jesus as political dissident is the blasphemy to which Christian orthodoxy feels a need to respond sharply – but, in the twentieth century, sensitively too. Catchpole therefore uses the methods of textual analysis, the *sitz im leben* of form criticism, to suggest that 'Jewish research into the Trial of Jesus cannot be understood apart from its setting in debate' (p. 261) – that is, though Catchpole does not say so, an understandable obsession with the Holocaust. Indeed, coolly appraised, the trial narratives of the gospels are not anti-Jewish at all, 'for to blame the Jews for the death of Jesus is not the same as being anti-Semitic' (p. 264).

Catchpole resumes where Josef Blinzler left off, after World War II but before Vatican II, with his attempt to produce a definitive Christian treatment of the issue. Blinzler is aware 'of the great wave of anti-Semitism of the very recent past',[47] but objects strongly to the notion that 'modern anti-Semitism was nothing else than the logical result of the Christian thesis that the Jews were guilty of the death of Jesus' (p. 4). Blinzler traces the history of Jewish writing on the issue from Joseph Salvador's *Histoire des institutions de Moïse et du peuple Hébreu* (1828), which took the uncompromising line that Jesus was justly condemned to death by due legal process, and encountered contemporary French legal process in consequence. In 1866 Rabbi Ludwig Philippson produced a simpler thesis 'that it was not the Jews but only the Romans who had condemned and executed Jesus. And in fact all Jewish authors have used the same method since' (p. 9), with the purpose of 'shaking the traditional view to its foundations'. Blinzler brushes aside most modern Jewish writing. 'As for the writing of modern Jews on the trial of Jesus, it is apparent often enough that their concern is to vindicate their forefathers rather than to reconstruct a historical event' (p. 8). He concedes that 'the story of the Passion of Jesus has truly become the story of the suffering of Jewry' (p. 8), but, nevertheless, on his first page, floats a possibility that the State of Israel might 'recapitulate the trial of Jesus and reverse the monstrously wrong verdict which was pronounced at the time'

(p. 3). Blinzler's conclusion is that 'the early Christian preachers' were right: 'the main responsibility rests on the Jewish side' (p. 290), and the death of Jesus was 'a judicial murder' (p. 293) – to which, however, Christians should respond as Jesus did, with forgiveness.

There is something shockingly ungenerous about such modern Christian formulations, that brusque and kindly desiccation simply an inadequate response to the horrific scale of lived Jewish experience, and blind to any worrying possibility that millions may have died for the truth shared by four partly conflicting narratives. That response intensifies when one turns to the greatest twentieth-century Jewish work on the subject, Paul Winter's *The Trial of Jesus*, with its dedication 'To the Dead in Auschwitz, Izbica, Majdanek, Treblinka, amongst whom are those who are dearest to me', and its biography of the author: a Czech Jew who went underground in 1939 on the annexation of Czechoslovakia by Germany, and managed to escape to Palestine, seeing active war service under British and American command. In 1945, Winter was charged with the repatriation of survivors from Buchenwald and other camps. He learned that 'his closest relatives, including his mother and his sister, to whom he was deeply devoted, had perished in Nazi extermination centres'.[48] He worked for refugees until 1947, but then returned to London and dedicated the rest of his life to writing on the trial of Jesus, the topic to which his history and the history of his century had led him, 'enduring a solitary existence devoid of every comfort, working in libraries by day, and by night earning a bleak livelihood as a railway porter, a watchman at a hostel for epileptics, a post-office sorter, and the like' (p. xl). His book was instrumental in affecting the Vatican Council's declaration on the relation between Christians and Jews, but Winter himself died, exhausted and in near penury, in 1969. The book is generous, brilliant and unpolemical in tone; and it has a moving epilogue that speaks nobly of Jesus and also wonderfully expresses Winter's sense of an ongoing text and of an exchange transaction:

> It is not over . . .
>
> Not Pilate's sentence, not the jostling of the soldiers who divided his garments, not even the cry from the cross was the last word.
>
> The accusers of old are dead. The witnesses have gone home. The judge has left the court. The trial of Jesus goes on. His is a trial that is never finished, and one in which the rôles of judge and accused are strangely reversed.
>
> Tribunals assemble. Tribunals disband. The bailiffs, the informers, the accusers, the witnesses, the governors, the executioners are still with us.
>
> Many have come in his name, and have joined the accusers; and there arose new false witnesses among them – yet even so, their testimony agrees not. Never spoken when Jesus was tried, the words 'His blood upon us and upon our children!' have come true – a thousand times. But no valid answer has yet been given to the question 'What will you that I do with the King of the Jews?'; only the cry 'Crucify him! Crucify him!' echoes throughout the centuries.

> Rabbi Eliezer ben Hyrcanus, Eliezer the Great, said of Jesus: He owns his share in the Age That Is Coming . . .
>
> It was not finished. Sentence was passed, and he was led away. Crucified, dead, and buried, he yet rose in the hearts of his disciples who had loved him and felt he was near.
>
> Tried by the world, condemned by authority, buried by the Churches that profess his name, he is rising again, today and tomorrow, in the hearts of men who love him and feel he is near. (p. 304)

The Jewish notion, then, is that the gospellers exploit the exchange transaction of blasphemy by having the Jews accuse Jesus in such a way that what the readers infer is blasphemy on the part of the Jews themselves, blasphemy represented in the narrative by their agency in the death of Jesus. Christian scholars have responded to this view as Christians have responded to blasphemy. I now want to put a parallel case rather than to arbitrate – a case where the roles are reversed, and where what is at stake has an almost Scriptural force. This time it is Jewish scholars who have found their orthodoxy challenged, and who have responded with some vehemence. The text is Josephus's account of the end of Masada – where, as he writes, at the end of a long siege the defenders realise that they can neither escape nor any longer resist. Their leader Eleazer then proposes mass suicide, rather than falling into Roman hands. Men kill their families and each other, until ten are left to kill by lots until the last kills himself. When the Romans enter Masada, they find absolute devastation, and learn of what happened only from two women and five children who had escaped death by hiding in a cistern. E. M. Smallwood argues convincingly that Josephus may have invented more than Eleazer's speech:

> The fire is a fact; abundant evidence of burning can be seen in the casemate dwellings and many of the public buildings. But this is no proof of Josephus' story. Is the truth the matter that when Silva's men broke in, they themselves fired the buildings and slaughtered everyone they found, that the few who hid out of their reach starved to death, and that Josephus' story is a myth serving the patriotic purpose of covering up the ignominy of the final Jewish surrender and at the same time the apologetic purpose of absolving the Romans of the barbarity of a final massacre of women and children?[49]

There is an extraordinary parallel with Jewish views of the trial of Jesus: the motive proposed for both is held to be apologetic, reflecting a need to exculpate and flatter the Romans. A cherished martyrdom of Jewish history is deconstructed in a manner that causes protests from orthodox historians.

However, in York in 1290 the two discourses meet. Hatred of the Jews as killers of Jesus blazes into violent hysteria, and the Jewish community of York, who have retreated for safety into Clifford's Tower, remember their Josephus and the commandment that Masada has become – and, according both to Christian chronicle and to Jewish sources, they put into effect the

Masada solution and commit mass suicide. What is the point here of distinctions between truth and falsehood? Past narratives, true or false, become the determiners of present history. It seems as if history itself, entering into the spirit of blasphemous reversals, indulges in a piece of carnival. The date of the York catastrophe was Palm Sunday.

As Winter understood, it is not just in Jewish history that the discourse of Christ's killing functions in our time. Norman Lewis, in *The Missionaries*, presents excerpts from the translation of the Bible by the fundamentalist New Tribes Mission for the Panare Indians of the Amazon in 1985. Since there are no Panare words for the essential Christian concepts, such as sin, this is a difficult task; but the New Tribes Mission solves the difficulty by translating key concepts into the Panares' own terms. What happens to the Passion of Christ is that there is no longer any reference to Pilate, to Romans – or to Jews. On the contrary,

> The Panare killed Jesus Christ
> because they were wicked
> Let's kill Jesus Christ
> said the Panare.
> The Panare seized Jesus Christ.
> The Panare killed in this way.
> They laid a cross on the ground.
> They fastened his hands and his feet
> against the wooden beams, with nails.
> They raised him straight up, nailed.
> The man died like that, nailed.
> Thus the Panare killed Jesus Christ.[50]

The new theology is used to predict the Panares' punishment; and that punishment is of course the destruction of their rainforest habitat and the traditional life-style that goes with it. God wants the Panare to wear American clothes, use soap, and have sweet-smelling orifices. The discourse of guilt for the Crucifixion is treated here as a transferable discourse justifying persecution and exploitation. Seeing it in this form, we can recognise it for what it is, and so identify the traditional role of the Jews in it. The Panare are non-Christians; they are therefore blasphemers, and so must be the subject of conversion whether they wish it or not. As blasphemers, they are able to assume the role of the Jews in the trial of Jesus. From the gospels onward, blasphemy is Greek for Jew.

Chapter 3

SPEAKING BLASPHEMY
The Later Middle Ages to 1600

The first two chapters of this book have attempted to characterise blasphemy in terms of certain themes and topics, and to provide an outline historical account of the discourse ranging from the Bible and councils of the early Church through to the Reformation. Detailed case-studies so far have been drawn mainly from the sixteenth and seventeenth centuries. I have explained in Chapter 2 that I subscribe, in the main, to Leonard Levy's argument that blasphemy in the medieval period is ancillary to heresy, and re-emerges as a primary discourse at the Reformation. There are, however, exceptions to this general case. It must be said that the only recent attempt to argue against Levy's thesis has misrepresented it though it valuably supplements his account by emphasising what Levy overlooked: later medieval Latin sources on sins of the tongue.[1] It remains true that blasphemy is not often used as a category separate from heresy, or from some other critique of sin as in the penitential manuals of the thirteenth century onwards.

There is a little more to be said than these positions allow. I want to establish in this chapter that there is a discourse of medieval blasphemy separate from that of heresy and more general dissent. It is of particular cultural importance in England. Writing about that discourse brings together various types of historical evidence and polemical, didactic and imaginative literature. I find too that the description of later medieval blasphemy I develop does not change substantially until the beginning of the seventeenth century. The Reformation and its aftermath play out the potential of medieval blasphemy. In the twentieth century, certain writers re-invent and partly rewrite it: Rushdie and Freud, but also Nawal el Saadawi, daughters as well as sons who would overthrow fathers. Continuities between medieval blasphemy and the Reformation are important, because they have been generally underestimated by historians and theorists working on later periods. Changes that occur during the seventeenth century have to do, to some extent, with the changing relation of Church and State on a European scale, whether Catholic or Protestant. In England, for example, blasphemy is held to be incorporated in common law after 1676. A major shift in the seventeenth century might also be seen to coincide with Foucault's notion of a major shift in episteme around that time and into the Enlightenment. However, I am as wary of this claim as I am of earlier claims for the originality of events in the early modern period. Both sorts of claim seem often to be grounded on a conviction, encouraged by some medievalists, that the Middle Ages are a period of such homogeneous and calm devotion that they cannot possibly have entertained ideas and social movements found to be interesting by later historians. In my view, two factors carry equal weight in the changes from the seventeenth century onwards: a change in theories of symbolisation and representation consequent upon a Protestant account of the Eucharist; and the transformed and freer types of exchange that follow upon industrial capitalism.

It is opportune here to recapitulate some definitions. In the end no absolute distinction is possible between heresy, blasphemy, sacrilege and apostasy. Isidore of Seville's definition of heretics as 'those who have withdrawn themselves from the Church' identifies heretics with apostates. Heresy, sacrilege and blasphemy come together in the following account of the London chronicle of 1466–7 – edited by Douglas Gray in *The Oxford Book of Late Medieval Verse and Prose* under the heading 'Heresy and sacrilege' – describing the opinions of the heretic William Balowe, burned at Tower Hill 'for he despised the Sacrament of the altar'. He also, consistently (he is a Lollard), refuses to confess to a priest and responds to the priest who attempts to get him

> at the time of his burning . . . to beleve in the hooly sacrament of the auter . . .: 'Bawe! bawe! bawe! What menythe thys pryste? Thys I wote welle, that on Goode Fryday ye make many goddys to be putte in the sepulker, but at Ester day they can nat aryse themselfe, but that ye moste lyfte them uppe and bere them forthe, or ellys they wylle ly stylle yn her gravys.'[2]

This outburst arises from an intellectual position but, at least as it is reported in an orthodox account, it is hardly comprehensible as one: its function is to excite shock, not thought. It works like an obscenity, not a logical proposition – and so it is blasphemy; but it is linked with Lollard views of the sacrament, heresy, and in orthodox eyes shows exactly the same brutal disregard for sanctified objects as in the robbing, that the account moves on to, from London churches of the boxes containing the consecrated Host.

So first, blasphemy is an act of language – in orthodox parlance, a sin of the tongue. Secondly, it differs from heresy in that it is not mainly doctrinal, as in my example, where the offensive speech is at one remove from a clear statement of the ideas that gave rise to it. From the New Testament on, one person's gospel is another person's blasphemy. If you are a Bogomil or a Cathar, you are likely to state your view of the Virgin Mary in a manner orthodoxy may find blasphemous; so will a Wycliffite stating a view on the

Host; and if you deny the efficacy of public prayer, you may get more than you bargained for by referring to the Lord's Prayer as 'bibull babill'.[3] Though in these cases the blasphemy follows from heterodox or heretical doctrines, it alludes to them by inference, without articulating them. Thirdly, blasphemy is a potent weapon in the armoury of heresy-hunters. It is satisfying as well as politic to impute blasphemous obscenity to heretics – while dancing naked, for example, they routinely defecated on crucifixes and stolen communion wafers (the charge is commonplace) – rather than articulating it fairly. Fourthly, and conversely, it is often a scandalised orthodoxy that gives both heresy and blasphemy wide currency – as in the extreme Muslim response to *The Satanic Verses*, or Calvin's outraged broadcasting of the anti-Trinitarian views of Michael Servetus. These are both permutations of the consequences of blasphemy's nature as a spoken act; they are a public ritual that confirms the fact of blasphemy, like the Jewish rending of the garments. Just as executing a murderer breaches a moral taboo against killing, so the accuser of blasphemy may feel a need to blaspheme.

Moreover, finally, blasphemy may be inherent not in the words used but in the nature of the user or the context in which they are used. Medieval parodies of the Mass routinely function in this way: the words are the right words, but the use and context are wrong. This is also the field of Chaucer's Pardoner: in certain circumstances, I can do most harm to something by repeating it. It follows that blasphemy, much more than heresy, is extraordinarily context-specific. Because this is so, blasphemy is a good perspective from which to see how *local* phenomena disturbed the *universal* claims of Catholic orthodoxy throughout the medieval period and beyond; it is also ideal territory for thinking about medieval popular religion and popular culture, for thinking one's way past the misleading opposition of popular and learned.

Above all, to reiterate the conclusion of the previous chapter, medieval anti-Semitism is culturally central. To quote Sander Gilman in *The Jew's Body*:

> It is Christianity which provides all of the vocabularies of difference in Western Europe and North America, whether it is in the most overt 'religious' language or in the secularised language of modern science. . . . Anti-Semitism is central to Western culture because the rhetoric of European culture is Christianity, even in its most secular form. This made the negative image of difference of the Jew found in the gospel into the central referent for all definitions of difference in the West.[4]

Blasphemy defines difference.

The connection between blasphemy and Judaism is present throughout the medieval period. It is the charge of heresy, rather than blasphemy, that is the standard from, say, the fourth to the fourteenth centuries, and blasphemy is often incidental to heresy in the way I have described, either as an activity or as an allegation. Heretics will be described as showing their true opinions or natures by attacking the symbols of orthodox Christian faith, the Trinity or the Cross: like Adelbert, or the Paulinians of the eighth century, or Peter of Blois, murdered by a hostile crowd in the twelfth century after he had made a bonfire of crosses.[5] Heretics will be described as blasphemers, like the beautiful girl who in the 1170s rejected the sexual advances of Gervase of Tilbury, with words associating loss of her virginity with her eternal damnation. She was reported by him and eventually burned for belonging to 'the blasphemous sect of the Publicani'.[6] But charges of blasphemy rather than heresy are brought mainly if infrequently against Jews or Judaisers: the condemnation in the synod of 754 of a man for propagating Judaism as a 'blasphemer' or 'pseudo-prophet';[7] the burning as a blasphemer of an English clerk who adopted Judaism in 1222, and another clerk, Robert of Reading, in the 1270s; the burning of a rich Jewish merchant of Norwich, Abraham fil' Deulecresse, as a blasphemer in 1279, and perhaps another such merchant in Nottingham at much the same time;[8] the sentencing of three Bulgarian Jews for blasphemy in 1360, one of whom recanted and was received into the Church, the second of whom was killed by an angry mob, and the third of whom had his tongue, lips and ears cut off in one of those calculated mutilations, like James Nayler's.[9]

The Jews, says the fourteenth-century *Life of St Theodosius of Trnvo*, 'blaspheme the images of Our Lord Jesus Christ and his most Pure Mother, . . . spurn the Churches of God and the sacrifices offered therein'.[10] Such anti-Jewish propaganda lies at the root of a broader discourse of blasphemy, such as the thirteenth-century account by Caesarius of Heisterbach of Albigensians in Toulouse, who 'led a prostitute to the holy altar and used her in front of the crucifix. Afterwards, they tore down the holy image itself, and broke off its arms' – blasphemies for which they will never, says Caesarius, be forgiven.[11] Did they really? Or is pious outrage here founded upon prurient invention? There seems to be no general rule to cover all cases, except that of the exchange transaction. There are more of those here, for sure. The obligatory orgy used as a charge against heretics is indebted, often verbally so, to Justin Martyr's account of the wild allegations levelled against the early Christians; and the sacramental outrages of the Albigensians – 'They have cast aside baptism; they blaspheme the sacrament of the body and blood of Christ' – are such as to make them 'worse than Jews or pagans', just as in their insults to the crucifix they 'behaved worse than Herod's soldiers, who spared the dead Christ and would not break his legs'.[12] Heretics attack God like Jews do. The English king, William Rufus, is represented by Eadmer as a blasphemer and as a friend of the Jews.[13] It seems reasonable to conclude that either one of these charges, true or not, could have given rise to the other, and they are, in discursive terms, tautologous.

Notions of swearing and of Christ-torture crescendo to reflect the piety of the twelfth and thirteenth centuries, as in Matfre Ermengaud's view that swearers are Jews, for blasphemous execrations against the Virgin and child re-enact the Crucifixion.[14] The association is licensed by Galatians 5: 20, but the concern with blasphemous oaths is constant in the discourse of blasphemy from the New Testament all the way to trials of the early twentieth century: profane oaths diminish respect for real ones, and the process of law is therefore brought to nothing. This is the orthodox view, and in the unstable exchange transaction of blasphemous discourse it rarely conforms to the reality of heterodox views: for example, Lollards such as Hawisia Moone express themselves in opposition to both legal oaths and profane swearing – in fact, they see legal oaths as a form of profane swearing.[15] The distinction is important to orthodoxy, not heterodoxy, and the binarism is therefore of orthodox imagining. So it is with the preposterous allegation that Jews go around stabbing the consecrated Host. In truth, one would only do this if one regarded the consecrated Host as the body of Christ and therefore as worth stabbing; in other words one would only do this if one were orthodox and confident of evading both legal process for slander and Freudian analysis. Underlying all such charges of attacks on Christ and on legal authority is the figure of the Jew, who in this discourse places himself where he had in fact been placed, outside the law. The blasphemer is outlaw, is Jew.

This is true of all periods of Christian history, at the level of ideology. St Athanasius condemned Arius as a blasphemer, and described Arians as 'Jewish blasphemers', 'modern Jews and disciples of Caiaphas'. In the Catholic prosecutions of the sixteenth century, we find a use of blasphemy as a means of condemning heresy as if from its own mouth. Ludwig Hatzer was executed in 1529 having been charged with offences against the doctrine of the Trinity and arguments against the worship of images: he was described as an 'Arian Jew'. Katherine Weigel was burned at the age of 80 in Cracow in 1539 for maintaining anti-Trinitarian beliefs which were described in her indictment as Jewish beliefs.[16] Luther pursued a tortuous route to full-throated anti-Semitism, for he began by embracing the Augustinian position that Jews, though their beliefs are blasphemous, should be tolerated as an index of the Christian difference and as a kind of final target for conversion. But he used the discourse of blasphemy – first, to attack the Catholic Church, then to justify the death penalty against Anabaptists, then to justify killing rebellious peasants (as blasphemers: to justify the peasants 'would be the same as to deny and blaspheme God, and to throw God out of heaven'), and eventually came full circle to a harsher view of the Jews as blasphemers:

> He urged that their synagogues, Talmuds, and prayerbooks be burned, their houses destroyed, their monies confiscated, their rabbis forbidden to teach,

and that no Jews be allowed to use the name of God under penalty of death. All must be put to forced labor, or, better still, exiled. Had he the power, he said, he would cut out their tongues because of their blasphemies and force them to accept Christianity.[17]

The shift in Luther's position reflects the major shift in the attitude of the medieval Church that, as Jeremy Cohen has, I think, demonstrated, came with the friars. Their view of the Church as a mystical body left no room for tolerance of Jews within Christian communities. Jewish beliefs were inherently blasphemous. All Jews did or wrote was 'blasphemous, sacrilegious, ridiculous and false' (not heretical); their blasphemies, as of the name of Christ, actively obstructed Christian belief.[18] So Jewish support was alleged for various Christian heretics. The Talmud was condemned, for instance by Pope Innocent iv in 1244, as the book of blasphemies, and it was ritually degraded and burned at the orders of St Louis of France. The choice of conversion or expulsion was offered by Ramon Lull. Obscene libels were alleged on Jesus and Mary (and on some of these inquisitors like Bernard Gui were in fact remarkably well-informed: there may have been some substance here); but there was no substance to the infamous blood libel – Jews killed and ate Christian children – which was disseminated by friars.[19] In all, the Jew is beyond humanity. In the words of Peter the Venerable: 'The Jews' refusal to submit to incontrovertible proofs and accept Christianity has placed them outside the realm of human reason, in the category of the beasts.'[20] The culmination, in European popular culture, is the image of the *Judensau* (Plate 2), as described by Isaiah Shachar.

A woodcut, instrumental in further disseminating the *Judensau* motif, was produced probably during the first half of the fifteenth century . . . and shows a large sow surrounded by nine Jews, of whom two stand in the background and seven are caressing or sucking the animal. The first two are bearded and are twice as big as the other, beardless, young Jews. . . . One boy, seated on the left, is caressing and kissing the sow's snout. . . . A group of four boys sit under the sow and suck. Another young Jew, the border of whose drapery is adorned with mock-Hebrew letters, sits facing backwards on the sow, holds up the tail and sucks its tip. Under the lifted tail another boys sticks out his tongue, caressing with his left hand the sow's hind-leg and pointing with his right to its rectum.

As it stands, the woodcut is a single big anti-Jewish joke centred on associating the Jews, in an intimate and obscene manner, with the animal they most abhor. The inscriptions make the joke quite explicit. The caption reads: 'This is why we do not eat roast pork. And thus we are lustful and our breath stinks.' While one Jew, probably the religious teacher, pronounces the exhortation 'This we should not forget – swine's flesh we must not eat', the other elderly man invites 'all the Jews' to 'behold what came to pass between us and the sow'. While most of the youngsters take the part of sucking piglets, one calls the sow 'our

2. *The Judensau*, woodcut. Germanisches Nationalmuseum, Nürnberg.

mother' and another encourages his brother to suck the tail so as to uncover the rectum. The tenor of the joke is profane and, while there are no allusions to Judaism as such, the Jews are explicitly the target.[21]

Exchange transactions are alive and well here: the attack on Judaism for blasphemy is itself a blasphemy on Judaism, in which one of its major taboos is subjected to scatological and demeaning etiological 'explanation'. In so far as it can be said to have a point, it is this: that Jews take to blasphemy the way that pigs take to dirt. There is a sort of historic justice in Freud's obsessive and scatological interest in blasphemy. The metamorphoses of the *Judensau* are beyond this chapter's scope, but there is evidence to dispute Shachar's conclusion that the motif is limited to Germany. There is an unpleasantly strong possibility that the exchange transaction of blasphemy is the marketplace of popular culture as studied by Stallybrass and White,[22] and their carnival pig is also a *Judensau*.

If the *Judensau* is a popular motif, the apotheosis of blasphemy, it nevertheless has learned manifestations. This is Matthew Paris's account of the death of Mahomet (Muhammad) in the *Chronica Majora*:

> By such empty discourses, this inveigler of souls, Mahomet, infatuated the minds of many persons. In his early life he was exalted and raised from the lowest condition by a noble woman named Adige, whom he had seduced and polluted by a clandestine connexion, and afterwards married; he then began to boast and exalt himself above all the powerful and wise men of the East, usurping the name and office of a prophet. The Lord therefore struck him with incurable epilepsy, and when it attacked him, he frequently fell down, as those who suffer from that disease usually do, on which, in order that he might not lose his accustomed authority, and thus be treated with contempt, he pretended that he was conferring and advising for the salvation of man with the archangel Gabriel, and could not endure his splendour standing. It happened one day, when surfeited with feasting and wine, in which, according to his preaching, he greatly indulged, that he fell on a dungheap overcome by illness, assisted, as was stated, by poison administered to him in his food that day by some nobles who were indignant at his pride. There he lay, in tortures, rolling about and vomiting, owing to his sins, and deprived of all consolation from his followers. Whilst lying there half dead, he was discovered by an ugly sow, with an unweaned litter of pigs, and being stuffed with food, the smell of which he breathed forth, and parts of which he had brought up in his sickness, he was by them smothered; and for this reason the Saracens till this day hate and abominate pigs more than all other animals.[23]

So much here is like the *Judensau* joke: bad breath, lechery, the Semite at the level of the pig; and the piece is an overt use of the discourse of blasphemy, in which Muslim taboos are used against Islam and actually explained etiologically as a sign of historic weakness, a cross between *The Satanic Verses* and a Just-So Story ('So we Jews do not eat pork . . .'). The conflation of Jew and Muslim is partly unconscious (they are both infidels, they both deserve death at the hands of crusaders – Jews in the Croxton Play of the Sacrament swear by Mahomet), partly strategic (a further exploitation of the exchange transaction), and partly a testimony to Western culture's particular concern with blasphemy in Spain, with its large Jewish/ Morisco population. This example shows the exchange energy of the topos. Quite rightly, the prevalent anti-Semitic value of medieval Christian culture is invoked today by those like Richard Webster who would extenuate Muslim response to Salman Rushdie's treatment of Muhammad. It is an irony, and a terrible continuation of the exchange, that apologists fail to see that the discourse of blasphemy adapted for use in condemning Rushdie is itself a product of that selfsame anti-Semitism.

The concern with possible blasphemy by the Morisco population of Spain extends well into the sixteenth century. Extensive records survive of the Inquisition in Valentia, where there are many more trials for blasphemy than elsewhere in Europe at that time. The Inquisition proceeded in Morisco communities with certain tests, such as saying the four canonical prayers, or making the sign of the Cross. Where these revealed possible problems, they enquired further into the speech acts of those under suspicion. The blasphemers they found were mainly male (blasphemy seems to have been more rarely committed by women), of reasonable family, most commonly small shop-keepers, and from a standard religious background (judged by knowledge of the Lord's Prayer, Creed, Ave and Salve). The most common blasphemies found are statements renouncing God, or expressing disbelief in him, denial of the Holy Name or of sacred tenets, non-observance of religious duties, and swearing by various parts of the body of God. The worst blasphemy is that against the virginity of the Virgin Mary. The Inquisition's punishments were graded according to the category of the offence, and whether the offence indicated or was likely to lead to heresy.[24]

The most developed use of the discourse of blasphemy in the medieval period before the Reformation occurs in England, where blasphemy gains a particular currency and vitality through the writings of John Wycliff. It is also the sharpest example of exchange at work before the Reformation, as Wycliff and his supporters battle for control of the discourse of blasphemy with the friars from whom Wycliff derives it and who will eventually succeed in using it against his supporters. The crux is again the consecrated Host. Wycliff's heresy grows out of a concern that the orthodox position is itself blasphemous, as Maurice Keen suggests:

> The friars live by a rule which is a human addition to Scripture: they sell absolutions and indulgences which are given by man, not by the Truth which speaks through Scripture; and they preach a doctrine of the mass which claims that man can make the body of God and which has no foundation in Scripture. The matter is always connected with putting the human above the divine, the cardinal sin and the error that is carnal by definition. What horrified Wyclif

most of all about the doctrine of transubstantiation was just this, its carnality. The priests who followed that teaching sold the host, which the eye can perceive is bread, as the corporeal body of God: they taught men to bow before what was material and corruptible, the very essence of idolatry; and they taught men to believe that they bit the body of Christ and were nourished bodily thereby, which was blasphemy.[25]

Gordon Leff adds:

[T]o identify the bread and wine with Christ's body and blood would be blasphemy in identifying him with what was material and corruptible; the priest would then be breaking Christ's body when he broke the bread; and an animal eating the host would be eating Christ. Above all, it would give the priest the power of making Christ's body when he celebrated mass.[26]

Wycliff's concern to avoid blasphemy does nothing, of course, to stop his reputation, when his followers have lost the battle for control of the discourse, as, in the words of Sir Thomas More, 'the first founder of that abominable heresye, that blasphemeth the blessed Sacrament'. Wycliff's views plainly prefigure the Protestant position, and are argued with a satiric vigour, especially in the vernacular. In the *Jack Upland* texts, exchange transactions become so circular that the Lollard texts attribute to the friars the Wycliffite position and attack them accordingly; it seems as if the exchange is more important than the substance of it.[27] However, it is of the essence of Wycliff's views that his Eucharistic position is bound up with his critique of the friars, in *De Apostasia* and *De Blasphemia*, as founding a private and irregular religion which brought the sacraments into a network of material and financial exchange. Wycliff accused the friars of bad faith: their sacramental teaching, he argued, was a deliberate and self-serving fraud.[28]

Vernacular Lollard treatises simplify but do not misrepresent in alleging that the friars have offered the sacraments for sale: they have become the usurers of the spiritual life.

They say that they have the keys of heaven and of hell, they may curse and bless, bind and unbind at their own will, in so much that for a bushel of wheat or xii d. a year they will sell the blisses of heaven by charter of clause of waranties, ensealed with the common seal.[29]

It is this intermixture of the financial and the spiritual that is the ground of blasphemy in Wycliff's own writing; and blasphemy is the ground of his writing. This may be seen very clearly from the *De Blasphemia*, which is the last treatise he wrote; it ends with an urgent recapitulation of the issues surrounding the Eucharist but develops the critique on this issue, on indulgences, on private religion and on papal power into the final and decisive demonstration that the Church of Wycliff's day is an institution of blasphemy. The entire discourse is that of blasphemy as I have described it, and behind it still stands the figure, or rather the spectre, of the Jew – both as consummate blasphemer and as usurer. This is why Dante places blasphemy and usury together in the third round of the seventh circle of hell (*Inferno*, Canto xiv); and why Langland in *Piers Plowman* (B, XVIII 92–109) has Faith suggest that living by usury is part of the thraldom of the Jews that is their punishment for murdering Christ. When proposals are made in seventeenth-century England for the return of the Jews, standard conditions mentioned are their perpetual abstention from blasphemy (teaching or profane swearing) and from usury. St Louis of France identified usury and blasphemy in his attacks on the Jews.[30] It is a crucial connection, and one that I shall explore further by showing how it is reversed in anti-Lollard polemic.

The Croxton Play of the Sacrament survives in a version designed for performance as played in Rome, we are told, in 1461. In outline, its plot is the standard anti-Semitic host-stabbing libel, and this is announced in the apparently processional banns constructed as a preliminary announcement. We learn that the events took place in Aragon, and concern a rich Christian merchant, Aristorius, who is persuaded by rich Jews, in return for £100, to steal and deliver to them the sacramental Host. This they attack with five symbolic stab-wounds, boil in oil and shut in a hot oven, all with unforeseen consequences: on the fifth stab-wound it drenches them with blood, the hand of the Jewish leader Jonathas sticks to the Host as he tries to throw it in the oil, with the result that his hand is torn off his arm and boiled with the Host in the cauldron that seethes as if with blood, and the oven itself bursts apart to reveal an image of the bleeding Christ who calls the Jews to repentance, asking them: 'Why blaspheme yow me? Why do ye thus?' (731).[31] And repent they do, immediately going to the Bishop to confess their misdeeds and be received into the Body of Christ. It has long been recognised that one element of the play is an attack on Lollardy, for the play uses the standard biblical injunction used in anti-Lollard propaganda, *Ite ostendite vos sacerdotibus*, and strikingly puts into the mouth of Jonathas the Wycliffite view of the Eucharist:

> The beleve of thes Cristen men is false, as I wene,
> For the[y] beleve on a cake – me think it is onkind –
> And all they seye how the prest doth it bind,
> And by the might of his word make it flessh and blode
> And thus by a conceite the[y] wolde make us blind
> And how that it shuld be he that deyed upon the rode.
>
> (199–204)

This is specific: the play represents an orthodox strong return of service in the Wycliffite contest of Judaising blasphemy.

However, there is a little more to say about it. First, it contains a genuinely popular element, the appearance of a quack doctor and his boy offering all sorts of guaranteed cure for the severed hand. This is a basic scene in the mummers' plays, and here is the earliest datable evidence for it. Here, the association makes for a redundancy in the text, for there are many stories that represent Jews as treacherous false doctors and in this context there seems little doubt that the Jews are confronted by another version of themselves (whom, however, they forcefully reject). If the carnival pig may be a *Judensau*, I am tempted by this example to argue that the quack doctor of folk drama is often a Wandering Jew. But what is of interest here is the displacement of Jewishness into more than one character, a process which is crucial in the case of the merchant Aristorius. Aristorius is given an opening speech that belongs to the genre of the brag: his trading covers the whole known world, both Christian and beyond. The speech also manages to convey the accurate sense that though Christendom may be universal, it is not infinite: it is in fact bounded by Semitic otherness.

That Other is defused at the end in two ways: by the conversion of the Jews and by the sentence that prohibits Aristorius from ever trading again. We have seen the moral danger of such merchandise in the scene where he contemptuously refuses the offer of £20 for stealing the Host, and again refuses £40, saying that he would not do it for £100 – but when Jonathas simply lays down £100, and the speech act is made into a material transaction, Aristorius takes it. At the end of the play, the priest is warned to be more careful, but continues to practise; the Jews are received into the community at the price of ceasing to be Jews; but Aristorius must cease to be a merchant, as if it is really his activities that have have occasioned the blasphemies of the play. Like Antonio in *The Merchant of Venice* (itself found in an earlier analogue in a friars' exemplum, where the true Cross takes the place of the Host in the Croxton play), Aristorius enables usury to enter the Christian community, and it is his activities that the play acts to curtail. He is the Christian fifth column who empowers blasphemy. There is a not entirely dissimilar moral ambiguity in Shakespeare's Antonio; and if there is a suggestion of homosexuality too, it is an appropriate one, for sodomy is what Dante places alongside blasphemy and usury: unnatural exchange of speech, goods or currency, and bodies. One might then think of the ambivalent position of merchants in much fourteenth- and fifteenth-century writing, and wonder if there is a connection between this and the discourse of blasphemy. Shylock's prototype is sentenced to lose his goods and his tongue. One might think of Valdes, who was a merchant and moneylender before he heard saints' lives performed by street performers and was moved to give up usury and blasphemy. I do not know how best to phrase the question to which all this leads. Does the exchange transaction that is blasphemy rest in part upon a fear of exchange itself, including that form of material exchange that requires speech acts such as promises and acceptance of conditions?

In discursive terms, are blasphemy and usury in fact interchangeable: a common discourse?

At this point a further theoretical step is needed. I should start with the interface between local and universal that I have mentioned at several points of my study. This is always a potential basis for misunderstanding, as the work of Carlo Ginzburg in particular has shown, but it is the coming of the friars that makes the issue impossible to contain, since the friars have and propagate a notion of universality so ambitious as to have been previously unimaginable. Using the work of Deleuze and Guattari, as well as Stallybrass and White,[32] I should like to show how the question is one of identity: identity, that is, as a functioning part of a Christian community. And the notion of identity, as Deleuze and Guattari enable us to see and verbalise, rests on a choice of incompatible models of the body – as organism, and as what they call machine. Ideologically, the orthodox view of the Church as Body of Christ rests on the notion of organism: thus a rebellious limb cannot be tolerated, and an (ab)errant local configuration must be attacked like a cancerous cell. But the real danger of such local growths is that they encourage an inorganic understanding of the body; because they can function separately, they reveal themselves to be potentially autonomous parts of a machine. What is offensive to orthodoxy is the thought that groups to be condemned as blasphemous can interact with each other and with other agencies without authorisation or mediation. Blasphemy is the product of a social machine, an institution of orthodoxy. And orthodoxy represses the knowledge of itself as an institution, reinscribing the notion of bodily organism in its very punishments: calculated mutilations of tongues, lips, ears, both punish the wayward parts of the blasphemer's body and mark the blasphemer symbolically as a wayward body part, now subject to the correction of the body politic.

It may prove possible to rewrite these distinctions so that usury occupies in the history of the machine the place that blasphemy occupies in the history of the Christian body. A society with hardly any vocabulary for conceptualising its own economic exchange moralises such exchange through a discourse that associates it with outlaws, Jews, even as the friars take on a competitive role in economic exchange and such activity becomes incorporated within the spiritual life of the Church, to fierce protests such as Wycliff's attack on indulgences. Different types of exchange transaction then revolve around the nature and propriety of exchange itself.

I want to avoid whatever the post-Marxist equivalent is of vulgar Marxism: because there is an economic exchange that is sometimes figured in the verbal exchange of blasphemy, it does not follow that the economic is somehow a deeper structure than the verbal. Nor, on the other hand, do I wish to privilege the role of discourse, as if historical events are spoken by it entirely to the bafflement of the actors within it. But I should want to argue that when Jeremy Cohen largely excludes the economic from his consideration of friars' attacks on Jews, his work is misleading, especially in view of the fact that friars are attacked by Wycliff for fulfilling within the Church the usurious role once fulfilled in medieval society by Jews.

In the second place, the homology of linguistic and financial exchange, the desire of orthodoxy is to prevent both. I have found very helpful Deleuze and Guattari's long fantasy on the history of civilisation in *Anti-Oedipus*, in a chapter that continually joins questions of representation and symbolisation with questions of social and economic organisation. They make a clear distinction between exchange and debt: medieval society admits debt rather than exchange. It is plausible, I think, to see medieval societies as amalgams of the two types of social organisation Deleuze and Guattari describe as anterior to modern capitalism, what they call the primitive socius and the barbarian despotic machine. So they are indeed societies whose institutions have a horror of both economic and semiotic exchange: exchange is 'that which must be exorcised, severely restricted, so that no corresponding value can develop as an exchange value that would introduce the nightmare of a commodity economy' (economic exchange) and 'lead to a decoding of flows' (semiotic exchange).[33]

In this light, it seems reasonable to argue that late medieval and early Protestant states (Calvin's Geneva as much as medieval Rome) seek to control both types of exchange in the name of transcendent value. There is no room for a neutral, empirical theory of language in a society grounded upon incarnate Word, and no real room for a material category 'debt' from which unregulated economic exchange might function when the term has already been reserved for sin and guilt, *debita nostra*. This may explain why there is no original medieval economic theory, and no language available to it: *Piers Plowman*, involuntarily rather than generically allegorical, sounds like a sermon or manual even when it it is trying to sound like what we would recognise as an economic treatise. And it explains what may seem to us the exaggerated and vociferous offence that orthodoxy takes at blasphemy: as in the notion that swearing tears the body of Christ, orthodoxy – behaving as the wounded organism – pointedly attributes to blasphemy the transcendent nature of Word, on which sacraments depend, and refuses to admit a more limited, material or instrumental possibility.

Why does the discourse of blasphemy focus on the Eucharist? Because exchange is semiosis, and the Church regulates it in order to perform it, uniquely, in the Eucharist, in the body of Christ which holds together the Body of Christ.[34] What is anathema is any proposal, or any rival practice that might conceivably signify, that the Host merely represents what incorporates it, and that the Eucharist is therefore a semiotic transaction like any other. The Church must be the mediator of exchange, semiotic and financial. According to Rossi-Landi, merchandisation is semioticisation.[35]

What does not accord with rigidly limited and controlled exchange is isolated from any other semiotic or cultural process, from any social or economic flow. That is why blasphemy cannot be heard; and why blasphemy can only be heard, never understood, as the report of it is decontextualised and desocialised.

What happens if the context gets free play? Then we should find something daring and dangerous, a literature based on blasphemy – and we find just such a thing in the *Canterbury Tales* of Geoffrey Chaucer, specifically in 'The Pardoner's Prologue and Tale'. The Pardoner himself is one of the most memorable characters of Chaucer's 'General Prologue'. He rides with his friend, the Summoner, singing 'Come hither, love, to me'; he has hair yellow as wax hanging as far as his shoulders, but thinly, in strands. He has eyes that glare 'like a hare's' and a voice 'as small as hath a goat'. He is beardless, now and forever: 'I trow', says the narrator 'he were a gelding or a mare' – a eunuch or a homosexual. Readers deduce from this enigmatic comment that the Pardoner is not a virile paragon of heterosexuality, but the alternatives we are offered seem generous to a fault. Chaucer does not tell his readers what to think; he simply constructs the impression of anomaly, of sexual difference. The portrait then moves on to the Pardoner's professional qualifications as a seller of indulgences. 'He was in church a noble ecclesiast' – a line that probably suggests the contrary of its obvious sense, and implies that like most pardoners, this is a lay official who nevertheless preaches – with great success, attributable in part to his collection of false relics: a pillowcase that he claims to be Our Lady's veil, a portion of St Peter's sail, a brass cross, pigs' bones, and a magic mitten. All his efforts are directed at self-aggrandisement; and this is the theme that the Pardoner takes up in the Prologue to his Tale, confessing: 'I preach of nothing but for covetousness.' The theme of his sermon is 'avarice is the root of all evils'. Thus, he says, he is able to preach against the very vice that he practises, avarice; yet he is able to make others turn away from it and sincerely repent. But that is a by-product of his own avarice. The cumulative details of the portrait and the Prologue suggest a response to the Pardoner stronger than amusement. For he is a figure of religious hypocrisy: 'Thus spit I out my venom under hue / Of holiness, to seem holy and true' (481–2). At the end of the Tale, he makes an attempt, good-humoured or otherwise, to sell his fake pardons to the pilgrims who have been the audience of his confession. The Host's response is one of the most famous outbursts of anger in English poetry: 'I wish I had your coillons [testicles] in my hand instead of relics', he says. He speaks of their being cut off and enshrined in 'a hog's turd'.

This ending is notoriously elusive, depending on whether one takes the Pardoner to be a eunuch or a homosexual. The joke turns on whether the Pardoner has any testicles to cut off: the Host either castrates him verbally or points out his existing gross deficiencies. The literary situation is further complicated by intertextual reference to the *Roman de la Rose*, where Reason responds to the Dreamer's complaints that she refers obscenely to 'coilles' ('testicles', but more like modern 'balls' in semantic register) by claiming that she has the power over language and can call things whatever she likes – she could have called relics 'coilles' or 'coilles' relics as she so pleased.[36] Relics become the category for verbal signs. The Pardoner's anatomy is therefore linked to the relics that he carries and the language that he employs: all are equally inauthentic. Other intertextual reference to the *Roman de la Rose* supports such a view. The portrait of the Pardoner is based on the figure of Faux-Semblant, False Seeming, the hypocritical friar. Yet the Pardoner, like False Seeming, is a literary contradiction: like the Cretan liar who says 'All Cretans are liars', he is candid about his dissimulation. And we do not quite know how to disencode his false appearance. Is he eunuch or homosexual? Is he layman or cleric? Is he an evil man who does good, or a totally corrupting presence?

The sermon the Pardoner preaches is impressive, in spite of the fact that it is identified in advance as the sermon on the theme 'avarice is the root of all evils' with which he feeds his own avarice. It begins with a setting: in Flanders there was once a company of young people who made a habit of folly such as debauchery, gambling, brothels and taverns – which they frequent day and night, eating and drinking beyond their capacity and swearing freely: 'they tear into shreds our blessed Lord's body' – 'it seemed to them that the Jews had not wounded it enough' (474–5). There follows a long and vehement excursus in denunciation of gluttony, seen here (as it often was in the later Middle Ages) as the keystone of sin and the cause of the Fall, including an attack on cooks who (in the language of eucharistic theology, and reversing its direction) 'turn substance into accident' (539). Blasphemy is a major consequence: and the Tale gives examples of false oaths ('By God's precious heart!'; 'by his nails'; 'by the blood of Christ'; 'by God's arms'). At length, the narrative resumes. At plague time the three figures of riot hear a funeral bell toll, and are informed that an old friend has been taken by 'a privy thief' called Death. They resolve to confront Death and slay him, and, swearing blood-brotherhood to each other and cursing horribly, they reel off in search of him. Instead, they discover an Old Man, who remains unidentified in the text and whose identity has been a topic of continual critical speculation: he is another enigma, to be added to those of the Pardoner's person, and some have even read in him the spiritual despair that supposedly characterises the teller. The Old Man wants to die but cannot, like the Wandering Jew; he roams the earth: 'And on the ground, which is my mother's gate / I constantly knock with my staff and say: "Dear Mother, let me in! See how I vanish – flesh blood and skin. Alas, when shall my bones be at rest?"' But the three simply insult him.

He then directs them to Death, and following his directions they find a huge hoard of gold under a tree. The eldest rejoices, and proposes how they may steal away with the treasure without attracting undue attention: two of them should guard the treasure while the third goes to town for bread and wine. They draw lots under the tree to determine which of them shall perform the mission to town; and the cut falls to the youngest. In his absence, the others plot his murder; meanwhile, he, in town, buys poison. On his return he gives his 'two brothers' poisoned wine; after they have murdered him, they drink it and die. The Tale ends with a rhetorical condemnation of 'mankind' for sin and blasphemy.

The Tale itself is an extraordinary essay in blasphemy. We know that some such story had currency in Chaucer's England, and that it was taken to allude to the three Persons of the Trinity: in the contemporary poem *Piers Plowman*, when an example is sought of blasphemous academic speculation, the text refers to 'clerics and lay people, in their cups at dinner, when minstrels are quiet', who 'speak about the Trinity, how two slew the third'. The Pardoner's Tale appears to be a version of this shocking motif. This is told against blasphemy as the rhetorical culmination of the 'cursed sin of all cursednesse' (899). The swearing of the rioters of the Tale wounds the body of Christ, so that they take on the role of his torturers. The three are a parody Trinity: 'We three be all one', they swear (696). The two older ones send the youngest one to town – more than one critic reads this as a parody of the Incarnation; and certainly the actions of all three then parody the Eucharist and the Crucifixion. The youngest returns with poisoned bread and wine, and he officiates over their final meal. Before it is over, he himself as victim lies dead under a tree, riven through the side by slayers who proclaim their sacrifice by a meal of bread and wine; the murderers who, when they had 'accorded to slay the third', promised to play at dice (824), like the soldiers at the Crucifixion. The Tale is told against blasphemy by a self-confessed blasphemer, the sexually anomalous lay Pardoner, who boasts of his skill in preaching and of taking the divine name in vain for his own profit – and who tells his tale toying with cakes and ale that are sometimes interpreted as being proleptic of the Eucharistic parody of this Tale. (The reason why gluttony in the late Middle Ages is held to include swearing, blasphemy, sorcery, witchcraft and devil-worship is itself to do with the Eucharistic perversions attributed to heretics and Jews.)

The entire combination of elements that I have listed in this chapter so far occurs in this tale: the Trinity, the Eucharist, Jews; blasphemy, sodomy (taking the Pardoner to be a 'mare'), and usury, the avarice of the Prologue and the attempt in the Tale to make gold grow by murder; merchandisation in the Prologue, in which God becomes a commodity on sale for profit, and semioticisation in the Tale; even the conjunction Goux sees as fundamental in his *Symbolic Economies* between gold and the phallus – the gold of the three rioters is fools' gold, and the Pardoner is a fool's phallus.[37] Yet the entire performance is typically context-specific: there is nothing wrong with the theology of the Pardoner's Tale except its environment – an environment that includes *The Canterbury Tales*. The Tale condemns blasphemy; produces blasphemy; and is blasphemy. And if Chaucer's purpose is to condemn blasphemy by showing two versions of it, then in order to condemn it he must first speak it. In this respect, the poet is like the Pardoner, which is why the Pardoner's Tale strikes so many critics as an unstable or parodic mirror of the making of *The Canterbury Tales*. Some critics see in the Pardoner's Tale Chaucer's return to the issues of classical rhetoric: can an evil man persuade an audience to do good? The fifteenth century thought not: beside the vastly effective peroration of the Tale, an appeal to mankind to cease being untrue to Christ, the scribe of the Ellesmere manuscript wrote *'Auctor'*, 'Author', presumably because he could not bear the thought of being moved by the ostensible speaker. But another variant of the same question would be: can a lay author preach? There is transgression here, resembling that of the Pardoner himself. The Tale induces a chronic instability, a crisis of voice and of reference, in the interplay between literal and metaphorical, truth and falsehood; and it seems to occlude the possibility that any language can escape the circle of paradox it establishes. Metaphoricity, like blasphemy, is here an infinite regression.

The Tale works as collapse of authority in terms of the rhetoric, and the theology, of the lie. Chaucer's interest in the lie occurs because he lacks a neutral term, and an easy distinction and defence, for 'fiction'. He must take authority over his readers and over language itself, in order to make room for his fiction – in order in the Pardoner's Tale to turn the substance of Latinate theology into the accident of vernacular fiction. The room is that of literary tradition in English, the room that Rushdie assumed was still available when he wrote *The Satanic Verses*; and Chaucer did more than most to construct it. One can as well ask the same question of Chaucer as Rushdie's detractors have asked: does his fiction itself not pervert religion for gold?

There is no doubt that the Pardoner's Tale is deeply shocking. The early Church and medieval Christianity took the Trinity as absolutely fundamental to the institution of the Christian faith, and Chaucer's parody of it is unparalleled until Apollinaire's story 'The Heresiarch' in the early twentieth century (see Chapter 6). The offence it might cause is as great, and potentially of the same order, as that felt by some Muslims in response to *The Satanic Verses*. But there is also a strikingly similar defence available to both Chaucer and Rushdie. In Rushdie's case, the counter-argument runs that the perversion of the Qu'ran is not that of the author, but that of the central character of the book, Gibreel Farishta, whose insanity is the subject of the book, and in whose mind we are unmistakably located. As Rushdie

stressed when he announced his return to Islam, the profanation of the
Qu'ran is Gibreel's psychodrama, and it marks the religious narrative of a
lost soul: 'a parable of how a man can be destroyed by loss of faith'. If this
struck some of Rushdie's liberal supporters as special pleading, they might
do well to read some Chaucer criticism. For the violence of the Pardoner's
Tale is there more often than not read as a projection of the Pardoner's own
evil and deadly literalism, as his whole Tale perverts theological and
sacramental truths by turning substance into accident.[38]

Certainly, the Pardoner is a product of his own discourse. The whole call
to repentance arises from the increased attention given to the sacrament of
penance after the Lateran Council of 1215, and the large number of
thirteenth- and fourteenth-century handbooks that addressed a tropical
profusion of interlinked sins. Recent work has shown how the homosexual
is constructed by such literature and its bodily prohibitions.[39] Sexual
misbehaviour is itself a form of blasphemy: the Pardoner is constructed
from the pages of the texts he writes. Whether or not he dwells too much
in the letter, he certainly exists too much in the body; and what he does
to the Trinity in his Tale is what Chaucer does to his description,
he over-embodies. The Host's violent retaliation, linking the Pardoner's
(disembodied) body parts with animal excrement, can plausibly be seen as
the winning return of service, orthodoxy's revenge for what the Pardoner
has done to God's body (or bodies) in his Tale. Chaucer does not merely
describe the Pardoner: both from the inside, in his confessions, and on the
outside he demonises him.

The way Chaucer represents the Pardoner is just the way that orthodoxy
represents a heresiarch as a diabolic and caricatured blasphemer. Bernard
Gui, for example, writing on Valdes and the Waldensians, tries unusually
hard to give a temperate account of their ideas – not out of any sympathy
for them, but in order to give fellow-inquisitors enough clues to catch them.
Waldensians hold that all oaths are forbidden by God; they deny
transubstantiation; they deny ecclesiastical authority and exalt the role of
the laity, including women, even to preach; they secretly subscribe to
receptionism (the Eucharist fails to change substance in the hands of a
wicked priest); they call each other brothers and live in a 'fraternity'; they
are committed to working in and through the vernacular; they advocate
celibacy, even for those who are married; they claim a direct mission from
God. So many of these allegations are conventional that it is hard to have
full confidence in such a listing, but it seems like an honest effort to entrap.
Every so often, however, Gui's aversion to the Waldensians tips into angry,
discourse-driven nonsense. These advocates of celibacy practise 'the
abominable and promiscuous coupling of men and women, under cover of
darkness, and concerning the apparition of cats, sprinkling with tail'.[40]
While Gui concedes that Valdes and his followers practised absolute

poverty, in other attacks we find more reversal: Valdes, the former usurer, enriched himself through the gullibility of his followers. He is therefore a discursive prototype of the Pardoner, a figure of the religious charlatan – to his followers, no doubt, a saint. Part of the reason for the richness of the Pardoner's Prologue and Tale is that many of the discursive markers of heretical Otherness as blasphemy are clustered in portrait or Tale or both: avarice; gullible followers; a concern with oaths (too many or none – equally transgressive in this economy); a mockery or parody of the doctrine of transubstantiation and of the Eucharist as religious event; sexual deviance (as with oaths, too much activity or none – the erotic range of geldings and mares); and, if the Pardoner is indeed a layman, the cardinal offence of the Waldensians, who 'infatuated with their own interpretation . . . presumed to preach the Gospel in the streets and public places'. The Pardoner's entire performance depends on 'this arrogant usurpation of the office of preaching'.[41] Chaucer's assemblage is therefore constructed from the discourses that also condemn a related activity, the one in which Chaucer is engaged: vernacular writing. Chaucer's project depends on the Pardoner's exchange, English for Latin – the institutional language of high culture, which is, by institutional definition, religious.

The discourse of blasphemy is therefore crucial to the production of a literary culture in the vernacular. The exchange transaction in the Pardoner's case is at work between Tale and teller, but it also continues between text and reader. Chaucer's semiotic programme is to take the mass audience of ecclesiastical discourse and appropriate it, as Walter Benjamin says of the modern novel, so as to 'produce a public of solitary readers in much the same way that modern political economy produces an aggregate of atomised individuals'.[42] It is a material space, Chaucer's characteristically political space of the ostensibly private, and a space made for secular writing, unauthorised yet drawing illicitly upon the luminosity of ecclesiastically licensed language. That cultural space, which we call literature, is made out of the discourse of blasphemy.

None of this is to imply that all vernacular writing on religious subjects in the later Middle Ages is potentially blasphemous. On the contrary, there are many approved works of devotion, or works whose function is to regulate lay behaviour in an ecclesiastically sanctioned fashion. During the course of the fifteenth century such works seem more and more destined for unmediated lay use – Chaucer includes one, the Parson's Tale, in *The Canterbury Tales*. Since, however, the reader represented in such texts is one who wishes to do nothing more than conform to ecclesiastical sanction, the distinction is unexpectedly academic. More challenging altogether is the large number of Lollard treatises, many of which seem to have won more general currency than might have been expected given their repression in Church and State. Their heterodoxy takes English prose into sophisticated areas of argument conventionally – that is, ideologically – left to Latin. The ideological prohibition is seen most clearly in the question of Bible translation: the Wycliffites produce one, and the Church activates the statute *De Heretico Comburendo* (1401) which provides that anyone found in possession of an English Bible translation should be burned at the stake. Here we see the basis of anxieties about vernacular blasphemy: Latin is God's language, not English.

Some vernacular works draw their safety from the fact that they were never designed for a general public and were addressed to readers whose views, tastes and abilities were already known to their writers. This applies to most of the writings of Walter Hilton, to many of the German mystics of the fourteenth century, and above all to the outstanding work of meditative counsel based on the teachings of the pseudo-Dionysius, *The Cloud of Unknowing*. In *The Cloud* and associated treatises, the vernacular is used, but not because it is easier to understand than Latin. On the contrary, the work is addressed to one who might be more familiar with such a discourse in its usual language. It might even be said that English is used because it is harder. The text is shorn of Latinate theological jargon, and the vernacular, in all its baffling unfamiliarity, is made to bear the personal spiritual experience of the reader, who by its use is deprived of an intertextual reference. The fact that use of the vernacular here is marked as a religious choice, and the vernacular is thereby raised to new heights in its struggle with difficult content, makes for a strange affinity between *The Cloud* and Lollard writings – albeit one visible only in the historian's hindsight.

More appealing still is the modern rediscovery of *The Book of Margery Kempe*, a work that seems never to have won a public in the fifteenth century outside the Charterhouse of Mount Grace in Yorkshire.[43] It appears to have been used there to license an expressive and highly physical form of devotional practice among the male recluses. Kempe, the pious entrepreneur and pilgrim, records a life of religious singularity: her desire to be excused from the embraces of an eventually compliant husband in order to accept the spiritual advances of her suitor Jesus, her troubles and tribulations in England and overseas, the behavioural consequences of her devotion (weeping, shouting, public swooning), and even a confessor's misunderstanding of the postnatal depression with which it all started. In spite of being mistaken for a Lollard, as she tells the story, Kempe is resolutely orthodox: her sole problem with the sacraments of penance and the Eucharist is her wish to partake of both more than once daily. Her style is vivid, particularly in its rendering of conversation, by no means wholly unlearned, and utterly memorable. Her book, which she says was dictated to her confessor, is rapidly becoming a classic of the late twentieth century. It is ironic and somehow fitting that from a century of growing lay containment and ecclesiastical control over religious affairs, of political orthodoxy and male dominance, the text that now stands out is the autobiography of a woman who would be religious.

Vernacular religious writing of this sort in the hands of a lay woman registers a shift away from exclusive clerical use, and as it were ownership, of the discourse. Is blasphemy then a danger? Wycliff thought so. His Latin treatise *De Blasphemia* (*Of Blasphemy*) begins with a false etymology of the word blasphemy as *blas-femina*, foolish and harmful woman.[44] The fifteenth-century evidence of Margery Kempe's book as a Carthusian treasure might indicate that it is not regarded as dangerous; but much writing on the book, since the rediscovery of the manuscript in 1935, has assumed the contrary. Kempe has been censured for 'a crude realism which intrudes in a very embarrassing manner' or for 'serious perversions of mystical concepts' supposedly arising from 'her consistent inability to differentiate between metaphor and actual experience'.[45] Scholars who have formed this view are thinking of passages in which Kempe imagines her spiritual marriage to Jesus. She has a vision in which Jesus presses himself upon her as her bedfellow:

> For it is appropriate for the wife to be on homely terms with her husband. Be he ever so great a lord and she ever so poor a woman when he weds her, yet they must lie together and rest together in joy and peace. Just so must it be between you and me, for I take no heed of what you have been but what you would be, and I have often told you that I have clean forgiven you all your sins.

> Therefore I must be intimate with you and lie in your bed with you. Daughter, you greatly desire to see me, and you may boldly, when you are in bed, take me to you as your wedded husband, as your dear darling, and as your sweet son, for I want to be loved as a son should be loved by the mother, and I want you to love me, daughter, as a good wife ought to love her husband. Therefore you can boldly take me in the arms of your soul and kiss my mouth, my head, and my feet as sweetly as you want.[46]

So strong is her love for Jesus that when the Father of Heaven proposes marriage to His Godhead, Kempe is reluctant: 'for all her love and affection were fixed on the manhood of Christ, and of that she did have knowledge and would not be parted from that for anything' (pp. 122–3). To modern eyes this teeters on the verge of doctrinal error: Margery Kempe's view of the Trinity goes too far, surely, in dividing the Persons. On the other hand, her distinction between the manhood of Jesus and the abstraction of God exaggerates in the direction of orthodoxy, not away from it, and she is not alone in her desire to emphasise, and revel in, the corporeality of the Son.

In fact, one cannot assess the issue of possible blasphemy here without taking in to account the genre in which Kempe is writing: the discourse of mystic eroticism that sweeps all before it in the twelfth century, and is associated with Saint Bernard of Clairvaux. The spiritual changes of that time quite suddenly shift their focus from Christ in Majesty to the immanent Jesus as infant and as tortured body suffering on the Cross. They foreground the Virgin Mary in an exalted role that she has not since lost in the Catholic tradition. Linked with these new cults is a renewed interest in the Song of Songs, read as the mystical book of spiritual love, and a plethora of commentaries upon it, of which the longest and most famous remains Bernard's – written in the form of a huge sermon cycle and preached to his community at Clairvaux. The dominant image is that of spiritual marriage, with the soul as the Bride of Christ, and, since this is always constructed as a feminine role, one might think that the discourse was more accessible to women than men.[47] There is a famous theoretical attempt to claim mystic eroticism as the genre par excellence in which women are privileged, by Luce Irigaray in 1974. Irigaray claims:

> This is the only place in the history of the West in which woman speaks and acts so publicly. What is more, it is for/by woman that man dares to enter the place, to descend into it, condescend to it, even if he gets burned in the attempt. It is in order to speak to women, write to women, act as preacher and confessor to women that man usually has gone to such excesses.[48]

As she characterises the quality of such women's writing, Irigaray's own writing enacts the heightened sexual excitement she recounts. Her language is appropriated from Georges Bataille, with its concentration on wound, ecstasy, flame and total immanence, as women discover their special relation to 'that most female of men, the Son' (p. 199) and act out the discourse in autoeroticism. The woman answers wound for wound, gazing upon 'the gaping space in your loving body' and touching 'the lips of that slit where I recognise myself' (p. 200). Irigaray's characterisation of the discourse extends to the later medieval women writers of Europe, who raise a masochist abjection to the level of sainthood, women such as Angela of Foligno, who drains with her mouth the pus from a leper's wound – and Irigaray sees in such conduct a form of transgression that disturbs orthodoxy in the form of her male confessors:

> This strength soon becomes exalted in such a flood of potency that she is taken to be possessed. Therefore she is condemned by confessors or inexperienced voyeurs who are horrified to see or hear her fall stricken to the ground, toss and turn, shriek, grunt, groan convulsively, stiffen, and then fall into a strange sleep. They are scandalised or anxious at the idea of her striking herself so terribly, thrusting sharp points into her stomach, burning her body to put out the fire of lust, searing her whole frame, using these extreme actions both to calm and to arouse her sleeping passions. The explosion of these passions strikes whoever witnesses them dumb. (p. 198)

Irigaray's is far from being a safe inference. When Satan wished to tempt Saint Francesca of Rome in the late fourteenth century, she reported that he appeared to her in the guise of her trusted confessor, Mattioti, offering to

write down her visions for her and promising her a 'big book' like Saint
Bridget's.[49] The evidence is not that confessors condemned such extreme
behavioural manifestations but that they showed an inexhaustible enthusiasm for them, and regarded holy women as a discursive site of mystic
eroticism available to men and women alike. Far from attempting to
suppress such discourse, confessors clamour for it with an insatiable
appetite: Margery Kempe is not alone in deploring the frequent exhortations
by her confessor to write down her visions. Like many of the women writing
in the vernacular, she dictates her visions to her confessor, whereas women
writing in Latin are held to write for themselves. Such scenarios do not tell
us of historical actualities; they are rhetorical figures of the hierarchy of
languages in the Church, and the need for vernacular writing to be
authorised. The desires of confessors for more text spans both Latin and
vernacular: Hildegard of Bingen records the same sort of pressures as
Margery Kempe, and like Kempe and others represents her eventual
production of text as the recovery from illness – illness that leads to vision.
Most of these women, then, represent themselves as *resisting* male urgings
to write; the holier they are, the longer and more intense is the resistance.

When they do write, all but Kempe write for a particular community. In
the cases of Saint Bridget of Sweden or Hildegard of Bingen, the women
themselves set up the religious communities that are to be their audiences.
No sooner has Hildegard consented to write when she produces a vision in
which Christ commands her to set up a new abbey at Rupertsberg, and she
insists on doing so with the full authority of divine instruction. For
Hildegard, vision and community are one and the same, and vision is
already cognate with writing. If writing is usually singular, the texts
produced by such women are always collective – a collectivity expressed by
Hildegard's music, written in order that all the voices of her community may
combine as one. Community, writes Jean-Luc Nancy, is prior to 'the division
of voices'.[50] Writing, for Hildegard or for Saint Bridget, is inseparable from
community: it is an act of foundation, of institutionalisation. When it is in
place, it becomes magic writing, like that of the book of Revelation – to
change one word is to be erased from the Book of Life: as the basis of an
order, it becomes a sacred text.

Margery Kempe is unique in apparently possessing no community.
However, she lives at a time when Lollards are becoming socially
treacherous, and in danger of death. She has to defend herself against the
charge of being one – and of being one at a time when there were many
outstanding Lollard women. In her behaviour, Kempe conspicuously does
everything that Lollards do not – confesses, takes the sacrament, goes on
pilgrimages, has herself authorised – as if in total reversal of the Lollard
programme (the Lollard William Sawtre was once her parish priest). The
places in which she had most trouble were Lollard centres like Leicester,
and the bishop by whom she had herself first authorised was the one

renegade Lollard to become a bishop, Phillip Repyngdon of Lincoln. It may therefore be that Margery Kempe's true community was the one that she denies, and by which she defines herself.

The point about women's writing applies to secular as well as religious work. There is a striking resemblance between two key scenes towards the beginning of major texts by the two greatest women writers of the medieval period, the German abbess Hildegard of Bingen from the twelfth century and the French court writer Christine de Pisan, from the early fifteenth century. In Hildegard's *Book of Divine Works*, she presents an account of her own vision in which three authoritative women identify themselves as aspects of God: Love, Wisdom and Humility. They speak to Hildegard and authorise her work. Similarly, in Christine's *Book of the City of Ladies*, three radiant women speak to her, identifying themselves as Reason, Rectitude and Justice; they authorise her work, and command her to build 'the City of Ladies' in the Field of Letters. In spite of the extraordinary resemblance between these two scenes, there is no question of direct influence from one text to the other. When Hildegard produces a Latin text for establishing a monastic community and Christine produces a French text for instituting a vernacular literature, both write their visionary justification by an allegorically feminised God – in fact, since in both cases the number three is conspicuously overdetermined, precisely by a feminised Trinity.

Still there is no question of blasphemy, only audacity, as both authors remain within the generic decorum of personification, in which the aspects of God are gendered as feminine, and within the existing structure, in which they construct a female enclosure: Hildegard's abbey in the Church, and Christine's City of Ladies in the Field of Letters. There is no question either of appropriating discourses, if by this is meant taking them for a different or subversive purpose: what we have here is not a new use of the discourse but new users. If Hildegard and Christine construct their writing as gendered, they do so as much by certain refusals as by specific inclusions. Hildegard, for example, eschews the discourse of mystic eroticism altogether in favour of something more intellectual and more sublimated in its theological harnessing of bodily energy. As for the discourse of mystic eroticism, it does not become exclusively or stably gendered in the hands of women. Where the authorship of a mystic-erotic text is unknown, the gender of the writing subject is often inscrutable to readers who do not simply assume a male voice. But there is no disciplinary problem with the use of such discourse by women – at least, the male confessors who solicited it did not seem to find one. An (outrageous) comparison would be with homily in the hands of the Pardoner: if there is any problem, it is specific to the user. Medieval women writers produce new communities of users.

This apparently negative conclusion about blasphemy is of the first importance. Well before the Reformation there can be no excuse for looking at medieval Christendom as if it were culturally homogeneous and unified, even in communities that were not, like Le Roy Ladurie's Montaillou,[51] overtly or covertly heretical. On the contrary, the universal Church was not only divided along the usual lines of race, gender and class, Latin against vernaculars: it also comprised a multitude of separate, sometimes enclosed, reading communities that shared and sometimes contested common discourses. This remains a harmonious model only where orthodoxy is prepared to share its discourses – as was the case with all the women writers I have discussed here. It is a truism of medieval history, however, that this preparedness varies according to time, place and, often, fortune. Valdes was condemned and Saint Francis was assimilated, yet the similarities between them outweigh the differences. Marguerite Porete was burned for her opinions as a heretic, yet the book she wrote, translated into Latin and her authorship forgotten, became an orthodox spiritual classic of the fifteenth century. When orthodoxy is disturbed by the use of its discourses – as it would say, elsewhere – it invokes blasphemy.

To invoke blasphemy in this way is to assert a single Super-Community – one might adapt Bakhtin's Grotesque Body and call it a Grotesque Community – against multiple communities. Such acts of assertion become progressively more absurd during the course of the Reformation, as Christianity splits into more and more sects. They are by nature political acts, and they continue to treat Christendom as a spiritual, theological and intellectual entity but also as a physical community, on the model of a society. The criterion for blasphemy in such circumstances is rebellion pure and simple. It is not a surprise that Luther should round on Germany's rebellious peasants and call them blasphemers, worthy of death. It is a standard function of the discourse of blasphemy, one anticipated in the accounts of the English Peasants' Revolt of 1381 by monastic chroniclers and, above all by the poet John Gower; and so far as these accounts allow one to judge it was perhaps a factor in the conduct of the peasants themselves, who executed the Archbishop of Canterbury. To rebel is to learn to blaspheme. And to learn to blaspheme is to learn to read – to read in a different way, or simply to be a new community of readers. The significance of reading to the rebels of 1381 is brilliantly demonstrated by Steven Justice in a forthcoming study.[52] The rebels assert their power as a community, including as a reading community. They are opposed by the Grotesque Community and its complicit discourses of blasphemy and public order.

From medieval women writers, whose communities remain incorporated within the Grotesque Community, and from the breaches undertaken by rebellious peasants, we learn that there are key connections between literacy, blasphemy and community. Their interactions form the subject of the next chapter.

Chapter 4

JUDGING BLASPHEMY
The Seventeenth Century to the Present

'Tis a weak Plea, to say, Error may be punish'd, but not Truth, when all sides take themselves for Orthodox; so that on this foot, Persecution must go round the Earth, *seeking whom to devour*. A Man had as good say plainly, 'tis a Sin for any Others to persecute, but that 'tis his sole Privilege to do it when he judges it fit.

THOMAS EMLYN (1719): 12

The purpose of this chapter is to examine briefly the State power to prosecute at law crimes against religion, and the propaganda industry that accompanies such power. I seek to present certain characteristics of such prosecutions and the cultural controversy around them, and to offer a typology of the most common cases seen in Western Europe from the breakdown of arguments for wide-ranging religious tolerance in the seventeenth century to the present day. I do not attempt either a comprehensive or a representative survey. Since it is my argument that local conditions are of paramount importance, no one case can provide a ready-made category for any other: there are major differences not only from country to country but from region to region, and even from town to town. The majority of examples here are again cited from England and Ireland. The place of blasphemy in common law, as announced by Lord Chief Justice Hale in the Taylor trial of 1676, makes English common law the custodian of Scripture and, to some extent, doctrine (especially the Trinity). This guardianship functions in a manner unparalleled elsewhere in Europe, where the churches retained some powers with the sanction of the secular arm, or where there was a stronger legal separation of Church and State, and for longer than in America, where the prosecution of offences against religion was held by some to conflict with rights of individual free speech as extended by the First Amendment. The English legal system represents itself as theocratic – 'the Scriptures are the common law of England'[1] – in the face of increasingly clear and decisive separation of Church and State and in spite of increasingly divergent social beliefs and practices.

Characterising the situation in one country, in which there is a greater degree of legal activity about blasphemy than in most others, has the advantage of linking like with like and of highlighting certain frequent recurrences in such cases, such as provocation. But the limitation is not meant to be exclusive: I have included important instances from other European countries, especially France, and I have neglected to mention much of importance from Britain. My concern is not with exhaustive recording of legal practices in the prosecution of blasphemy but with the issue of what such divergent practices all signify, the use of power through law to construct a notion of community that sets out to override and neutralise actual community difference, and the reasons for such constructions, including the perceived lack of any plausible non-religious alternative. Without religion, the law has no community.

In 1855, the trial took place of the Catholic Redemptorist father, the Reverend Vladimir Petcherine. I shall quote from the account of the trial, *A Special Report . . .* , published by his Dublin supporters the following year. Petcherine was charged with blasphemy in that

> disregarding the laws and religion of the realm, and devising and intending to bring the capital Holy Scriptures of God, in the Authorised Version, in the English language, appointed to be read in churches, and generally received by Her Majesty's subjects professing the religion of the United Church of England and Ireland, as by law established, into disregard, hatred, and contempt, among the people of the United Kingdom, on the fifth of November, at Kingstown, by causing a certain printed copy of said Scriptures, in the Authorised Version, &c, consisting of the Old and New Testaments of our Saviour, to be contemptuously burnt, profanely and in the presence of divers of Her Majesty's subjects, and with the view to the destruction of said copy, did cause and procure to be thrown, and did cast and throw said copy into a certain fire until it was burnt, to the high displeasure of Almighty God, and the great disrespect, discredit, and dishonour of the religion established by law. (p. 10)

This charge sets out the nature and distinctive position of the Authorised Version, but the indictment was nothing if not inclusive and incorporated seven other counts, one of which referred to the Holy Scriptures in general 'irrespective of any particular version'. The circumstances of the case were simple. Petcherine, a distinguished Russian academic who had embraced Catholicism and exile, came to Kingstown as a Redemptorist missionary and set out with his colleagues to evangelise the people:

> Having ascertained that a large number of grossly immoral books were circulating through the town, they, as usual, exhorted the people to bring all such works to them for the purpose of destruction; and their request was promptly complied with. A large quantity of the filthy periodicals, continually issuing from the London press, reached Father Petcherine's lodgings; and he resolved to enhance the moral effect of their destruction, by burning them

publicly on the last day of the mission. Accordingly, on the 5th of November, he caused them to be conveyed in two open barrows to Kingstown chapel-yard, and there destroyed. (pp. 6–7)

News of the impending bonfire (which of course occurred on Guy Fawkes' Day) reached local Protestants in the town long plagued by 'sectarian controversy', and numerous of them congregated at the site, led by 'a Methodist preacher named Wallace'. A crowd moved freely through the yard where the books were piled for burning. One Catholic boy held up a penny-dreadful novel, called out that it was a 'Protestant Bible', and threw it on the fire. Perhaps as a result of such badinage, the rumour spread that Bibles were being burned, and after some hours, a copy of the Bible was actually pulled from the flames and fragments of it seized by 'Mr Wallace and friends'. After a public campaign largely orchestrated by Wallace and his followers, Petcherine, who had organised the bonfire but supervised it fitfully and infrequently, was charged with Bible-burning blasphemy.

Petcherine was tried by two judges and a jury of twelve men, the case against him being led by the Attorney-General and Solicitor-General – a clear sign of the seriousness with which it was regarded. In his opening speech the Attorney-General immediately regretted that a clergyman should have 'been subjected to such a charge', and cunningly foregrounded the fact that Petcherine was not British:

> Gentlemen, I have told you that the traverser is a Roman Catholic clergyman. I have furthermore to tell you – and I do it without the slightest desire to prejudice in any way your judgment against him – that he is not a native of this country. In stating that, gentlemen, if it were to have any effect whatsoever, our laws and institutions – and I think we may feel justly proud of those institutions – provide against any distinction, unless it be in favour of a foreigner who is put on his trial. I therefore made that statement in no expectation, with no desire, that the circumstance should in any way prejudice him in your mind. On the contrary. . . . (p. 11)

The Attorney-General made no attempt to question the ostensible motive behind the bonfire. If the fathers' efforts 'were directed to induce the Roman Catholic people to bring in and abandon the reading books of an immoral tendency', works of 'a light and trivial character – some were novels, some romances, others weekly or daily publications', then 'no man would have a right to make any complaint whatsoever on the subject. . . . It was creditable, it was meritorious to preach against immoral publications' (p. 13). Thus the British government sanctions book-burning. However, the Attorney-General continues in an ironic mode that undermines his apparent professions – as in the case of Petcherine's 'foreign' extraction. Just as preaching against immoral publications is 'creditable and meritorious', so is zeal: 'Zeal, especially in the practice of religion, is creditable and meritorious, but zeal may degenerate into fanaticism – and the darkest pages of history are the records of fanaticism' (p. 13). Thus Petcherine crosses a line that is cognate with being foreign, from zealot to fanatic. And the Attorney-General is in no doubt that Bibles were conveyed to his lodgings, and that Petcherine had them conveyed to the bonfire. At this point, indeed, and uniquely in the course of the trial, the Attorney-General questions the wisdom of book-burning, if only in the name of community standards:

> Now, I must say, gentlemen, although it might be no offence against the law, yet a cooler judgment, a calmer discretion might have suggested that the burning of any books, the piling up of any volumes in that public manner, was most calculated to give offence to the surrounding inhabitants. (p. 14)

The distinction is artfully made between British Protestants, who merely would like to burn immoral books, and foreign Catholic fanatics who actually do so, though the Attorney-General promptly denies it: 'Does the history of the world teach us that fanaticism is ever confined to any particular denomination of Christians?' (p. 15). The Attorney-General's main appeal is to xenophobia. The facts, such as they are, are clear: 'The very pieces of the Sacred Volumes themselves' that were plucked from the flames will be produced in evidence, and the question will only be that of intention: 'Did he or did he not mean to treat the copy of the Sacred Writings with disrespect?' (p. 15).

For the Attorney-General, what matters is the legal status of the Authorised Version itself, and its relation to the Constitution. The ground of the relation is again the oath, the legal oath that blasphemy always imperils:

> What was the volume which you took in your hands this day? To what were you referred as you advanced to be sworn to do your duty, and upon the evidence to find a verdict between the Crown and the traverser? Was it not the Authorised Version of the Sacred Scriptures? What security has any man in this country for life and property that is not sustained by an appeal to the Authorised Version of the Sacred Scriptures? By what sanction will the witnesses who shall come on the tables presently be controlled? Will it not be by putting into their hands a copy of the Authorised Version of the Scriptures, and swearing them upon it to give true evidence between the Crown and the traverser, whence arises our confidence in the due administration of the law?

The Attorney-General must purport to argue that the significance of his case overwhelms mere 'sectarian differences' in the Irish community, since 'all join in reverence and respect for the Sacred Scriptures that are common to all' (p. 17).

His actual case depends on an appeal to two other cases, both of which are markedly different from the current one, and on the evidence of witnesses: the boy from whom Father Petcherine solicited a wheelbarrow, a Protestant policeman, a Protestant coachman who claimed to see a Bible on the barrow, and five other Protestant witnesses including the coachman's brother, whose evidence was less than impressive. Asked how he knew that the book he saw was a New Testament, he replied: 'It was newly bound' (p. 25). During his cross-examinations by one of Petcherine's juniors, Judge Crampton revealed a clear prejudice. When the witness was asked whether he was 'a follower of the Rev. Mr. Wallace', the judge intervened: 'These questions are only wasting public time' (p. 25). Wallace himself, the North of Ireland Orange minister, was the key witness. Under cross-examination, he agreed that he had published three letters in the newspapers protesting against the scandal, all under aliases:

> an 'Eye Witness', 'An Observer', and the letter 'C'; I preached on the subject of the Bible burning on Sunday the 12th November; I had that sermon printed in the course of the following week; I believe I gave away some copies of it; it was circulated largely; the fourth edition is out at present (*laughter*); the first edition was out on the 20th of the month; there were five hundred copies in each edition; I gave the last edition into the hands of the publisher on last night or this morning. (p. 29)

Reading from Wallace's sermon established that he asserted, without proof, that the Bible had been 'committed to the flames by the Redemptorist fathers' – a claim met by 'loud and general expressions of disapprobation throughout the court' (p. 30). In spite of this, Wallace insisted on several occasions that his claim was 'not in the least degree calculated to prejudice the case of the party charged' (p. 30).

Mr O'Hagen, for the defence, made a long and florid preliminary speech that lasted for three hours. He began with a skilful undoing of the Attorney-General's linkage between 'stranger' and 'fanatic':

> A stranger he is – if he can be called a stranger, who for a large section of the life of man, has dwelt within this empire, doing the noblest service to the religion and the morals of its people. A zealot or fanatic he is not. (p. 33)

He protested: 'The cause has been misjudged', drawing attention to street demonstrations, allegations in the press and even denunciation by 'a Protestant archbishop' (p. 34). O'Hagen then himself exploited the discourse of xenophobia: the charge 'is founded on the old common law of England', and rests on a misconception that 'the Catholic Church is the enemy of the Holy Bible – that she fears and hates its divine teachings, and would utterly destroy it if she could' (p. 36). In refuting this representation in detail, O'Hagen was able to suggest that English Protestantism, and so the law under which Petcherine was charged, was hopelessly prejudiced. He then cast aspersions on the Authorised Version itself, condemned, he would have it, by the best Protestant opinion 'as having been executed in a spirit antagonistic to the true spirit of Christianity' (p. 41) – a tactic tantamount, in the Attorney-General's terms, to challenging the justice of the legal system under which Petcherine was charged. To make the point as unequivocally as possible, and to the best moral advantage, O'Hagen then compared friendly comments on the Authorised Version by Irish Catholic archbishops with seventeenth-century English statutes requiring the burning of 'Popish missals and the defacement of crucifixes'. Yet O'Hagen regretted all such sectarian difference: some of his best friends were Protestants ('I have been from earliest days, the familiar friend of Protestants', p.46). When he attacks Reverend Wallace for cowardly and unmanly prostitution of the pulpit, O'Hagen is careful to speak of him as 'a minister of religion – I know not, and I care not, of what special persuasion' (p. 55). O'Hagen's defence depends, indeed, on a form of sectarian even-handedness: he contends that the sole Bible demonstrably found on the bonfire was put there unknown to Petcherine by a zealot of one side or other, either by a Catholic truly hoping to attack the Protestant Bible, or by a Protestant seeking to discredit the Redemptorist fathers: 'if any man – I cannot too often press the question – a zealot on one side or the other, cast a Bible on that heap of books, is Father Petcherine to be made answerable for the act?' (p. 52). But in his attempt to give equal rein to these two possibilities, O'Hagen's presentation is unbalanced, and builds into Catholic outrage:

> There are Protestants whose scorn and hatred of Catholicism know no control of moral restraint or social decency or Christian love. And there are Catholics who have been roused to answer scorn with scorn, and hatred with defiance, and stung to fierce retaliation by the sectarian scandals which darken the annals of our time – by continual slanders against all they deem most venerable, against priests and prelates, and the holy women who have given their lives to Charity and Heaven – by outrage on the effigy and profanation of the name of the Supreme Pontiff, whom they revere as the chief of their Church, and Christ's Vicar upon earth – by insult to the images of their canonised Saints, and the Mother of their Redeemer, – by impious assaults upon the Cross itself, and sacrilegious desecration, in the open day, of the Holy of Holies, before which they worship with trembling love, and awful reverence! (pp. 48–9)

The trial takes place in Dublin, and O'Hagen's speech is 'greeted with outbursts of applause, again and again repeated, withstanding the efforts made by the officers of the court to repress it' (p. 60); the Attorney-General, not O'Hagen, makes reiterated reference to his confidence that the jury will do its duty regardless of religious affiliation. It cannot be assumed therefore that O'Hagen loses control when he reveals his strong bias, for all his sorrow at living in 'a country tortured by miserable feuds' (p. 57).

It is as well that O'Hagen's address was effective, for the next day he was prevented from calling any of the witnesses he had hoped to produce to establish Petcherine's motive in urging the surrender of immoral books. Judge Crampton objected at once, and sustained his opposition in a ruling. Whether this was legally accurate or not, Judge Crampton's bias was evident from his interjection on behalf of Reverend Wallace's supporter the previous day, and showed again later at the end of the subsequent trial of John Hamilton, the boy who had teased Protestant spectators by claiming to throw a Protestant Bible on the flames. In spite of the fact that Hamilton had been acquitted, implying the jury's disbelief that he had done any such thing, Judge Crampton discharged him with an inflammatory instruction: 'Take care and do not meddle so with the Protestant Bible any more.' On the other hand, his fellow judge, Baron Green, behaved impeccably, and summed up without undue prejudice. The summing up occurred quickly after Crampton's ruling, since the defence then decided to call no evidence and rely on the jury's good sense. The jury, in the event, took 45 minutes to acquit Petcherine, to loud cheers; and he then burst into tears.

I have quoted from the account of this case at some length for one reason: its banality and pettiness are all too characteristic of legal process against blasphemy in English-speaking countries during the nineteenth and twentieth centuries. Compared to the drama of cases examined in this book so far, the Petcherine case is typical of later proceedings in the apparent thinness of the charges and the anecdotal uncertainties with which they are heard. The trial actually lacks the kind of ritual, almost consensual quality of, say, the Nayler case, where everyone agrees in finding Nayler's entry into Jerusalem portentous, and the trial is a conflict of interpretative power. In the Petcherine case there may be no sign at all, only the flimsiest attempt to counterfeit one: the simulation of a simulacrum. The blasphemy may exist at the level of intention, or merely at that of frame-up. Yet the case is typical of later proceedings in other respects too. First, it takes place in Ireland, in, as O'Hagen comes close to conceding, a hopelessly divided community. The entire basis of the proceeding is viciously sectarian: not only in the activities of Reverend Wallace and his supporters, but in the trial itself. The Attorney-General claims that Petcherine's Catholicism is, as it were, incidental to the offence – Catholicism itself is not on trial; yet he calls only Protestant witnesses and he links fanaticism with foreigners, as if to contrast it with the native Anglicanism protected by common law. O'Hagen's speech is, as I have shown, rhetorically unbalanced – it takes sides in a community schism, and it wins over the jury by doing so. Nor is there any particular ground for confidence in the verdict, which is itself likely to be sectarian and predetermined. The entire legal process therefore responds to community schism and amplifies it without resolution. The very fact that proceedings are brought shows the bias of the government, and one of the two judges does his best to reinforce that bias. Bad and prejudicial behaviour by judges is a common feature of blasphemy cases, even more than in other kinds of trial: Lord Chief Justice Ellenborough, for example, was particularly flagrant in his persecution of William Hone.[2] Since the charge depends on English common law, and English common law claims a Scriptural basis, it is virtually impossible for the law to be neutral in a matter of blasphemy: hence the Attorney-General's sustained reference to the Bible as the basis of legal oaths, and so of the trustworthiness of justice. The entire judicial process becomes a forum that refuses to admit what is being transacted within it: everyone here claims, for example, the issue of Catholic versus Protestant is not active within the courtroom, when in fact hardly anything else is. The trial becomes self-reflexive: Protestantism is made to stand in the charge itself for the justice system that sustains it, so that an acquittal becomes a nationalist gesture towards subverting that system.

The nature of the crime depends on the subjective judgment that represents itself as in some sense a 'community standard'. Blasphemy is judged by the offence it causes. Hence public opinion needs to be mobilised, not only by skilful advocates within the courtroom, but by expert provocateurs outside it. If biased judges are a common feature of blasphemy trials, organised provocation is an invariable one. Here the provocateur is the Reverend Wallace, with his cronies at the burning and his pamphlet-eering after it. In Britain the most common source of external provocation was the Society for the Suppression of Vice, founded by William Wilberforce in 1802 and later successfully transplanted to the United States. It is one of the great ironies that Wilberforce, who fought to give freedom for slaves overseas, should have worked so zealously to block freedom of thought at home. It is a political irony, and it was appreciated at the time: for example, in *Vindiciae Britannicae*, a series of public letters addressed to Wilberforce by one 'Christophilus' in 1821, maintaining that Wilberforce was allowing himself to be used by a cynical government. The central charge that blasphemy is a convenient catch-cry for repressive governments is heard elsewhere, in, for example, George Edmonds's complaint against the Poor Law in 1836. In fact the rhetoric of 'Christophilus' implies a conviction that Wilberforce knew what he was doing: that the Society for the Suppression of Vice was an instrument of political repression. It functioned by organising press and crowd protests against whatever it deemed offensive, with the express and often successful purpose of persuading those in authority to prosecute. Its function was imitated by the Salvation Army later in the nineteenth century, and was copied by a host of moral campaigners well into the twentieth century, including Mrs Mary Whitehouse in England and John S. Sumner and Anthony Comstock in the United States. William Wilberforce is the spiritual father of Yusuf Islam and Dr Siddiqui, and as a genius of provocation could have achieved even more than them given, say, Saudi financial backing. Public opinion exists to be manipulated, and is the sole arbiter of the offence that is held to establish blasphemy. Blasphemy in common law is a provocateur's charter, and the judicial process abets it.

The issue of blasphemy normally arises in a community that is divided, and it normally arises because the community is divided. It makes little sense in such a situation to appeal to some abstract community standard, however flexible, and it turns such appeals into the improvisatory construction of one hegemonic viewpoint. Blasphemy, that is, becomes a power struggle in which government, which has the right to prosecute, both defines itself by the exercise of power and seeks to marginalise or preferably eradicate what threatens it: Protestantism in a Catholic country and vice versa, deism, unitarianism, radicalism, atheism and socialism. It makes such interventions in multiple sites of discourse: not only the church but also university, theatre, street corner, mechanics' institutes and, above all, in all areas of the press and book trade. The connection between blasphemy and censorship is intimate, and the rest of this chapter documents it as it documents the other claims made in this paragraph. The book trade is policed by recourse to blasphemy charges, which are a recourse to common law, and 'the Scriptures are the common law': in other words, a culture of the Book licenses the repression of books.

The most striking feature of the Petcherine case is the universal acceptance, only slightly qualified by the Attorney-General on grounds of discretion rather than policy, that burning bad books is a worthy occupation; and bad books, as we have seen, comprise 'novels', 'romances' and 'weekly or monthly publications'. Mr O'Hagen has a more colourful way of describing them: 'infamous periodicals, which are the daily food of the common mind of England – translations of sensual novels from the French, and vile English novels, whose very names are an abomination', 'immoral works', 'scandalous books, creeping too fast amongst us', which are

> devilish agents for the destruction of the bodies and the souls of men . . .
> deforming the body and destroying the grandeur of man's moral nature and
> making him a brutal sensualist and a godless reprobate, whilst they sap the
> foundations of social order and the authority of law, which have their only
> security in the high sanctions of the nation's virtue and religion. (p. 44)

Mr O'Hagen produces a copy of a penny-dreadful called *The Mysteries of London* and shows it to the jury as the lynch-pin of his case for Father Petcherine as cultural hero:

> I have looked through portions of it; I had never seen it until I entered this
> court today; and I tell you, that it presents a mass of bestial and revolting
> impurities adequate, if sin can do so, to bring down God's avenging wrath
> upon the unhappy people who, in thousands and tens of thousands, week
> after week, delight to wallow in them. Look at these obscene pictures; regard
> the tales of worse obscenity which they illustrate; consider the effects they

must produce on the heart and understanding of the multitude; remember that they circulate through the length and breadth of England, and tell me if he is not a benefactor to our country who forbids the diffusion of their poison here? Of such books as these – more devastating than the pestilence, more terrible than internecine war, because they pollute the spirit of man, and kill his immortal hopes – my client has been the enemy.

O'Hagen's language here is that of biblical prophecy and of the book of Revelation. It is an invocation of the language that in a previous chapter I identified with the discourse of blasphemy, and it successfully takes control of it on his client's behalf. Petcherine is not a blasphemer but a blasphemee. He objects to what we should now call 'popular culture': as ever, the discourse of blasphemy is anti-cultural, both high and low. The gross indecency of the works he describes belongs at least as much to the discourse employed to describe it as to any inherent property of the work itself. No doubt a devotee of high culture might have found penny-dreadfuls distasteful, but the degree of O'Hagen's horror is as excessive as the effects he attributes to such literature. This is in fact another generic characteristic of blasphemy trials, here displaced from the target of legal attack to another type of writing altogether. Lord Scarman supposed that the idea of homosexuality and the love of Jesus could have been considered in the same poem had that poem been sober and respectable, that James Kirkup's poem 'The love that dares to speak its name' just happened to be disgusting, depraved and calculated to corrupt. It had to be: for that is only to say that Scarman found it blasphemous.[3] Kirkup and Rushdie are in good company: equally sweeping denunciations, in similar terms, have at one time or another characterised Shelley's *Queen Mab*, Thomas Paine's *The Rights of Man* and Hobbes's *Leviathan*. An apocalyptic register of execration goes with the territory, expressing moral and political disapproval and the determination to exercise tight cultural control in the spirit of Holy War.

When the spirit of blasphemy walks in the land, books are never the only casualties. So, for example, when the Nazis burned books, they were drawing upon a discourse of blasphemy, and the same discourse, with awesome predictability, sanctions the killing of Jews. There is surprisingly little distance between burning books and killing people. We have seen how Michael Servetus is burned together with his book, which is strapped to his thigh, a scene which suggests that the book and its author are synechdoches of one another. The desire of power to commit violence in the cause of cultural orthodoxy quickly learns to adapt the discourse of blasphemy in order to suppress the unthinkable and limit the imaginable. It is no accident, then, that the Inquisition burned Menocchio, the miller of Friuli, and Giordano Bruno in the same year 1600. Menocchio's potential for damage was strictly on a local level, and his blasphemy seemed to have won him no disciples but to have been incorporated into the numerous conflicts of village life. On the opposite end of the cultural spectrum, the situation with Bruno was not dissimilar: he did not represent any kind of movement or diffused menace to the Catholic Church, and his writings were esoteric, more likely to strike his readers as impenetrable than inflammable. Both men were killed, like Admiral Byng, *pour encourager les autres*, and the message from Bruno's death is not one of careful textual judgements on his ideas but of vehement refusals to tolerate unorthodox writings of any kind. We have seen how Servetus was burned in effigy by Catholics and in the flesh by Protestants. Consistently, Bruno was censured for his ideas in Geneva, and burned for them in Rome. It is not, in the final instance, that particular ideas are weighed carefully and found offensive: the offence is taken at the very existence of books and writer. Blasphemy is a pronouncement on the books, and apostasy is used to seal the writer's doom. Bruno was a renegade Dominican, whose thinking about the Trinity and the Eucharist had caused him to remove himself from order and from sacrament.[4] But any believer who transgresses against orthodoxy stands apostate in orthodoxy's eyes – ideas and the body both ripe for burning. The association between blasphemy and apostasy is therefore generic, and does not arise for the first time with Rushdie. In the Petcherine case it is the subtext, for example, of the Attorney-General's play with special regret at having to charge a clergyman with blasphemy.

All over Europe from the seventeenth century, religious orthodoxy redefines itself as, and even substitutes for itself, cultural conformity, repressing dissidence in both high and popular cultures. One consequence was in the increasing distance between the opinions of intellectuals and the cultural norms upheld by State power: in England, the greatest poet, philosopher and scientist of the late seventeenth century – Milton, Locke, Newton – all shared Bruno's disparaging view of the Trinity. Thomas Hobbes's writing on religion in *Leviathan* led Parliament in the early Restoration to debate revising the statute *De Haeretico Comburendo*, in which case Hobbes would have shared the fate of Bruno. There is some irony here, for Hobbes, while making clear his personal scepticism, argued the need for an established Church precisely as a means of social and cultural control. He re-authorised, and provided with its own rationale, the very institution that sought to punish him. Associated with such marginalising of intellectuals and their views is a narrowing of community. Community no longer ostensibly incorporates everyone, as in the ideology of the Church, but functions as a kind of enclosed middle ground set against social and intellectual extremes and dedicated to their continued separation. What is held in common is law, in England common law, which becomes the expression of an exclusive rather than an inclusive ideal of community, an elevated abstraction from which comes the standard used to judge transgression.

Social control therefore exercises its vigilance by a number of means, legal or literary (the writing of propaganda) or both, and on a number of fronts (the number itself being a potential cause of embarrassment, since blasphemy may appear an indiscriminate charge to level against so many diverse viewpoints). One target is Catholicism, discrimination against which changes in law between 1689 and the Restoration of an English Catholic hierarchy in 1850, but which is misrepresented throughout the period with unremitting vehemence. William Crashaw, writing against Jesuits in 1641, offers 'The Points of New Divinity in this Gospell'. They include 'That the Milke of Mary may come into comparison with the blood of Christ'; 'That the best compound for a sicke soule is to mixe together her milke and Christ's bloud'; 'That her Milke, and the merit and vertue of it, is more precious and excellent than Christ's bloud'; and editorialises: 'a blasphemy whereat the Angels will shrinke, and the very Divels tremble, and yet no doubt we shall finde Jesuites will defend it'. Crashaw's attack sounds a generic note of provocation:

> Having observed this blasphemy twenty yeares agoe, I held my tongue, expecting it would be discovered and reproved by some that could doe it with more Authority, but failing of my hope, I long conceal'd my labours to now, that the necessities of these times doe force it from mee.[5]

Reluctance to utter thus builds into complaint against government in action. The mode and substance of attack alike are blasphemous. Sir Edward Dering, writing in response to a Catholic in 1641, makes little attempt to conceal the sort of government action he would like: 'Is not this language worthy of the faggot, without a recantation?' He asks whether the Catholics and Protestants serve the same God or not: 'Did ever any of us deny, or disclaime your *God* to be *our God*? . . . Is *the God of the Protestants your God*? How dare you then revile him? If he be not *your God*, you then do serve the divell.'[6]

So, lazily, does blasphemy build discursively into apostasy. If both Catholics and Protestants serve the same God, there is yet no notion of reciprocity in the discourse, which uses blasphemy to commit slander. What purports to be an English translation of the Missal, *The Romish mass-book*, immediately places itself in an apocalyptic context: 'and who cannot but see unless they are bewitch't by the Sorceries of the *Whore of Babylon*, that the whole Mass of their Worship is a meer Medley of Blasphemy, non-Sense and Irreligion?' The writer's 'observations' are a concentrated distillation of every cliché such discourse has to hand: mummery by mountebanks, conjurors' enchantments, diabolic arts and drunken debauches with whores: 'all the Repeated Blasphemies of these Wretches!'; 'Here are almost as many Blasphemies as Prayers.' This licenses a simple reverse transaction: Catholics are confounded from their own mouths, and their own missal proves 'that your God is a corrupt, rotten filthy Idol'.[7] Ritual is deconstructed into theatre:

> Here to be sure the Priest chuses the largest Cake to make a lustier God for himself . . . and then eats him (washing it down with his Blood), but not a drop for the people. His God is a large one, and Capers about as a spiritual Magician Charms, while the other little Diminutives lie sneaking until the grand Wafer makes its Exit into the Priest's unsanctified Guts. But O what a Comedy is it to see how many Freaks, Gambols and Antick-Tricks our God-Maker plays, what Tossings, Cringings, Postures, Adorations before the poor God is devoured. This is a mere Comi-Tragedy. (pp. 8–9)

> The Priest like a Stage player, hath his capital Part by heart, that he may the better act it: O mimick Religion. . . . That is, (monkey-like) he must put a good face upon't, and so he had need . . . he is reputed the devoutest that's most dexterous at their Apish Bobtayl'd grimaces. (p. 3)

The treatise ends with a crescendo of hatred that desecrates without any sense that the damage may extend to Christian belief of any kind:

> If your Sacrament could speak, (and doubtless it wou'd if it were *alive*) it would cry out O! I am bitten, I am swallow'd, I perish, I mould, I am kept in a Box for fear of Rats, if you leave me out all Night I shall be devoured before Morning, If the Mouse gets me, I am gone, I am Bread, I am no God, don't believe the wretches – murder, murder, murder! (p. 150)

This is virtually an empty discourse, fatuous, corrosive and infinitely adaptable to anything that falls foul of orthodoxy or government. Thus Hogarth's depiction of Methodism as *Superstition, Fanaticism and Credulity* belongs in the same framework as the attacks on Catholicism from which I have just quoted. In the first draft of the etching, which was never published (Plate 3), Hogarth bases the preacher on the figure of George Whitfield, who

> has a harlequin's robe under his gown and the tonsure of a Jesuit under his wig, thus equating Methodists and Catholics according to a popular prejudice of the time. He holds two puppets: the first, God with angels from the Stanza d'Eliodoro in the Vatican, the second a Devil holding a gridiron. Other puppets, Adam and Eve, Peter with his key pulling Paul's hair, Moses and Aaron await their turn.

The picture has as its text II Corinthians 11: 23, 'I speak as a fool.'

> A thermometer in place of an hour-glass gives the key to the reactions of the congregation, ranging from Luke-Warm to Convulsion Fits, Madness and Despair. Prominent among the congregation are Mother Douglas, the pious bawd, having convulsion fits, and a Jew in the Manner of Rembrandt, with his Bible open at the Sacrifice of Isaac. At the window a Mohammedan Turk is amazed to see such strange manifestations of Christian piety.[8]

3. William Hogarth, *Enthusiasm Delineated*. First state of *Superstition, Fanaticism and Credulity*, engraving, British Museum.

If it is not fanaticism, it might as well be atheism. The Archbishop of York, Sir William Dawes, published his *Anatomy of Atheisme: A Poem* in 1694 under the pseudonym 'A person of Quality'. Dawes had intended to versify all the thirty-nine articles of the Anglican faith, but found it too much work. Thus he converted positive into negative and published a verse attack on atheism instead. The point of the example is that Dawes characterised the atheist in terms of a common definition of blasphemy:

> His fatal Crime is of the deepest dye
> 'Tis Treason 'gainst the highest Majesty.[9]

So William Assheton, chaplain to the Duke of Ormond, writes in 1690 'to vindicate the Great Majesty of Heaven from the Malitious lections of a Blasphemous Tongue': his aim is to defend divine revelation and the historicity of the Scriptures in order to uphold the existence of hell and the certainty of eternal torment.[10] Though his target is obviously the conservative deism of Charles Blount (1654–93), Assheton presents his essay in blasphemy as an attack on atheism. This is clearly more than rhetoric: the orthodox of whatever flavour could not conceive that those of radically different religious views could be sincere or, indeed, Christians at all. But the purpose is provocation, a continual badgering of government to do something. The Bishop of Rochester, Francis Atterbury, published in 1706 his compilation of 'the Prophaneness and Blasphemy that abounds in some Late Writings' entitled *The Axe laid to the Root of Christianity*. It is an open letter to an English gentleman with whom he had recently dined. Both agreed that they would always continue fast friends to 'Liberty', but Atterbury was surprised to find his host 'so ill-inform'd' of the contemporary situation in England, where 'liberty is indulg'd too far' and 'degenerates into such a Boundless License as shall undermine the foundations of Religion and Government'. His host 'could hardly, I remember, believe that such Blasphemies have been printed, because you had never heard that anyone had been punish'd for them'.[11] Atterbury simply lists examples, and disseminates their blasphemies by quoting from them copiously: including the deist Blount, who 'profanely Scoffs at the manner of our Saviour's Entry into Jerusalem a little before his Passion, which he calls *the making his Cavalcade upon an Asinego*' (p. 2); and John Asgill's demonstration that 'Man may be translated from hence into that Eternal Life, without passing through Death, although the Human Nature of Christ could not be thus translated, till he had pass'd through Death' (p. 3).

Until the nineteenth century, however, the major target is not Catholicism or Methodism, deism or atheism, but, as ever, anti-Trinitarianism, socinianism or unitarianism. It is on the issue of the Trinity that orthodox fears of deist or atheist were fixed, as is shown by John Howe's *A Calm and Sober Enquiry concerning the Possibility of a Trinity in the Godhead* (1694). Howe's work was written to arbitrate the rival Trinitarian positions taken up by William Sherlock and Robert South, and it concludes

> That not only a Trinity in the Unity of the Godhead is a Possible thing, but that it is also possible that the Father, Son and Holy Ghost may be sufficiently distinguished to answer the frame and design of Christianity.
>
> And that will equally serve my purpose. For so however, will the scandal be removed that may seem to lye upon our Holy Religion, through the industrious misrepresentation which is made of it, by *Scepticks, Deists and Atheists* as if it were made up of inconsistencies and absurdities, and were fitter to be entertained with laughter than faith. . . .[12]

In the *Compend of the Letters of the Reverend Mr John Brown*, published in 1797, we find a preface by one William Fletcher that adumbrates a connection between orthodox doctrine and the conduct of civil magistrates. Fletcher runs together scepticism, Quakerism, infidelity and atheism in his argument against 'modern reforms' whose error is to teach that 'Christian magistrates' shall no longer govern by the law of God:

> It is absurd to suppose that God can give men a power, which he hath not himself, and shocking blasphemy to suppose him possible of giving man a right to counteract his own law as their rule, or his own glory as their chief end, in everything they do.

Magistrates must prevent the teaching of blasphemous errors and the practice of 'abominable idolatries' for 'a positive or authoritative toleration proclaims to men a liberty to sin'.[13] For this writer, too, there is no mystery about the doctrine that must be enforced: 'Gross errors and blasphemies are so plainly condemned by the word of God, that persons of common capacity may easily discern them' (p. 21). As so often, fundamentalism quietly awards itself a discretion to apply the rules as circumstances vary. I cite this example, as I have cited other writings by minor clergymen, for its representative quality. For it is such opinion that explains why the civil power, as late as the nineteenth century, continued to persecute unitarianism.

There are more important cases, even in Britain, than may be reviewed here. As early as 1645 a Member of Parliament, Paul Best (1590–1657), was charged before Parliament with blasphemy in denying the Trinity and Christ's divinity. Best's socinianism was an acquisition on his travels in Germany and Poland. He wrote no book but was informed against by friendly clergymen. Parliament sentenced him to death, but he was released in 1647, probably at Cromwell's behest.[14] There was no such readiness by the Protector to intervene in the case of John Biddle (1615–62), whose *Twelve Arguments against the Deity as the Holy Ghost* was burned by the hangman on 8 September 1647, by special command of the Parliament. Biddle became the rallying-point of anti-Trinitarians in England, and his followers in later generations identified themselves as 'unitarians', who were a partly native development of European socinianism. Biddle's fate lay in the hands of the Puritan Parliament for a long time: eventually, in 1656, he was sent in exile to the Scilly Isles. After the Restoration, he was again imprisoned, and was one of many religious prisoners to die during his internment.[15]

An actual death sentence was carried out on the 18-year-old Scottish student Thomas Aikenhead, who in 1695 had spoken to a few friends of the exciting, free-thinking ideas to which he had recently fallen subject: the Trinity was a nonsense, Moses was an Egyptian magician (had Aikenhead been inducted into freemasonry?), Christianity was a delusion. In spite of his tearfully recanting and doing penance, Aikenhead was hanged at the urging of the Edinburgh clergy.[16] This was at the time in England of the Sherlock–South controversy, and of Archbishop Tillotson's private opinion of the Athanasian Creed: 'I wish we were well rid of it.'[17] However, William Whiston's attempt to remove it in his *Primitive Christianity Revived* (1711) was unsuccessful. Whiston's Arianism deprived him of the Chair of Mathematics at Cambridge, where he had been Sir Isaac Newton's successor. His friend Dr Samuel Clark (1675–1729) tried to reconcile an Arian position with Anglican doctrine and a revised liturgy, but aroused the active suspicion of Parliament in 1714. Enforcement of orthodoxy against unitarianism therefore extended into the highest ranks of Church and University – and continued to do so into the nineteenth century. William Frend was deprived of his tutorship and income, then dismissed from his fellowship at Jesus College, Cambridge, in 1793, for his public disbelief in the Athanasian Creed and a pamphlet ironically entitled *For Peace and Union*. The Master of Jesus told Frend that his pamphlet prejudiced the clergy in the eyes of the laity, degraded the rites and doctrines of the Church of England 'in the publick esteem' and found 'that there is a tendency in the said pamphlet to disturb the harmony of Society'.[18] The College Visitor, the Bishop of Ely, supported the college, and Frend was then tried in the Vice-Chancellor's Court, and in the Court of Delegates, accused of defaming the liturgy of the Church of England, calling the Church idolatrous, arguing that 'all ecclesiastical ranks and titles were repugnant to spirit of Christianity', profaning the most holy offices of the Church and violating the laws of the university. All these charges were denied, and all found proven. Frend commented:

> Then will a future generation scarce credit the report that a celebrated university was employed, like a Spanish inquisition, eight days in investigating the question whether one of its members, for publishing some remarks on ecclesiastical affairs, should be subjected to the sentence of banishment.[19]

In fact, if Frend was indeed the author of the 1788 pamphlet later attributed to him, *An address to the members of the Church of England and to Protestant Trinitarians in general, exhorting them to turn from the false worship of three persons to the worship of One True God*, his views are best described as uncompromising and unlikely to conciliate. The style of the pamphlet is energetic: 'Trinity is a Latin word not to be found in the scriptures. The notion annexed to it in your creed of three persons, each of whom is God, making but one God, is rank nonsense.'[20] It is not only irreligious, but 'highly criminal' to pray to the Trinity: 'Consult common sense. Could God be in the womb of a woman? Could God expire on the cross? Could God be buried in the grave? Shocking suppositions!' Moreover, Frend was a political radical who had rapturously welcomed the French Revolution, and his unitarianism combined with such radicalism to make him a prime candidate for expulsion. When in 1791 the 'friends of the Revolution' (who at that time included Wilberforce) held a dinner in Birmingham, an angry mob destroyed the home of the great unitarian radical and scientist Joseph Priestley, who left for America in 1794 after preaching a farewell sermon on 'the Use of Christianity, especially in difficult times'.[21]

What Priestley would have found in America, though more tolerant than the legal system he left behind, was also highly variable. In Pennsylvania, naturally, anti-Trinitarianism found a congenial home: Penn's book *Sandy Foundations Shaken* (1668) – dubbed by Pepys 'Penn's book against the Trinity' – caused the arrest of his printer and his own imprisonment in the Tower of London, though the matter was never taken to court.[22] In Rhode Island, Roger Williams had founded a state based on complete toleration and freedom of conscience; but he first had to be expelled for exactly those ideas from Massachusetts. In the eighteenth century, Virginia became the site of a struggle for religious liberty that culminated in the Act of Toleration adopted in 1785 and championed by James Madison and Thomas Jefferson. Jefferson was a fierce opponent of Hale's doctrine that Christianity is part of the common law. He was able to show Hale's declaration, though based on no cited authority, depended on a mistranslation from the Anglo-Norman of Chief Justice Prisot in the fifteenth century, who was held to declare that common law was grounded in the Scriptures, when in fact he referred to 'ancien scripture' – that is, to old writing. Jefferson commented on this '*judiciary forgery*': 'What a conspiracy this, between church and state!! Sing tantararara rogues all; rogues all; sing tantararara, rogues all!'[23] Jefferson was passionately anti-Trinitarian, maintaining that Calvin 'blasphemed' God, and really worshipped 'a demon of malignant spirit'.[24] However, the Virginia law as finally adopted does not depend on such a position but on a fine discrimination by Madison that goes to the heart of all such arguments to this day. Madison objected to the Bill of Rights adopted in 1776, with its guarantee

> that all men should enjoy the fullest toleration in the exercise of religion, according to the dictates of conscience, unpunished and unrestrained by the

magistrate, *unless under the color of religion any man disturb the peace, the happiness, the safety of society.*[25]

Madison objected that the Bill substituted for the right of religious conscience a form of qualified permission. He proposed an amendment that foreswore all legal 'emoluments or privileges' on the one hand and 'penalties or disabilities' on the other, instituting in law the exercise of conscience 'under the direction of reason and conviction only, not of violence or compulsion'.

That basic difference – between 'violence or compulsion' and the absolute contracting out of the State from all matters of religion ('unless under cover of religion the preservation of equal liberty and the existence of the State be manifestly endangered') – remains the major line of combat in Britain, and ceased to be so in the United States only after Justice Felix Frankfurter ruled on behalf of the Supreme Court in 1950 that the First Amendment applied to the affective as well as to the cognitive content of words: a landmark decision that signals a unique legal acknowledgement of the nature of language, and calls the bluff of an orthodoxy that had often represented the cognitive ('Jesus was not born by virgin birth') as if it were the affective ('Jesus is a bastard, son of a whore'). Until then, prosecutions for blasphemy were not uncommon in some states, predictably enough with a strong political flavour. Anthony Bimba was tried for blasphemy and sedition in Brockton, Massachusetts, in 1926, having preached the overthrow of government and God. In the report of one witness,

> Ministers and priests tell us there is a God in the clouds somewhere, which there is not and who can prove it? Bimba tells us there is no such thing as God. He said Christ was a coward and was afraid to die and that communists were braver than Christ. He said there were still fools around for 2,000 years and the workers got nothing out of it.[26]

Bimba was found not guilty of blasphemy and was fined $100 for sedition, and the entire prosecution was abandoned when he appealed. One might think this sort of outcome, together with the publicity for dissident views, entirely counterproductive, but the desire to prosecute is born of the conviction that the State is bound to uphold institutionalised truth. There are any number of American John Browns – not the friend of slaves, but the Scots scourge of blasphemers. Noah Porter (1781–1866) in 1813 argues 'that gross impieties and immoralities are proper subjects of legislative prohibition. . . . In this, every real friend of his country, not to say every faithful servant of God, will lend a cheerful concurrence.'[27] 'Every real friend of his country': in the American way, as Republican presidents have recently maintained, God is for patriots.

Curiously, the mixed American experience differs less in its practical results from the English than legal comparisons might suggest. The discourse of blasphemy is still in use, and its availability tends to blunt the effect of attacks on cults that may have been factually based but still sound as if they are discourse-driven. An example might be the attacks on Mormonism by the Utah judge Cradlebaugh (1819–72), who had investigated the massacre of men, women and children carried out at Mountain Meadows in 1857. Cradlebaugh, sounding like Conan Doyle in *The Sign of Four*, concluded that 'Mormonism is one of the monstrosities of the age in which we live', a faith that sanctifies falsehood, degrades women and sanctions murder. Cradlebaugh quotes Brigham Young as saying: 'I could refer you to plenty of instances where men have been righteously slain in order to atone for their sins.' He editorialises: 'Brigham is both Church and State. True, the atrocities committed in Utah are not committed by him with his own hands, but they are committed by his underlings, and at his bidding.'[28] True or false? One is almost certain to impute Cradlebaugh's strictures to genre and convention, to a discourse of beast-baiting that is really a form of crying wolf. No doubt such scepticism is justified. Yet there are still shadows on the fringes of Mormonism, such as the followers of Ervil Le Baron (1925–81), a dissident practitioner of polygamy, 'celestial marriage' (Mormonism embraced monogamy and statehood together in 1890), who organised at least twenty-five murders among his fellow sect members in the self-assured knowledge that he was the Prophet of God, a member of the Godhead itself (a plural godhead goes with plural marriage) and secure in the knowledge that the government of the United States performed his bidding. Le Baron's *Book of New Covenants* was, in fact, a hit-list of those he felt had betrayed him. Had it been published, it would probably have been protected under the First Amendment.

Certainly, nobody who has had inflicted upon them in the USA free publications of stunningly crude and violent racism or anti-Semitism can have absolute confidence that the First Amendment is the right antidote to blasphemy laws. It is probably true to say, ironically, that legal religious freedom in the United States has served to protect and stimulate the growth of particularly aggressive and intolerant types of cult. The renunciation by government and law of 'violence or compulsion' in religious matters has produced an exponential increase in violent fundamentalism (is there any other kind?).

In the Britain that the persecuted Priestley deserted, the operative fundamentalism was belief in the Trinity: a belief that subsisted not only in the creeds of the Church but also in the New Testament, especially on the basis of the spurious, forged verse 1 John 7: 'there are three that bear record in Heaven . . .'. Modern biblical scholarship is in no doubt about its inauthenticity, but the first man to urge it in print was ruined on a charge of blasphemy. Thomas Emlyn (1663–1741) was a gentle Presbyterian minister in Dublin, whose doubts about the Trinity were specifically aroused by the controversial works of the 1690s, by Sherlock and by South, in its support. His destiny resembles that of the atheist William Hone, who, as an orthodox youth of 13, was given by his father a copy of Bishop Watson's *Apology for the Bible*, a book that 'gave William the ideas which the Bishop sought to refute'.[29] For many years Emlyn avoided reference to the Trinity in order not to disturb the faith of others, but was eventually taxed with the omission, and forced, as an honest man, to admit his honest doubt. He offered to resign from his church, but at once became the subject of vigorous sectarian provocation. He was driven to seek refuge in England,

> though with great Inconveniency, thus hastily leaving my House and Family, with two small Children: lately become Motherless to my great Grief, which was then very fresh, and heavy upon me, though it gave such a check to all earthly delights as made me more easy under all that followed.[30]

After ten weeks, intending to move permanently to England, he returned to collect his family and to publish a brief and temperate tract in his own defence, *An Humble Inquiry into the Scripture Account of Jesus Christ* (1702). This referred to his conclusions on 1 John 7, later to be amplified in his 1703 tract, *The Case of Mr Emlyn in relation to the Difference between him and some Dissenting Ministers of the City of Dublin which he supposes is grossly misunderstood*, and again in several tracts of the period 1715–20. But Emlyn was arrested and prosecuted under common law on a charge of blasphemy.

Notwithstanding later legal opinion that the law in Ireland never incorporated the doctrine of the Trinity,[31] Emlyn was convicted after a spectacularly unfair trial, even by the standard of blasphemy trials, with two archbishops sitting on the bench. In his *True Narrative* of 1719 he records his difficulty getting Counsel, 'and those whom I did retain were at the beginning so interrupted and borne down that they would not attempt it more' (p. xxvii). The Chief Justice, sentencing him to a year's imprisonment and a fine of £1,000 (more than Emlyn could ever have paid), wistfully reflected that in Spain or Portugal the prisoner's fate would have been death by burning ('but then, 'tis to be consider'd', wrote Emlyn, 'that they act upon Principle, though a Wicked one'). Emlyn was in gaol for more than two years before his friends secured his release after the fine was reduced to £70. Bishop Hoadly's summary of the case is well known: 'The Nonconformists accused him, the Conformists condemned him, the Secular power was called in, and the cause ended in an imprisonment and a very great fine: two methods of conviction about which the gospel is silent.'[32]

Emlyn records his mortification at being charged with blasphemy, 'a scornful and spiteful reproach utter'd in design'd Contempt of God', rather than heresy, 'when false Opinions unwittingly and by mistake are received':

> but *Heresy* was not punishable at Common Law, and so it must be Blasphemy, though never so unjustly called so. But my Counsel wou'd say nothing on this

head, on my behalf; and they would not let me speak for myself; when I offer'd it, the Queen's Counsel turned upon me and cry'd, *Speak by your Counsel.*

After the Lord Chief Justice summed up ('with great Anger'):

> the Jury as men afrighted never considered how unable they were to judge of such Controversies, nor how little reason they had to suppose a *Malicious* Intention in me, and that there was only Presumption of the Fact itself, as was own'd by the Queen's Counsel and Judge. After a little time, the Court sending to 'em to hasten 'em, they brought in a *Verdict* (some of 'em were afterwards sorry; the *Foreman*, and one other, came to me in Prison, ready to help me, what they cou'd, when it was too late).

The pillory was due, said the Lord Chief Justice, but not inflicted 'on a Man of Letters'. It is a tribute in which the Chief Justice spoke better than he knew. Emlyn's is the most moving work against a charge of blasphemy I have read in preparing this book, and I include some longer extracts from it as an appendix to this chapter.

Emlyn's experience gives substance to the claim of a later campaigner against blasphemy laws, Hypatia Bradlaugh Bonner, the daughter of the first atheist member of the British Parliament, Charles Bradlaugh. In an 1882 booklet of stultifying simplicity she assembles a feeble collection of writings under the heading *Blasphemy versus Religion*, with an articulate 'blasphemy' counterpointed by particularly brain-damaged pieces of orthodoxy from Salvation Army sources:

> I have purposely chosen outrageous folly for the religious specimens because I want to put forcibly before my readers this all-important fact, that the law which condemns the eloquent and thoughtful blasphemy of the heretical extracts has nothing to say against the debasing immorality of the Salvation-ists.[33]

Fired as it is by such triumphant non sequiturs, Bonner's work nevertheless identifies an important shift away from Church and University into the schoolroom and on to the streets, based on a realisation that religious orthodoxy and political conformity have to defend themselves more frequently in an age of mass publication and mass reading. This is the age of Father Petcherine and his book-burnings. Authors of blasphemies are still punished: Holyoake, for instance, in 1842, atheist and socialist (Chapter 1), or George William Foote in 1883, given twelve months' hard labour by Mr Justice North, who called it 'a sentence worthy of your creed'.[34] Holyoake responds with genuine puzzlement: 'I am told I may hold opinions, but must keep them to myself';[35] and he cites the counsel in another case who argued 'that if the government were consistent in carrying out prosecutions for blasphemy, Shakespere, Milton, Byron, Shelley, Southey might be prohibited' (p. 47 – Shelley's *Queen Mab* was in fact acted against). This is absolutely the point: Holyoake is no great writer, and it is his very humble station that constitutes his danger. As the American prosecutor of Abner Kneeland put it:

> There have been other infidels – Hume, Gibbon, Voltaire, Volney, &c. but the works of those persons were read only by men of literary habits – necessarily a few – and to men of sound understanding they carried their antidote with them. But here is a Journal, a Newspaper, cheap – and sent into a thousand families. . . .[36]

The Attorney-General, prosecuting the bookseller Henry Hetherington in 1840, made play of the price and availability of the offending texts, *Haslam's Letters*, sold by Hetherington. As Hetherington argued in his defence:

> the true crime is that Haslam's Letters are sold at a penny. Why should two-guinea blasphemers be tolerated and penny ones prosecuted? How can the learned Attorney-General, whose shelves are, doubtless, adorned with Drummond's Academic Questions, Voltaire, Gibbon, Volney, and Shelley, uphold this prosecution; and what must that law be which can find the crime not in the contents of a book, but in the fact of its being sold for a penny? They might for two guineas buy a magnificent book full of blasphemy. The Attorney-General, in his opening speech, had told the jury that such works were 'dangerous to society if addressed to the *vulgar*, the *uneducated*, and the *unthinking*'.[37]

The point was important enough for the Attorney-General to respond to in his right of reply, flattering the jury and playing on their class antagonisms at one and the same time:

> The Defendant accused him of not objecting so much to the matter of the publication, as to the price at which it was sold. Notwithstanding what the Defendant had said on this point, he, the Attorney-General, contended that the low price at which it was sold made the publication doubly mischievous, as it caused it to circulate among the working classes of society, who were, from their habits, incapable of thought or discrimination; their time was so entirely occupied that it was impossible they could devote sufficient time to reading to guard themselves against the evil tendency of such works; while the Jury, and men in their class of life, were, from their education, furnished with an antidote to the poison. If attacks on the Scriptures were to be permitted, what was to prevent the pious feelings from being outraged? Suppose a man were to carry a board through the streets on which was inscribed in large characters, that 'Christ was an imposter'? Could it be tolerated? Yet this, according to the Defendant, was only free inquiry?
> (pp. 20–1)

Much of the Hetherington case is familiar. The charge – that Hetherington, 'being a wicked, impious and ill-disposed person, and having no regard for the laws and religion of this realm, most wickedly, blasphemously, impiously and profanely devising and intending to asperse and vilify that part of the Holy Bible which is called the Old Testament' sold and published Haslam's 'scandalous impious and blasphemous libel' on the Old Testament – is close in language to the Petcherine indictment. The Attorney-General's summing up calls on the jury 'by the oaths they had taken on the Holy Gospel' (p. 22), and presents Haslam's work as an attack on 'the institution of private property'. Notwithstanding such similarities to many other cases, Hetherington's case is one of several that marks a movement in orthodox defences. It matters less what is said and written, and by whom, but how and by whom it is read. The government's target is cheap publication, and the victims are therefore printers and booksellers more than writers: Thomas Williams (1797) and Richard Carlile (1819) in the case of Thomas Paine's *Age of Reason*, Daniel Eaton (1812) in the case of Paine's *The Rights of Man*, George Houston (1813) in the case of *Ecce Homo, A Life of Jesus Christ*, though Houston later confessed himself the writer.

The blasphemy laws in this kind of use take their place alongside obscenity laws, theatrical censorship and Customs regulators as means of controlling the popular circulation of ideas. Boccaccio ran into trouble in both twentieth-century America and Australia; *Ulysses* was banned or charged with obscenity, or, where obscenity failed, with irreligion, successfully in Britain and unsuccessfully in the USA. E. J. Harmon, Australian Minister for Customs in 1927, showed the depths of his mind and morals by urging that *Ulysses* 'holds up to ridicule the Creator and the Church. It ridicules the whole moral standard of civilisation, citizenship and decency. Such books might vitally affect the standards of Australian homelife.'[38] Ireland, to be on the safe side, banned virtually everything.

In a real sense, such controversies continue the coded exchange of a discourse of blasphemy in which both sides agree what is at stake – in this case, two entirely different models for reading communities. In the nineteenth century prosecutions and bans, right to the mid-twentieth century, what is at stake is books, or the Book. Law takes the side of the Bible because the Bible and the law are cognate if not identical. In any case, in the words of a mid-century Australian judge: 'There is enough infidelity in this world without people publicly proclaiming the Bible as a mass of lies.'[39] The trial of Hetherington continues to function as a useful, and representative, example. To begin with, Hetherington's defence was a disaster. Faced with prosecution under a law he clearly sees as illegitimate, Hetherington does what many others have done – he lies, claiming to be merely a poor bookseller 'who never read a line of the book till his attention was called to it by this unjust prosecution' (p. 9): 'it is a great hardship and injustice to hold a bookseller responsible for the contents of the books he sells. I am a general bookseller, so great is the competition, and so fully is my time occupied, that I have no time to spare for reading the various works in my shop . . .' (p. 18). The defence might have succeeded had

Hetherington's name not appeared on the work as its co-publisher, and is not assisted when Hetherington then goes on to defend its contents in detail – after making the gleeful point that the prosecution has made the book a smash commercial success. Haslam's work cannot be 'insulting to God' because his very ground for rejecting the Bible is that it contains passages insulting to God. Having attacked the Bible, Hetherington then uses it in his defence: Old Testament prophets spoke without fear or favour, and so should 'the proclaimers of new truths, and new subjects' (p. 12). Those who prosecute him are like the persecutors of Jesus. In his reference to the trial of Jesus, and in his criticism of the Old Testament, Hetherington agilely invokes the usual anti-Semitism: 'why should *Christians* persecute man for disbelieving the *Jewish* Scriptures, when, according to Dr Adam Clarke, the Jews disbelieve parts of the Old Testament themselves?' (p. 13). Even so, Hetherington's extraordinary defence is markedly less insulting than the work he defends as quoted in the indictment:

> What wretched stuff this Bible is, to be sure! What a random idiot its author must have been! I advise the human race to burn every Bible they have got. Such a book is actually a disgrace to ourang outangs, much less to men . . . I renounce it as a vile compound of filth, blasphemy and nonsense, as a fraud and a cheat, and as an insult to God.

We return, then, to blasphemy and to Bible-burning.

There is a parallel case in America in 1887, when Robert B. Ingersoll defends Charles B. Reynolds against an allegation of blasphemy based on the ideas in Reynolds's pamphlet *Blasphemy and the Bible*. The pamphlet accuses the Bible of giving 'blasphemous representations of God':[40] 'Is it possible to concede more horrible blasphemy than this holy Bible contains?' It urges that the best things in the Bible come from the wisdom Moses gained from the Egyptians (Acts 7: 22): Reynolds too was most likely a freemason. 'The Bible is simply a barbarous history of a barbarous people' (p. 5), with a 'silly story' for an account of Creation (p. 7), and a parodic rendering of the Bible's teaching, especially on the incarnation and life of Jesus:

> Now, reader, take time, and calmly think it over. A Jewish girl becomes the mother of God almighty, the mother of your God. The child of this young Jewess was God. Christ is God. God cried and screamed, squealed and kicked; God flung about his little arms; God made aimless dashes into space with his little fists; God stared foolishly at his own little toes; God smiled when he was comfortable and howled when he was pricked by a nasty pin; God was nursed at Mary's breast; God was wrapped in little diapers; God lay in a cradle and was rocked to sleep; God was quite sick when cutting his little teeth; God caught the measles, mumps, whooping cough, and scarlet fever; God learned to walk and often tumbled down, bumped his forehead, and made his little nose bleed; God was spanked when he was naughty, etc. etc. . . . . Reader, if

you read such absurdities and contradictions in any other book would you regard it as divinely inspired? (pp. 12–13)

Secularism here becomes the alternative to having a God with a Jewish mother. On such unpromising ground Ingersoll constructs what remains the best and most reasoned defence of blasphemy produced in a court of law. He tells the jury: 'The question to be tried by you is whether a man has the right to express his honest thought':

> How has the church in every age, when in authority, defended itself? Always by a statute against blasphemy, against argument, against free speech. And there never was such a statute that did not stain the book that it was in, and that did not certify to the savagery of the man that passed it. Never. By making a statute, and by defining blasphemy, the church sought to prevent discussion, sought to prevent argument – sought to prevent a man giving his honest opinion. Certainly, a tenet, a doctrine, a dogma, is safe when hedged about by a statute that prevents your speaking against it. In the silence of slavery it exists. It lives because lips are locked. It lives because men are slaves.[41]

Ingersoll retaliates with the claim that there can be no blasphemy: 'No man can blaspheme a book. No man can commit a blasphemy by telling his honest thought. No man can blaspheme a God, or a Holy Ghost, or a Son of God. The Infinite cannot be blasphemed.'

There is a further and fascinating parallel between these two cases. Both defences consider the function of Christian missionaries. Hetherington characteristically fumbles his ideas:

> Gentlemen, the enlightened Christians of the present day, by sending out Missionaries to propagate Christianity, are guilty of blasphemy against the established religion of heathen countries. It would be considered in England very unjust and cruel if the natives were to seize our Missionaries, and imprison them and ill-treat them. If in this country we are in the habit of sending out Missionaries to proclaim new truths to foreign countries – is it not grossly inconsistent and unjust while doing this, to punish persons for free investigation at home? (p. 14)

Ingersoll, on the other hand, discovers cultural relativism – and does so with such persuasiveness that I have quoted his remarks as the epigraph to this book. His weighing of the rival claims of Christianity and Islam in the hands of their proselytisers breaks through the equally proselytising aggression of the work that he defends, and invents a genuinely dialogic viewpoint in the midst of the monologic warfare for and against the Book – 'In other words, what we want is intellectual hospitality. Let the world talk.' It is still the best defence of books I know.

When Christian religious leaders support Islamic demands for an extension of blasphemy legislation to cover all religions, the suspicion remains that the cause of the Book against books still lives, even if the hope of victory is now with the Qu'ran rather than the Bible. This is not a pluralism that says 'Let the world talk' but, in Ingersoll's terms, an extension of slavery. Any such new law would still be designed to protect the interests of the religious community of readers against all others, a law to express only the shared values of the Petcherine case, a law for book-burners.

In any case, however, we should be cautious of renewing, still less reinforcing, links between State power and the punishment of blasphemy. Blasphemy and patriotism are already related, and make a dangerous combination. We know too that the discourse of blasphemy is transferable, and can be activated even in the formal absence of the Book. The Stalinist show trial perfected a fundamentalist genre of unassailable guilt. Its American counterpart, the quasi-hysterical invention of communists, is not called a witch-hunt for nothing: the Rosenbergs died in perfect accord with Stalin's victims and those of the Inquisition. One might also say that they died for America, since, as E. L. Doctorow has it in *The Book of Daniel*: 'Every man is the enemy of his own country.'[42]

Reference to comparable French history may clarify the issue. Is it true that, more than their British or American counterparts, French writers tend to be religious non-conformists (Voltaire, Stendhal) or political rebels (Victor Hugo, Zola, Sartre) or sexual dissidents (Proust, Gide), or all three (Genet)? If so, modern French history has some part to play in the explanation. Not since the late seventeenth century has British society experienced funda-mental, top-to-bottom community schism. France has endured not only the Revolution but also the conflict of republicans versus imperialists (twice), monarchists versus republicans versus imperialists (three times), clericalists versus anti-clericalists, fascists versus communists versus democrats, Vichy collaborators versus the Resistance, supporters of French Algeria versus decolonisers, and so on. Such fundamental rifts and choices lie in living memory, and they are enough to give the lie to the rather lazy consensual notion of community that against all odds persists in underlying many Anglo-Saxon assumptions. The French experience is true to a world in which Yugoslavia may fall apart into warring communities divided by language or religion or both, and sometimes, but not always, race as well – a world at which Anglo-Saxon politicians wring their hands and commentators express astonishment. Yet one might as well deduce that Balkanisation is the reality of community – except where conformity to an ideology overrides it. Anglo-Saxon ideals of community, what is 'common' in common law, may be nothing more than the surviving fragments of the medieval ideal of the universal Church. That may be one reason why British lawmakers are reluctant to give up blasphemy laws: these articulate the last real connection with the foundation on which the subsequent legal notion of community is built, undefined in Britain by any Constitution or Bill of Rights. A law of blasphemy is not incidental to such a community but integral to it. It invokes a mythical 'community standard' as a kind of quasi-sacrament. In nineteenth-century France, by contrast, cultural and political norms changed so drastically and so quickly – one moment anti-clerical, and the next fervently Jesuit – that one can be under no illusion of any true consensus: the model is that of conflict. French laws are frequently rewritten throughout this period, and religion is subordinated to morals, that is, to custom: 'outrage à la morale publique et religieuse et aux bonnes moeurs' was the charge against both *Madame Bovary* and *Les Fleurs du Mal*, both in 1857. H.-R. Jauss argues that the acquittal of Flaubert marks a decisive shift in readers' 'horizon of expectation', but this mystifies community into consensus once more.[43] The conviction of the one, and the acquittal of the other, is most obviously interpreted in terms of different dynamics of community. I assume that those who disapproved of *Madame Bovary* disapproved as much after the verdict as before it: the trial did not express change but enacted conflict. Such conflicts show precisely how 'every man is the enemy of his own country'.

Given this historical background, modern French cultural theorists have shown a great deal more interest in the notion of community than their Anglo-Saxon counterparts. The first of them was Georges Bataille, whose worry about community led him to set up a society, the Acéphale. Bataille, who did not always sit securely in the discursive saddle, even worried about the need for a real human blood sacrifice with which to consummate it: the idea goes with his fascination with Sade, his insistence on the literal reality of Sadean orgies and the medieval Black Mass, and reveals an intimate connection, inside and outside his work, in the idea of community and the discourse of blasphemy. It may be that secret societies, communities of the shadows, have long played a key part in French intellectual life. We know that Freemasonry was radically involved in the politics of the Enlightenment: Voltaire and all the major Encyclopédistes were Masons, as were the leading English figures of the Royal Society in the late seventeenth century, such as Newton, Wren and Locke; it is more plausible than not that the rites of the order are an invention of that period, bringing together Protestants and Catholics, Christians, Deists and Jews in their avoidance of any reference to Christ and cementing a free-thinking community in a kind of enlightened parody of religious ritual. This sort of history would locate Freemasonry where the contemporary Church did, in the business of blasphemy, but it is likely to remain secret as long as official Masonry implausibly insists on its direct continuity from King Solomon's temple by way of Canterbury and Chartres. At any rate, Masonry conforms to the model of community that Bataille mentioned, one that has recently been refined and restated by Maurice Blanchot (1988) and in a major book by Jean-Luc Nancy: small compared to the total population; exclusive, not inclusive;

and religious in character. For all three theorists, 'community' is a Christian concept cognate, as etymology suggests, with 'communion'. Bataille's preferred model is the monastic order. Community is therefore the conceptual common ground between accusers and accused in the circus of blasphemy. Where religion loses its social cohesiveness, community as a notion loses its coherence. The twentieth century is therefore the age of community crisis, in a different sense from the usual one, the age in which the term 'community' has suddenly, and dramatically, lost its meaning.

Modern experience of community is therefore that of multiple rupture. Hence Nancy's sense that:

> The Book is no longer. (I am not saying 'there is no longer a Book', for there is undeniably, to the same extent that there is divine service, in every temple, church, synagogue or mosque; but I am saying *the Book is no longer*, as we ought to know since Mallarmé and Joyce, Blanchot and Derrida.) It is not in vain that the text has proliferated, has become scattered and fragmented in all our writings.[44]

Indeed, Nancy's final chapter is characterised by an almost elegiac nostalgia for the sacred, which remains in art – the sacred desacralised – and is lost to religion since the Reformation (through schism). There is an obsessive and aphoristic review of the properties of different religions:

> Judaism is an atheism with God. Protestantism, on the other hand, is a theism without God. Catholicism is the worship of all gods in God, or the loss of God in all gods. Islam is the pure proclamation of God to the point where it becomes an empty clamour. Buddhism is the worship of God in all small gods or the loss of all small gods in God. (p. 128)

In such a review, with its sense of the relative, there is only loss:

> if there are no more gods, there is no more community. That is why community has been capable of becoming horrifying, massive, destructive of its members and itself, a society burned at the stake by its Church, its Myths or its spirit. Such is the fate of community without god: it thinks it is God – (p. 143)

– the fate of Gibreel Farishta.

After God, after community, remains only blasphemy – all that remains of the hope of keeping God and community alive, even where its life now depends on the last possible resurrection, Nietzsche's, done only to declare another death but unable to accomplish it. 'This God who quickens us beneath his clouds is mad', writes Bataille. 'I know, I am he.'[45] Such blasphemy, caught between tenderness and pastiche, bears with it the last vestiges of community.

The ramifications of these ideas for modernity form the subject of the next two chapters, and in Chapter 6 I return explicitly to their relevance for Rushdie and the world in which community meets hyperreality. It is enough to say now that it challenges those whose religion is literature as much as it does those whose literature is religion. The most common model we have for the reading of texts, that of the sovereign and individual 'private' reader, appears not only inadequate but discredited. Readers are not singular, they are communities; and the history of reading is one of the conflict of interpretative communities. The history of blasphemy is a valuable corrective. We are not united by what we read. We are divided by it. Our reading divides us, on the level of community rather than that of the individual subject. Those who would recuperate reading by legislation do not understand reading or community.

What are we to do? The community to which I wish to belong would accept the advice of Theodore Schroeder:

> Equality before the law . . . requires all of us to submit to ridicule and contempt from the unbeliever when that is directed against our conception of God, or against our religion, just to the same extent that the Christians have the right to hold the contrary convictions of heathens and Atheists up to ridicule and contempt; that is, so long as it is free from a criminal, malicious intent.[46]

One might even strive to give up the highly coercive and religious category of intention. Of all the literature produced by the *Gay News* trial of 1977, the most congenial is the 'Buddhist reflections' of Sangharakshita, who argues that for Buddhists in Britain 'there is no such thing as blasphemy'.[47] It follows, first, that 'the law of blasphemy should be abolished altogether. It should not be extended to cover other religions. Buddhism itself does not, in any case, require the protection of any such law'; secondly, that there 'should be a complete separation of Church and State'; and thirdly, 'Blasphemy should be recognised as healthy, and as necessary to the moral and spiritual development of the individual. Far from being prosecuted, it should be encouraged' (p. 24). This is not irresponsible libertarianism: it is the only principle that guarantees my freedom to read what I and those like me wish to read.

Why else is blasphemy 'healthy'? Because, I think, it often registers the irruption of a new reading community, though such a community through its very particularity is rarely capable of mobilisation and will lose a really determined contest for control of the streets to any half-competent fundamentalist. Blasphemy is not infrequently such a community's rite of passage. That is why blasphemy occurs more often than usual in work that is dissident in some other way as well, such as Genet's work or Rushdie's. Women's writing has been an important site of blasphemy in the twentieth century, as in the later Middle Ages. Within a Christian, or Jewish/Christian, cultural tradition one thinks of Radclyffe Hall's *The Well of Loneliness*, with its transvestite Christ figure named appropriately Stephen, and of women's writing that challenges theological orthodoxy – as here, on the creation of woman, where God is shown as falling in love with his new creation:

was it then he conceived
of himself
having a son

as he laid her
across his knees
to carve the long line
of spine down
to the smallest part
of her back
this time he was more concerned
with symmetry
a balance of buttocks
with breasts
how to give her two mouths
so he spread and slit her
slow work
then to dig out
a passage
for pleasure
a crevice
as wonderful as thunder
as dangerous as a fault
in the earth
as red within
as the innocent
apple

yes. god made man
and it was good
but this was better[48]

The point is even more valid in Islamic cultures, in, for example, the work of Nawal el Saadawi, whose *The Fall of the Imam* shows the Imam as father and rapist as well as spiritual leader and political tyrant. The author's preface explains:

I could not allow him to exercise absolute power in my story just as he had done in everything else. I said to myself, at least where my novel is concerned I should enjoy some freedom, exercise some control over the Imam, and not let him do just as he likes.

So Saadawi calls her heroine 'Bint Allah', daughter of God:

the name of Bint Allah gave me a lot of anxiety and kept me awake long nights. I tried to find another name for her. Her name seemed to violate what is most sacred, to encroach on the holiest of holies. How could a girl dare to bear the sacrilegious name of Bint Allah (she also dared to bear a child without a father)? Christianity has permitted a male, Christ the Messiah, to be called the Son of

God. But no one has ever heard of Bint Allah, the Daughter of God. And one day, right in the middle of the novel, she asked me a question. What if I was the Virgin Mary and had borne a female child instead of a male? Would she have become Christ the Messiah?

This made it difficult for me to change the name of Bint Allah to something else. Besides, since the moment she was born until the moment she was stoned to death, people had always called her Bint Allah. Then came the day when I came upon her, a lifeless body, lying face downwards on sand and rock. I decided to banish her from my life, to forget.[49]

As she tells it, Saadawi is unable to forget. The novel she writes is the witness to God's daughter in Islam, who is raped by the Imam and murdered at his behest, and who reveals on the first page of the novel as she lies dying: 'My father is the Imam. They screamed: Not another word. May your tongue be cut out of your head' (p. 1). And so it is, this being Islamic law. The novel unwrites such law, and rewrites it literally to incorporate woman. The blasphemy here, of which stoning is the expression and murder the outcome, is the realisation of Islam's own treatment of its daughters. The novel is not a rational plea for liberation. It makes sense only as desecration, violation of the masculine sacred that represses women, Islamic blasphemy.

In Christian and Islamic cultures, then, certain sorts of fiction tend to blasphemy for the reason that they set out to assert the rights of the new community outside existing law. Religious orthodoxy has always recognised the danger in such assertion and taken it seriously: hence, in both Christian and Islamic cultures, a seemingly endless sequence of allegations, trials and killings, judicial and otherwise. It is not God whom such fictions would affront but the religious community that they seek to transform, and which exercises whatever power it can wield to resist a transformation. A community, not God, is the recipient of blasphemy: a community that by its violent response identifies itself as fundamentalist. For fundamentalism is the necessary violence with which to discipline readers. All readers are potential enemies to their own community.

Appendix to Chapter 4: Extracts from the *True Narrative* of Thomas Emlyn (1719)

If the great End of publishing this *Narrative*, had been to disburden my Mind of any uneasy Resentments of my ill Usage, or to load the Authors of it with Reproach, I should not have delay'd it for so many Years; Passion is more in haste, than to bear fifteen or sixteen Years voluntary Restraint. 'I thank God I have no revengeful Disposition towards the keenest of my Enemies; and am so far from any Uneasiness at the Remembrance of my Sufferings, that no Scene of my Life yields me more solid Satisfaction: The *Peerless Unequal'd* Majesty of the One *God and Father* of all, appears to me both so evident and so important a Doctrine in the Christian Religion, and so directly impugned in later Ages, that if ever I would be tempted to glory in any Suffering, it should be in so noble a Cause, which is the very basis of Christianity. . . .

And indeed where Charity is esteem'd, as with St *Paul*, the greatest of Virtues, even *greater than Faith* in all Mysteries, there Persecution, the most cruel uncharitable thing in the World, must needs be deem'd the greatest of Crimes; for which reason, that Apostle reproaches himself as the *Chief of Sinners*, because he had been, though with good Meaning, a Persecutor, the worst of Criminals. I think 'tis less wicked in the sight of God, for the matter of the Sin, to rob a Man on the Road from Necessity, than to spoil him of his Goods and liberty, and to afflict him with Tortures and Reproaches for not making a Surrender of his Conscience; the one aims to rob a Man of his Money, the other of the Peace of his Mind, and his Eternal Salvation; it looks like a sort of Malice against God himself, and is certainly a worse Heresy than any differing Opinion about the Sense of a Text of Scripture. . . .

'Tis a weak Plea, to say, Error may be punish'd, but not Truth, when all sides take themselves for Orthodox; so that on this foot Persecution must go round the Earth, *seeking whom to devour*. A Man had as good say plainly, 'tis a Sin for any Others to persecute, but that 'tis his sole Privilege to do it when he judges it fit. (p. ix)

Might not any Protestant, then, all these things considered, venture upon a serious Examination of Modern Creeds by the light of Revelation, the Words of Christ's own Mouth, and the Writings of his Inspired Apostles? Or might not I, who had been brought up in a different Study of the Scriptures, and admitted to be a Teacher of others, justly expect the liberty of declaring what I judged to be the Doctrine of the Gospel, though rejected by others not more infallible than I?

I am sure that I was under too serious Impressions & Concern of my Soul to treat the Argument with ludicrous Derisions, or indecent Scurrility, or any real token of designed Contempt of the Holy Jesus. I wrote my *Humble Inquiry* &c. as one grieved in Spirit and afflicted, forsaken of my People, and my Friends, and abandoned to the Reproaches, Indignation or Contempt of all round about me; cast out as a despised broken Vessel, in which is no Pleasure; so that I had nothing to support me in this Case, but that I was maintaining the Cause of the God of Gods, and the Truth of Jesus his Son. And though I had given all the proof of my acting conscientiously, that a man could give, in quitting my beneficial Station among the Dissenters quietly and easily; retiring from all the Respects, and even from all further Acquaintance of my Friends, into a silent and neglected Obscurity; and this in the very vigour of my age (at 38 years) when, if ever I was capable of signifying anything, I might most have expected it: yet was I numbred among the vilest Transgressors and Blasphemers. The Pulpits pounded with Heresy and Blasphemy, to beget abhorrence; and I was prosecuted and treated as if I had written with the profanest Scorn in derision of Christianity; nor could I ever hear of any other Precedent the Lord Chief Justice offer'd, but of one M-----, who had been convicted of Blasphemy, for calling our Saviour a Bastard or Son of a W-----, and my Case must be like his; and so under Forms of Law, I was made a *Gazing-stock, and a Companion to them, in Bonds, and suffered the spoiling of my Goods*; but with this allay, that it was in hopes of a more enduring Substance. (p. xii)

Chapter 5

WRITING BLASPHEMY
Freud and the Wolf-Man

I am anxious not to be misunderstood.
SIGMUND FREUD (1918): 238

The Wolf-Man keeps howling: Six wolves! seven wolves! Freud
says, How's that? Goats, you say? How interesting. Take away the
wolves and all you have left is a goat, so it's your father. . . . That
is why the Wolf-Man feels so fatigued: he's left lying there with all
his wolves in his throat, all those little holes on his nose, and all
those libidinal values on his body without organs.
GILLES DELEUZE AND FELIX GUATTARI (1987): 38

At least until the Rushdie affair, it might have seemed to many in America,
Australasia and Europe that blasphemy had grown less virulent in the
twentieth century: in Western societies, those who would ban or burn books
and people still express themselves fiercely, but there are fewer of them
than, say, in the twelfth or in the seventeenth century, and their chances
of gaining legal sanction, outside the Islamic world, are slighter than ever
before. If this impression is at all true, there are some outstanding
exceptions; moreover, Western law continues to engage with heterodoxy,
but often at the level of obscenity rather than blasphemy. Nobody who
believes it to be true should be altogether confident that the situation is
irreversible: the freedom to dissent is always in danger. Whether it is true
or false, its currency might be seen as evidence of the further loosening of
ties between Church and State, religion and law. A cynic might even
conclude that religious tolerance grows most securely in inverse proportion
to religious enthusiasm. Such a conclusion is itself a construct of modernity;
it is a Freudian conclusion, grounded in Freud's lifelong attempt to show
religion as a childish thing: a basic drive, a powerful and often sinister force,
but one to be outgrown in a civilising adolescence. Religion, like perversion,
is pre-cultural. Freud is far from being irreligious: much of his coolness
towards Christianity is attributable to his Jewish background, but in his
passionate relation to Judaism his role model could almost be a Christian
heretic. To adapt Jonathan Dollimore's observation about André Gide,
whose ethical essentialism is simply too close in type to that of the Church:
organised religion encounters in a blaspheming rival 'a proximity rooted in

144

their differences'.[1] It is my purpose here to portray Freud as master blasphemer, with blasphemy at the very core of his enterprise.

The metaphor I have just used – a revelation made at the core of something or someone – is classically Freudian. Freud sets out to show that psychoanalysis reveals truth, the truth of dreams and early childhood experience, in a form that can be disencoded by the analyst as scientific outsider. The truth does not come from the analyst; it is discovered by him in the psyche of his patient. This is the essentialism of Freud's work: not for him postmodern fragmentation, the thesis that 'the unconscious represents nothing, creates no symbols or signifiers, no veiled or distorted wishes that call for interpretation'.[2] That way madness lies. In establishing the validity of his claim, and of subsequent psychoanalytical procedure, Freud's most famous case is that of Sergei Pankejeff, identified by Freud only as the Wolf-Man. This case was made all the more important by proving intractable, and so extending throughout, and beyond, Freud's career. It is in his reports of this case that Freud develops his theory of the primal scene and, over time, modifies it: at the root of neurosis is a childhood catastrophe, the truth of which may be subjected to analysis (especially of dreams), whether that truth takes the form of fact, as he first thought, or is the 'truth' of fantasy refracting fact, as he came to think. It is Wolf-Man to whom Freud writes for factual confirmation of some of his key ideas, based on Wolf-Man's own case, when they are under attack by Adler: the 'primal scene' is a dialogic fiction constructed in the consulting room by analyst and patient, and testimony to the 'will to power' of both. Moreover, Wolf-Man's dream of five wolves is actually Freud's reverie of himself and his five pupils, including Adler and Jung. That is one objection Freud must answer, together with Jung's attack on his over-personalised analysis of dreams and their symbols. The controversy – which resembles nothing so much as the bitter religious feuds of the seventeenth century – is conducted across his ongoing report of the Wolf-Man's case. That report is therefore a defence against others' blasphemy, a description of Wolf-Man's own childhood blasphemy, and a product and deliberate construction of Freud's own blasphemous system.[3]

From the History of an Infantile Neurosis was first published in 1918, with an introductory note recording that it was first written 'shortly after the termination of the treatment in the winter of 1914–15. At that time I was still under the impression of the twisted reinterpretations which C. G. Jung and Alfred Adler were endeavouring to give to the findings of psychoanalysis.' He adds that 'no alterations of any importance have been made in the text of the first draft', the publication of which was held up by 'the Great War' (p. 187). However, the fourth chapter, 'The dream and the primal scene', had already been published in an essay on the occurrence in dreams of material from fairy tales, and, as the introduction noted, Freud's *Introductory*

Lectures on Psychoanalysis, given in 1916 and 1917, had already dealt with many of the points of the history relating to the primal scene; with the result that Chapter v, translated as 'A few discussions', concludes with a long authorial interpolation that effectively undoes Freud's reading of the case to date, and which leads to notes in the rest of the work that attempt to bridge the disparity (for example, note four of the sixth chapter, reading simply 'Assuming the reality of the primal scene', or note six of the seventh chapter, which supplements the text – 'what else could he have supposed when at the age of one-and-a-half he was a spectator of the scene?' – with the notorious addendum, 'Or so long as he did not understand the copulation of the dogs'). There is a further long interpolation, justifying his view of the Grusha scene and the support it gave to his previous hesitation about reinterpreting the primal scene. In his second year of life, did Wolf-Man see his parents copulate, or did he watch two dogs doing it? This is the key issue presented by the whole account, but it connects with Freud's resolute response to Adler and Jung:

> I admit that this is the most ticklish question in the whole domain of psychoanalysis. I did not require the contributions of Adler and Jung to induce me to consider the matter with a critical eye, and to bear in mind the possibility that what analysis puts forward as being forgotten experiences of childhood (and of an improbably early childhood) may on the contrary be based upon phantasies brought about upon occasions occurring late in life. . . . On the contrary, no doubt has troubled me more; no other uncertainty has been more decisive in holding me back from publishing my conclusions. . . . If, in spite of this, I have held to the more difficult and more improbable view, it has been as a result of arguments such as are forced upon the investigator by the case described in these pages or by any other infantile neurosis. (p. 296)

The major alternative readings of the primal scene that Freud presents in this account, which will be examined below, are wildly inconsistent with each other and their inconsistency is probably a source of embarrassment to most readers; but Freud seems well content with their diversity, since both depend on childhood experience of one sort or another, rather than adult imagining in collaboration with a gifted psychoanalyst.

The Freudian case-history is constructed in a way that supposedly enacts, as if mimetically, the difficulty for both patient and analyst in producing it by a series of fragments adduced and assembled over time, a difficulty on which Freud as narrator eagerly focuses at the beginning of the later chapters:

> I must beg the reader to bear in mind that I obtained this history of an infantile neurosis as a by-product, so to speak, during the analysis of an illness in mature years. I was therefore obliged to put it together from even smaller fragments than are usually at one's disposal for purposes of synthesis.
> (Chapter vii, p. 261)

It happens in many analyses that as one approaches their end new recollections emerge which have hitherto been kept carefully concealed. Or it may be that on occasion some unpretentious remark is thrown out in an indifferent tone of voice as though it were superfluous; that then, on another occasion, something further is added, which begins to make the physician prick his ears; and that at the last he comes to recognise this despised fragment of a memory as the key to the weightiest secrets that the patient's neurosis has screened. (Chapter VIII, p. 281)

The second of these artfully suggests that the bewildering changes and contradictions in the course of the writing are representations, and therefore validations, of the psychoanalytical process itself, and of the analyst's role of reader through prior re-readings. Thus the literary task of narration endorses, albeit opaquely, the narrator's experience as participant. It is therefore the case itself that sets the limits of writing:

I am unable to give either a purely historical or a purely thematic account of my patient's story: I can write a consecutive history neither of the treatment nor of the disease, but I shall find myself obliged to combine the two methods of presentation. (Chapter II, p. 195)

This, at the very start of the case-presentation, claims for the literary difficulty a role at once reportorial ('it happened this way') and heuristic ('this leads to final understanding'). The rhetorical balancing of Freud's functions as narrator and actor is reiterated at the start of the ninth and final chapter, 'Recapitulations and problems':

I do not know if the reader of this report of an analysis will have succeeded in forming a clear picture of the origin and development of the patient's illness. I fear that, on the contrary, this will not have been the case. But though on other occasions I have said very little on behalf of my powers in the art of exposition, I should like in the present instance to plead mitigating circumstances. (Chapter IX, p. 297)

The major circumstance is one that again testifies to Freud's double skill: 'the case itself was not a particularly favourable one'. The final chapter now ends with a note added in 1923, revolving around the reality of the primal scene and the wolf dream. Here, however, Freud concedes so much to the reader's difficulty as, at the very end of the work, to give a brief chronology: 'I will once more set out the chronology of events mentioned in this case history' (p. 316). It is inadequate – less than forty lines long – and calculated at best to be a basic grid for re-reading. Nevertheless, I follow that grid here in an expanded recapitulation of Freud's account.

For the first time the note clearly identifies Wolf-Man's nationality, with what is evidently a rhetorical disclaimer; 'It will have been easy to guess from my account that the patient was a Russian.' Certainly, the grounds for guessing are there; what is surprising, however, in so long a case-history is that until this addition the straightforward statement was never made. Its absence is part of the decontextualising by Freud of the Wolf-Man's life; his history is used as a reference for his psyche, but it is hard to see the Wolf-Man through Freud's eyes as open body and soul to history itself, even as dramatic a history as that of the 'Great War', to which the text here makes only its second allusion since the Introduction. The war has been a factor in Wolf-Man's life, we learn (was it not in everybody's?); and so it merits a mention that wryly mixes compassion with an unpredictable moralism. After his return to Freud in Vienna during the war's course,

> the patient has felt normal and has behaved unexceptionably, in spite of the war having robbed him of his home, his possessions, and all his family relationships. It may be that his very misery, by gratifying his sense of guilt, contributed to the consolidation of his recovery. (p. 316)

Yet in the very paragraph that identifies Wolf-Man as a Russian, there is no mention of the Russian Revolution itself, or of his future as a displaced person. The case still belongs to Freud, not to history, to the looping and backtracking structure of Freud's prose rather than to a sequence of events.

'Born *on Christmas Day*'

This is revealed in Chapter II of his account, when Freud notes that his patient had the first of his tantrums 'one Christmas, when he was not given a double quantity of presents – which was his due, because Christmas Day was the same time as his birthday' (p. 196). The detail is introduced casually, and in a subordinate position. Its development in the unfolding of the account is held back. There is no overt association with the mention of pieties, and blasphemies, that follows, except that Christmas Day marks the child's transition into behavioural naughtiness.

'1½ *years old: Malaria. Observation of his parents' coitus or of the interview between them into which he later introduced his coitus phantasy*'

A major element in the narrative is treated in one sentence as if it were unproblematic. The primal scene is not introduced until the fourth chapter of the case-history, where it again follows a reference to Christmas: the tree of the wolf dream is identified as a Christmas tree. The primal scene is invoked, indeed, in the explanation of that dream; but there is no sense that it follows at all easily: 'I have now reached the point at which I must abandon the support I have hitherto had from the course of the analysis. I am afraid it will also be the point at which the reader's belief will abandon me' (p. 221). In the discourse written by Freud it is less that the primal scene explains the dream than that the dream, a datum of analysis, justifies the introduction of the primal scene: 'What sprang into activity that night out of the chaos of the dreamer's unconscious memory-traces was the picture of a coitus between his parents, a coitus in circumstances which were not entirely usual and were especially favourable for observation' (pp. 221–2). And out of the chaos of Wolf-Man's life springs a dazzlingly specific and audaciously detailed ur-narrative. The child witnessed the coitus at (possibly) five o'clock in the afternoon – this is a number taken from the wolf-dream and later interpreted in Roman numerals, by way of a butterfly, as the splay of his mother's legs in the usual position. But in this first rendition what the Wolf-child sees, as he wakes in his cot in the room to which his parents had retired in white underclothes, 'half-undressed, for an afternoon siesta', is no missionary activity but 'a coitus *a tergo*, three times repeated: he was able to see his mother's genitals as well as his father's member' (p. 223). The unexpectedness of the 'coitus *a tergo*' is perhaps dissipated by the three occasions, and by a footnote in which an amused Freud records that Wolf-Man at first, and of course erroneously, accused Freud himself of having made up the number. Was the child old enough for unconscious perception? How was the memory then stored? Freud raises the doubts and dismisses them. What justifies Freud's certainty as to the position? (A scrupulously qualified certainty: 'the evidence does not require that the coitus should have been performed from behind each time'.) Nothing, it seems, except a strange exegetical literalness: the dream concerns animals, and this is how animals couple – buttocks high, *more ferarum*. It sets the child thinking of lions and wolves, and the illustrations of wolves in fairy-books may later, speculates Wolf-Man, have reminded him of his father during the constructed primal scene. Certainly, for Freud, the father is the wolf. It is also theologically and socially orthodox: 'the man upright, and the woman bent down like an animal' (p. 224). Because of the intertextual confusion with fairy-tales, two parents come to be figured in seven wolves: so from two come three, five, seven.

Yet no sooner is this adamantine hypothesis erected than another substitutes for it. Perhaps as well as his father's backside he also saw his mother's face? (The mother's gaze is important in this case, though repressed in a manner to delight a Lacanian.) Perhaps, then, he first saw 'a coitus in the normal attitude, which cannot fail to produce the impression of being a sadistic act' (p. 231). Freud's generalisation here borrows the woman-crushing brutality he detects in the scene. He is to go on: 'He understood now that active was the same as masculine, while passive was the same as feminine' (p. 233) – an understanding that contributes much to Freud's mature philosophical system. Such a vantage point would have given the child (this perceptive 18-month-old child) a better view of the vagina; and he, not of course the adult analyst, would immediately have construed it as a wound, as castration, the precondition of coitus with his father. 'He could no longer confuse it with the bottom': in which case, actually, it may appear surprising that his heterosexual activity is to express itself in a lifelong fetishising of buttocks. Indeed, Wolf-Man's proclivities for bottoms and *a tergo* penetration must be attributed to his witnessing the primal scene: 'It seemed necessary to trace this predilection back to the coitus which he had observed between his parents' (p. 244). Perhaps his sister also saw it, for she spoke of people standing on their heads during sexual intercourse (p. 245). A chapter of digression, rejecting any notion that these are fantasies of patient or analyst, leads to a defiant challenge on Freud's part: the reader must take it or leave it.

> It must therefore be left at this – I can see no other possibility – either the analysis based upon the neurosis in his childhood is all a piece of nonsense from start to finish, or everything took place just as I have described it above.
>
> (p. 224)

All is true or all is false.

It is all the more astonishing that within a page we are given a radically alternative reading. 'It is true that we cannot dispense with the assumption that the child observed a coitus, and his later predilections leave us no choice but to conclude that it must have been a coitus *a tergo, more ferarum*', the only position that affords a spectator 'the possibility of inspecting the genitals'. In a bold use of Occam's razor, Freud suddenly suggests that the child might never have seen his parents in this position at all: 'Perhaps what the child observed was not a coitus between his parents but an animal coitus', specifically between dogs, in which case the primal scene is 'only a phantasy' made out of the 'transference from the copulating dogs onto his parents' (p. 246). In face of so drastic a revision, such transference is necessary to nothing but Freud's theory; it both maintains the good manners of the parents ('We need no longer suppose they performed a coitus in the presence of their child . . . which was a disagreeable idea for many of us', p. 247) and preserves the notion of the primal scene even as the interpretation of the dream on which it is based is suddenly rejected. As the reader collapses into the imploding argument, Freud expresses a narrator's modest pleasure in the further interpretative complications yet to come: 'I can well believe that I have now laid myself open to grave aspersions on the part of the readers of this case history' (p. 248). Since interpretation is here enacted as fundamentally torn, there seems almost a gloating rhetoric in his foreshadowing of what follows. 'The case history is not yet at an end; in its further course a factor will emerge which will shake the certainty which we seem at present to enjoy.' The reference to certainty is a Freudian joke.

If, as seems likely and as already predicted, that new factor has to do with the Wolf-Man's bowels, it appears altogether impervious to the interpretative chasm that precedes it. Freud cannot resist an explanation of the Wolf-Man's lifelong bowel trouble (haemorrhoids and an over-active but irregular colon): it is a sign of repressed homosexuality, the mark of one identifying with his mother in the desire to be penetrated by the father – an identification which arises from the primal scene, because of 'what the father has done to her' (p. 266): 'A conclusion', adds Freud, 'which was probably not far from the truth', later adding only that cursory and notorious palinode: 'Or as long as he did not understand the copulation of the dogs', as if small children might have so much more trouble doing this than appraising primal scenes at a glance. Why bowel trouble? Because faeces are both a child's sign of sexual excitement and a child's most loving gift – even a child's child, since, as Dr Freud assures us, 'children, like faeces, are born thorough the anus' (p. 274). But the most important reason depends on a literal level of the primal scene: 'the child finally interrupted his parents' intercourse by passing a stool, which gave him an excuse for screaming' (p. 271). Primal scenes always end this way. It is the infant's rite of passage into creativity, an initiation – so we shall see – into that apotheosis of excrement, the divine, where the primal scene is seen to yield place to Christmas trees, buttocks and full-scale quadrupeds.

'Just before 2½: *Scene with Grusha*'

Late in the history, in Chapter VIII ('Fresh material from the primal period: Solution') there emerges, 'timidly and indistinctly, a kind of recollection' of a nurserymaid of whom he was fond and who, as Wolf-Man initially recalls, had the same first name as his mother. This turns out to be a false verbal association. It recalls another and later identification, when his sister rejects his advances in puberty, and he, with 'an intention of debasing his sister', turned his attention to

> a little peasant girl who was a servant in the house and had the same name as his sister. In doing so he was taking a step which had a determinant influence upon his heterosexual object-choice, for all the girls with whom he subsequently fell in love – often with the clearest indications of compulsion – were also servants. (pp. 204–5)

The young nurserymaid is therefore a prototype. Wolf-Man arrives at her true name by associating her with a pear, the word for which, 'in his language' (even at this late stage Russian is still not mentioned explicitly), is her name, Grusha. What Wolf-Man chiefly remembers about Grusha, in Freud's reconstruction, is, again, a bottom: the child observes her 'kneeling on the floor, and beside her a pail and a short broom made of a bundle of twigs; he was also there, and she was teasing him or scolding him' (p. 283). Freud proposes that the reason for her scolding him – which is a threat of castration – is that the child had involuntarily urinated on the floor when seeing her in this provocative attitude:

> When he saw the girl upon the floor engaged in scrubbing it, and kneeling down, with her buttocks projecting and her back horizontal, he was faced once more with the attitude which his mother had assumed in the coitus scene. She became his mother to him; he was seized with sexual excitement owing to the activation of this picture; and like his father (whose actions at the time he can only have regarded as a form of urination), he behaved in a masculine way towards her. His urinating on the floor was in reality an attempt at a seduction, and the girl replied to it with a threat of castration, just as though she had understood what he meant. (p. 284)

This is vintage Freud: confident, circumstantial, prurient. Particularly astonishing here is that Freud arrives at this reconstruction by way of a verbal and visual clue of the most indirect kind: Wolf-Man does not actually remember a particular moment of enuresis, and at the age of 2½ might well not have invested it with external significance had he done so. Freud's object of attention or fetish here is Grusha's broom of twigs; he associates this with Wolf-Man's recalling his interest in the bundles of faggots by which John Hus was burned at the stake in 1421. Freud notes: 'his sympathy for Huss [*sic*] created a perfectly definite suspicion in my mind, for I have often come upon this sympathy in youthful patients' (p. 285). Hus, then, is the patron saint of bedwetters. Hence Freud's conjecture of urination, and his (less than plausible) association of this with the father's penile activity.

The context is especially rich in visual associations and puns: Grusha, the yellow-striped pear, is associated with a swallow-tailed butterfly with yellow stripes. Its open wings form a Roman v, which patient and analyst take to symbolise the mother's outstretched legs in intercourse and confirm the time of the primal scene at 5 p.m. The fear of the butterfly, like the fear of the wolf, is a castration fear; and the Wolf-Man then conflates the yellow-striped butterfly with a wasp, misremembering the German name (*Wespe*) as *Espe*: his own initials, S. P. All these associations cluster around Grusha, for two reasons. First, the episode is held to explain, or support Freud's explanation of, Wolf-Man's adult sexual habits: violent copulation with servant-girls from behind, or with servant-girls with whom he has fallen in love from behind, antedates his rejection of the sister and attaches to the mother. Even Freud here recognises misogyny when he sees it: 'an endeavour to debase his love-object' (p. 286), 'his desire to debase women' (p. 288). But in the 1922 additions he seeks to extenuate it in terms of a rather general reference to the patient's history. Secondly, as the 1922 addition spells out, the Grusha episode – so ingeniously reconstructed – affords support to the reality of the primal scene:

> It affords me a justification for having refused on an earlier page to adopt

unhesitatingly, as the only tenable explanation, the view that the primal scene was derived from an observation made upon animals shortly before the dream. The Grusha scene emerged in the patient's memory spontaneously and through no effort of mine. (p. 288)

In fact, the extent of Freud's mediation in arriving at the published account of the Grusha scene is considerable. There is nevertheless still room for narratorial uncertainty, though that the boy urinated at the sight of Grusha is now a 'fact' (p. 289), doubtless arrived at without any help of Freud's. The only question is whether the urination testifies to the child's sexual excitement: 'On these issues I can venture upon no decision. I must confess, however, that I regard it as greatly to the credit of psychoanalysis that it should even have reached the stage of raising such questions as these' (p. 289). At last, however, he arbitrates in favour of reality, albeit an empirical one, this case as opposed to other cases:

> I cannot deny that the scene with Grusha, the part it played in the analysis, and the effects that followed from it in the patient's life can be most naturally and completely explained if we consider that the primal scene, which may in other cases be a phantasy, was a reality in the present one. After all, there is nothing impossible about it. (p. 289)

The Grusha episode, then – however apparently gratuitous and over-determined in its collapsing of all loved women (sweethearts, mother, sister) into kneeling servants – is a major prop to Freudian orthodoxy and it meets the blasphemous challenges of Adler and Jung. It does so at the cost of a major inconsistency. The mother, as we shall see, is the main object of reverence in Wolf-Man's life; the second object, incidentally, is always a servant-woman. The identification of the servant with the mother is logically at odds with the desire for the servant's physical debasement – at least, that is, if we accept Freud's reading of the child's horror at the violence of the primal scene. In the process, another heroic struggle of orthodoxy and blasphemy is decontextualised with a casual violence: John Hus's martyrdom becomes a mere parable of faggots and bedwetting. The decontextualisation is again typical of the account, especially when it related to the patient himself. Early in the account, the first mention of a butterfly is in a context of fear and loathing; and what he feared and loathed as a child – beetles, caterpillars – he tormented or cut to pieces. 'Horses, too, gave him an uncanny feeling. If a horse was beaten he began to scream, and he was once obliged to leave a circus on that account. On other occasions he himself enjoyed beating horses' (pp. 198–9). Did young Russian men of Wolf-Man's class always distinguish scrupulously between horses and servant-girls? There is no attempt to look at Wolf-Man's social reality at that time, as the pampered boy-child of rich landowners in pre-revolutionary Russia, or to contextualise his activities in the light of the sexual practices of his gender and class. What of his place in history we learn, that 'the exciting cause of his later illness' was contracted from a peasant girl when he was 18 years old, we learn in a subordinate clause. The narrator prefers the role of rhetorician to that of historian. The possible relevance of gonorrhoea to Wolf-Man's later mental history is ignored.

'2½: Screen memory of his parents' departure with his sister. This showed him alone with his Nanya and so disowned Grusha and his sister'

Freud's highlighting of this memory in the note takes longer than its telling in the text (Chapter ii, p. 196), and is not the only sign of second or third thoughts. The first memory of the case is Nanya, 'an uneducated old woman of peasant birth, with an untiring affection for him'. She is also one source of his childhood piety. In Muriel Gardiner's late memoir, the elderly Wolf-Man retains his old servant-woman, Fräulein Gaby, long after she has ceased to be able to work for him in his flat in Vienna, when he himself is in very straitened circumstances. With his mother, who comes to live with him in her old age, he finds the closest and most successful relationship of his life.[4] It is not just Grusha and his sister who are disowned, but young women in favour of old ones.

'Before 3¼: His mother's laments to the doctor'

This too is little emphasised in its original position (Chapter ii). It is the confirmation of his mother's weak health, in consequence of which 'she had relatively little to do with the children' (p. 196). Only death can restore her to health and beauty. In a letter to Dr Gardiner after his mother's death, in May 1953, Wolf-Man remarks that he had never seen her look better than she did in her coffin: 'For I have never before seen my mother looking so sublimely quiet and peaceful, yes, almost of classic beauty.'[5] Freud's account of the infantile neurosis places greater emphasis on his father's more serious, nervous illness, which the child came to understand much later than 'before 3¼'.

'3¼: Beginning of his seduction by his sister. Soon afterwards the threat of castration from his Nanya'

Both these elements also occur in Chapter ii. It is not clear whether 'Nanya's threat of castration' is a reconstruction; certainly, it appears to be an overstatement, of a warning that she (may have) issued against masturbating. The 'seduction' by the sister is certainly an overstatement, and it is the term that Freud habitually uses. The importance of the sister in Freud's account is great, yet her life and death are dealt with in the briefest compass within the first half of this chapter and Chapter III. She embodies the threat of castration: by owning a picture book which first provoked her brother's fear of a wolf (looking at the book, he was 'afraid of the wolf coming and eating him up'); by her suicide; and by the 'seduction'. Their initial congress is anal: hence Abraham and Torok's play on the sister's name, Anna.[6] In the lavatory, 'Let's show one another our bottoms'; and later, 'his sister had taken hold of his member and played with it'. She was forward and sensual; when she was 4 or 5, she sat on a male cousin's lap and opened his trousers (p. 203); she was also boyish. In puberty, however, she rebuffs young Wolf-Man's advances, and he turns to the little peasant girl for sympathy and a lifelong heterosexual career of sister debasement. She had male admirers, to whom she was genuinely much superior. In her early twenties, she travelled to relieve depression, but 'poisoned herself and died far away from home' – proof of long-standing mental instability on both sides of her family. Freud records Wolf-Man's admission that he had to fake sorrow at his sister's death ('he was able quite coolly to rejoice at having now become the sole heir', p. 205); but Freud extenuates this as being a symptom of Wolf-Man's own mental illness, and also records later acts of displaced grief. For his part, Wolf-Man in his autobiography more simply states that he was unable to show the deep grief he felt at his sister's death, a very different matter.

Freud's claim that Wolf-Man's relationship to his sister sets the pattern of his future sexual relations actually contradicts the logic of the 'primal scene', in which the boy's identification with his father focuses on his mother. Wolf-Man's father is also to die suddenly, and perhaps by suicide; there are strong grounds for suspicion but here the account, ever fluctuating between terse discretion and prurient amplification, is coy. Trying to align the formative influence of the sister with the father's role in the primal scene has led Torok and Abraham to suppose that the Wolf-Man represses, or the account suppresses, incest between the father and the sister. Their scenario, as fear or fact, is by no means wholly implausible. It is, however, playing a Freudian game, albeit playing it in a permutation that Freud conspicuously avoids. For him, the significance of the sister's 'seduction', linked as it is with the beginning of the wolf-phobia, is its basis in hard fact: 'his seduction by the sister was certainly not a phantasy' (Chapter III, p. 203). It thus has a corroborative bearing, Freud claims (though one is a memory while the other is remembered only as a dream!), on the authenticity of the primal scene. Late in the essay, in the second addition of 1922, he asks again whether the primal scene was fantasy or not, and replies: 'With my patient, his seduction by his elder sister was an indisputable reality; why should not the same have been true of his observation of his parents' intercourse?' (p. 290). The sister's death is the precondition of such reality.

In narrative terms, Freud and the Wolf-Man are accomplices in misogyny. The scenario of the Wolf-Man's seduction by his sister blames the sister. She is blamed for seducing him in childhood, and then she is blamed again for declining his sexual advances in adolescence. Her death is their revenge for one or other or both, and it is this revenge against women that is truly to determine Wolf-Man's future sexual relations – though this is totally unacknowledged and perhaps unseen by Freud, who is intent at this very point on denying Adler's thesis that sexuality is a symptom of the will to power.

'3½: *The English Governess. Beginning of the change in his character*'

The English governess, in whose care the Wolf-child is left for the summer, is the major influence on his change from being 'a very good-natured, tractable, and even quiet child, so that they used to say of him that he ought to have been the girl and his elder sister the boy'. Being herself an eccentric and quarrelsome person, and 'moreover addicted to drink', and because of her implacable opposition to Nanya, she makes him 'discontented, irritable, and violent' (p. 197): that is, she makes a man of him. Manhood, good and bad, is conferred or taken away by a series of foreign (multilingual, multicultural) teachers and tutors. His Latin master at secondary school, of whom he was afraid, happened to bear the name of Wolf – a coincidence that Freud is honest enough to record, and which drives him to a defensive footnote on the theme of falsely projecting backwards. Young Wolf-Man is cured of religion by a German tutor, under whose influence 'he developed an enthusiasm for military affairs, for uniforms, arms, and horses', and thereby 'under a man's influence . . . found himself for the time being on fairly normal lines' (Chapter vi, p. 258). Uniforms, arms, horses and 'German things (as, for instance, physicians, sanatoriums, women)' – Freud here prophesies himself and the Wolf-Man's marriage – are antidotes to womanly passivity and to the influence of the father alike, and represent health. Religious affiliation, as noted at 3½, represents sickness.

'4: *The wolf dream. Origin of the phobia*'

A number of white wolves sit in a tree and watch Wolf-Man watching them. There are five in his drawing, six or seven in the telling. The tree is a walnut tree in the telling, any old tree in the drawing, and turns into, or out to be, a Christmas tree as analysis and Freud's text proceed. Freud asks almost every possible question and dwells on every imaginable detail. Why are the wolves white? Interestingly, despite his musing on the parents' white underwear during the primal scene, Freud does not consider two obvious associations: the scene takes place in White Russia, and brides, who to

Wolf-Man are as threatening as wolves, wear white. Why so many? Why is there variation in the numbers? There is no point in further commentators introducing new folkloric or literary analogues, though many do: Wolf-Man thought of it first, and Freud mentions many, Little Red Riding Hood, Reynard the Fox and the Seven Little Goats.

Goats? In what follows, Deleuze and Guattari struggle hard to produce a *reductio ad absurdum*:

> Who is ignorant of the fact that wolves travel in packs? Only Freud. Every child knows it. Not Freud. With false scruples he asks, How are we to explain the fact that there are five, six, or seven wolves in this dream? . . . The wolves will have to be purged of their multiplicity. This operation is accomplished by associating the dream with the tale, 'The Wolf and the Seven Kid-Goats' – only six of which get eaten. We witness Freud's reductive glee; we literally see multiplicity leave the wolves to take the shape of goats that have absolutely nothing to do with the story. Seven wolves that are only kid-goats. Six wolves: the seventh goat (the Wolf-Man himself) is hiding in the clock. Five wolves: he may have seen his parents make love at five o'clock, and the Roman numeral v is associated with the erotic spreading of a woman's legs. Three wolves: the parents may have made love three times. Two wolves; the first coupling the child may have seen was the two parents *more ferarum*, or perhaps even two dogs. One wolf: the wolf is the father, as we all knew from the start. Zero wolves: he lost his tail, he is not just a castrater but a castrated. Who is Freud trying to fool?[7]

This dream is the canon of the Wolf-Man's case-history, the text upon which Freud's exegesis is practised. One canon begets another:

'4½: *Influence of the Bible story.*
Appearance of the obsessional symptoms'

My treatment of this stage in the chronology, however, is deferred: it belongs, in my view, with the rest of Freud's and the Wolf-Man's blasphemies. I therefore concede Freud's structural point: chronology should not be allowed to get in the way of a good argument. His placement of the Bible story and obsessional symptoms in parallel sentences is rhetorical, a mini-argument.

'Just before 5: *Hallucination of the loss of his finger*'

This occurs exactly as Freud describes it. While playing in the garden near his nurse, the Wolf-child was carving with his pocket-knife in the bark of one of the walnut trees featured in his dream. He noticed that he had 'cut through the little finger of my (right or left?) hand, so that it was only hanging on by its skin' (p. 276). This is set down immediately as a castration fantasy, but Freud's exegesis of it is particularly cultured: based on a reference to Tasso's *Gerusalemme Liberata*, Freud opines that 'the tree meant a woman' to the Wolf-child. 'Here, then, he was playing the part of his father, and was connecting his mother's familiar haemorrhages with the castration of women, which he now recognised – with "the wound"' (pp. 276–7). Freud deduces from this a fear of castration by the father at a time of identification with the mother, but this is, on the face of it, a surprisingly complex reading. In terms of Freud's own symbolic system, a more obvious reading would be a man's castration as a result of intercourse with a woman. In contrast with that more obvious reading, Freud here substitutes a woman's genitals for the man's.

There is an acute analogy with Freud's reading of the case of Dora, where Freud puns on the interpretation of one of Dora's two dreams on various meanings of the German word '*schmuck*', jewels, and then notes a linguistic connection: the jewels become a jewelcase in the dream, and the term 'jewelcase', '*schmuckcasten*', is 'a term commonly used to describe female genitals that are immaculate and intact'. Sander Gilman points out:

> In Viennese urban dialect, borrowed from Yiddish, 'Schmock' has another meaning. 'Schmock' even in German urban idiolect had come to be a standard slang term for the circumcised male penis. . . . Hidden within the female genitalia, (the 'Schmuckcasten') is the image of the male Jew as represented by his genitalia (the 'Schmock').[8]

In the context of the Dora case, too, Freud is discussing Dora's apprehension of the passing of the father's syphilis to the mother, and so perhaps to the daughter.

There is no mention of venereal disease at this stage of the Wolf-Man account, but it is not difficult for a modern reader to guess at exactly what the code of communicable mental instability might intimate: it claims the lives, after all, of father and daughter. I do not wish to exaggerate here by reading repressed connotations as evident meaning. Nevertheless, venereal disease, its symptoms still confused with those of leprosy, is seen in the nineteenth century as a direct physical threat to the existence not only of the penis but also of the fingers, as in the hallucination, and of the nose. At the least, finger and nose are cognate in Freud's system as penis symbols.

We might now consider Ruth Mack Brunswick's account appended to Wolf-Man's autobiography of the illness which he suffered between November 1923 and February 1927:

> In November 1923, the patient's mother arrived from Russia. When he met her at the station, he observed a black wart on her nose. In reply to his question, she told him that she had been to various doctors, most of whom told her to have the wart removed. However, the doctors were themselves

uncertain of its nature, because of its curious way of coming and going. At times it was present and at times it was not. Therefore she had refused to have it operated on, and was now very glad of her decision.[9]

Shortly after, Wolf-Man begins to have trouble with his teeth, and has two extracted by a dentist who has the distinction of being named Dr Wolf. Anxiety about his teeth leads to worry about his nose, a long-standing cause for concern: 'At the age of puberty, a nasal catarrh had caused sores on his nose and upper lip, requiring salves for their treatment. These were prescribed by the same doctor who later treated him for another catarrh, namely, the gonorrhoeal' (p. 269). This association between catarrh and venereal disease replicates that of the Dora case-history. Wolf-Man's observation of the wart on his mother's nose leads him to an obsession with the purity of his own nose – a nose in which he already takes pride because it is small, a snub-nose, and differentiates him (guesses Dr Brunswick) from 'his many Jewish contacts' (p. 269). Of course, prolonged examination of his own nose for blackheads and the like reveals the existence of a pimple. Visits to dermatologist and dentist ensue, with teeth and nose becoming confused. The nasal symptoms reappear when he is sitting alongside his wife in a park and, using her pocket-mirror, notices 'a new swelling'. This time the dermatologist squeezes his pustule, and it explodes in a moment described by Wolf-Man as yielding 'acute ecstasy'. Dr Brunswick here encodes, albeit discreetly, the Freudian identification of nose and penis, and constructs a sudden orgasm of relieved good health.

This is not the end of Dr Brunswick's tale. For the symptoms recur, again becoming mixed with a renewed dental problem and leading to work by a second dentist, also named, incredibly, Dr Wolf. At the same time Wolf-Man is receiving money from Freud – both are in Vienna – and deceiving Freud, whose payments are charitable in nature and made in ignorance that Wolf-Man now has adequate money from other sources. Indeed, Dr Brunswick notes the difficulty she found in believing that this was the Wolf-Man described by Freud, 'a reputable, compulsively honest and conscientious individual, absolutely reliable from every point of view. The man who presented himself to me was guilty of innumerable minor dishonesties. . . . Most striking of all was his total unawareness of his own dishonesty' (p. 279). Her analysis is skilful, and suggests an unconscious identification on Wolf-Man's part of his dermatologist, Professor X (who dies suddenly during the treatment), and Freud himself, thus introducing Freud as a factor in Wolf-Man's delusion about his nose. These have common ground in the figure of his father (readers of the case-history and Wolf-Man's autobiography will recall a similar financial meanness in Wolf-Man's response to the deaths of his father and Professor X, as well as to the prospect of Freud's own death). Money is implicated with the father and the pustule on his nose, a symptom he 'catches' from his mother.

But it is not only Wolf-Man's mother who has a wart on her nose; so does his wife Therese. Dr Brunswick notes this early ('his wife had had a wart on her nose for years', p. 269), and provides the story of its removal: when Wolf-Man realises that Professor X, the dermatologist, has diagnosed him as a hypochondriacal nuisance,

> [he] decided to have his wife, who, it will be remembered, had a wart on the tip of her nose, accompany him to professor X, whom he was afraid to visit alone. X, extremely cordial, immediately removed the wart. When, however, the patient approached him with his familiar query as to the future of his own nose, X became irritated. (p. 274)

There is thus a medical and narrative association between Wolf-Man's nasal pustule and his wife's wart, as well as an origin of the phobia in his mother's own nose. Again, a narrative concerning Wolf-Man appears over-determined. Why should Wolf-Man develop fear of nasal disfigurement from his mother, and regard his wife's nose as relevant? We are told that at the same time 'certain changes occurred in his sexual life'. Wolf-Man reverts to his old ways, following working women on the street: 'He now frequently accompanied prostitutes to their lodging where, on account of his fear of venereal disease, his relations with them were limited to masturbation in their presence' (p. 272). It is a significant concatenation, and suggests a common factor. The fear of castration – injuries to finger and to nose – is linked to the father in Freud's account, and occurs as a contagion from the mother in Dr Brunswick's. There may be more to this than the gender of the analysts. A comparison with the Dora case might lead a reader of Freud's work to wonder whether here too – at least as an anxiety, and contemplating his mother's face – the contagion may not be derived from the father; and whether Wolf-Man does not play the role of his father by infecting his own wife with nasal warts (their dental manifestation is 'gumboils'), that is to say, with the venereal disease we know (from Freud) he had.

'5: Departure from the first estate'

The traumatic move from the Wolf-child's first home is caused by financial difficulty, and thus associates his later meanness with the fear of homelessness. It also sets a pattern for his future.

Wolf-Man is not only to lose his first home: he is destined to lose everything, including any hope of abode in his native land. He is to be an exile, a wartime refugee, a nomad – a gypsy. His life is therefore to enact what he describes in his autobiography, in a disturbingly passionate comment on what seems a picturesque incident, as his first childhood impression of hell:

> This estate was well known throughout the surrounding countryside, because

part of our land was used as a marketplace where fairs were held every now and then. As a small child I once watched one of these Russian country fairs. I was walking in our garden and heard noise and lively shouting behind the garden fence. Looking through a crack in the fence, I saw campfires burning – it was wintertime – with gypsies and other strange people clustered around them. The gypsies were gesticulating wildly, and everyone was loudly shouting at the same time. There were many horses, and the people were evidently arguing about their price. This scene created an impression of indescribable confusion, and I thought to myself that the goings-on in hell must be pretty much like this. (p. 5)

In the autobiography, this image of nocturnal and unregulated horse-trading immediately precedes Wolf-Man's memory of the sale of the estate, the very next sentence reading: 'My father sold this estate when I was about five years old.' The sale and the hellish gypsy existence are therefore connected by Wolf-Man himself.

Less than four pages later, Wolf-Man remembers his first drawing lessons, with his sister. 'At first we used to draw trees', but Anna drew them better; so Wolf-child gave up drawing trees and tried instead to draw horses. This too was unsuccessful: 'unfortunately every horse I drew looked more like a dog or a wolf than like a real horse' (pp. 9–10). In the most famous drawing of the Wolf-Man's that survives – his drawing for Freud of the wolf dream – he draws a tree, and in it what are supposed to be wolves but look more like fat dogs. What if they were really horses? Then the dream would express a nightmare vision of his own future as an involuntary gypsy, stateless, rootless and homeless, condemned to poverty and to make money as gypsies must, by haggling, wolfishly; a future that resembles, as Wolf-Man's life did, 'the goings-on in hell'.

'After 6: *Visit to his sick father*'

Freud recounts that the father is not seen for many months. The mother takes the children to town and promises to show them something that will please them: 'She then took them to a sanatorium, where they saw their father again: he looked ill, and the boy felt very sorry for him' (Chapter VI, p. 256). The boy sees his sick father as the 'prototype of all the cripples, beggars and poor people' in whose presence he has developed a habit of deliberate exhalation. This occurs in the middle of Freud's longest discussion of the Wolf-Man's religious symptoms, and the role of the father in these is discussed below. It also occurs in the context of the boy's 'homosexual libido'; his 'libidinal expectation' in early childhood has already shifted to the absent father ('at that time away from home', p. 210). Much later on, as Wolf-Man himself confirms, the sister's death becomes a turning point in relations between father and son. 'My father, who had previously paid little attention to me, had since Anna's suicide developed an active interest in everything I did' (p. 38). When at the age of 21, Wolf-Man boards a train from St Petersburg to Munich, suddenly, 'I was reconciled to life again and I felt in complete agreement and perfect harmony with the world and with myself' (p. 46).

Again, the moment of wholeness prefigures death: 'There were only a few minutes left before our departure, and my father had to leave the train. I did not know then that when I bade him farewell, it was to be farewell forever' (p. 47). As Therese comes into Wolf-Man's life, his father quits it: dying suddenly, again far from home (just as Anna died), in a Moscow hotel room. In death, his ties with his daughter are again emphasised; he is buried next to her. Otherwise, he remains out of focus or context. 'As my father had held various honorary positions and had actively participated in public life, there were funeral orations and eulogies in his recognition' (p. 64). This is the closest we come, and a lot closer than we ever come in Freud's account, to knowing that the father was one of the leaders of Russia's liberal party and a major political figure. Freud's suppression of this is characteristic: one might compare his suppression of the fact that 'Dora's brother, Otto Bauer, was one of the founders of the Austrian Socialist Party'.[10] Both can be ascribed to necessary professional tact, but not all doctors publish their cases: the point is that Freud seems to think such details irrelevant to the reader's, and so his own, judgement of the cases. But there is a more immediate disturbance to the reader of Wolf-Man's autobiography who comes to it from Freud's case-history. When describing the shock of his father's death, Wolf-Man goes out of his way to insist that his father never had a day's illness in his life:

> For us the news of his death was the more unexpected as my father was only forty-nine years old and enjoyed perfect physical health. I cannot remember that he ever, even for a single day, stayed home with a cold or a grippe, or that he ever had to stay in bed. It is true that he suffered from insomnia and regularly took veronal before going to sleep. Perhaps his premature death was due to an overdose of this sleeping medicine. (p. 64)

Does this hint at suicide? That is a minor question. The major question is the conflict of evidence: if the father had never been ill in his life, what caused his removal for several months in Wolf-Man's childhood to a sanatorium? The possible explanations, mental illness or venereal disease, are not necessarily compelling.

Ruth Mack Brunswick again supplies an invaluable gloss, one which picks up other questions, already discussed, of castration, money and noses. Wolf-Man storms out of analysis with her 'in a rage at Freud' (p. 285), and has a dream 'in which his father is obviously castrated':

> The patient's father, in the dream a professor, resembling, however, a begging

musician known to the patient, sits at a table and warns the others present not to talk about financial matters before the patient, because of his tendency to speculate. His father's nose is long and hooked, causing the patient to wonder at its change. (p. 286)

The begging musician also looks like Christ. Dr Brunswick comments:

> The begging musician who looks like Christ and the patient's father, and is at the same time a professor, is obviously according to his nose a Jew. Since the nose is throughout the symbol for the genital, the change in the father's nose making it Jewish denotes circumcision – castration. Also a beggar is for the patient a castrated person. Thus from the anger against the father, due to unrequited love, we come to a castration of that father. . . . (p. 286)

This is the son's 'death-wish against the father' arising not from 'masculine rivalry' but from 'passive, unsatisfied, rejected love'. Wolf-Man has lately seen Freud after Freud's first bout of cancer, and been shocked by his appearance (thus re-enacting his childhood visit to the sanatorium). He has parted from Freud calculating profit and loss, whether Freud's death, in the event of a legacy to Wolf-Man, would be of more advantage than his survival and ensuing continuation of his annual payments: 'The patient had profited so enormously by the death of his own father that it is not surprising that his expectation of inheritance should triumph over his rational calculations' (p. 286). But he has also conflated Freud with his dermatologist, Professor X, at the news of whose recent death Wolf-Man cried out, to Brunswick herself: '"My God, now I can't kill him any more"' (p. 283). For Wolf-Man blames Freud-father-Professor X for his nasal injury, and wishes for vengeance: 'But if the patient's nasal injury can only be avenged by death, that is a sign that castration is the equivalent of death. In that case the castrated father is the dead father, killed, presumably, by his son' (p. 286).

The son who kills a father kills for money, kills for love, kills for revenge. Dr Brunswick understands that her role is as much one of priestess as healer. The father's function approaches the theological: sacrifice. At this point, the remaining heading can be joined with that postponed earlier, in an overtly theological discourse.

'4½: *Influence of the Bible story. Appearance of the obsessional symptoms*'

'8:
10: } *Final outbreaks of the obsessional neurosis*'

Chapter II, Freud's general survey of the patient's history, defines his childhood attacks of obsessional neurosis as, initially, religious. Wolf-child would pray 'for a long time' before going to sleep and would 'make an endless series of signs of the cross'. He would 'make the round of all the holy pictures' in his room, standing on a chair in order to 'kiss each one of them devoutly'. At the same time, however, 'he recollected some blasphemous thoughts which used to come into his head like an inspiration from the devil. He was obliged to think "God-swine" or "God-shit".'

Freud's account immediately jumps to an adolescent experience in which the words 'God-shit' are made material, visual and theologically orthodox in number:

> Once while he was on a journey to a health-resort in Germany he was tormented by the obsession of having to think of the Holy Trinity whenever he saw three heaps of horse-dung or other excrement lying in the road. (p. 199)

To this period too Freud ascribes the Wolf-Man's habit of deliberate exhalations 'when he saw people that he felt sorry for, such as beggars, cripples, or very old men'. These revelations are the climax of Freud's initial unveiling of the case, and they lead him to the 'fear of his father'. The last paragraph of the chapter asks a series of questions about the origins of the Wolf-Man's phobias, the final one of which is: 'How did he arrive at his obsessive piety?' (p. 200).

Freud's discussion of the case then turns to the primal scene, and other episodes from Wolf-Man's childhood, from which we learn only that the tree of the wolf dream is a Christmas tree and that Wolf-Man's birthday 'was' Christmas Day. Not until Chapter VI, 'The obsessional neurosis', do we return to the patient's piety, with his introduction to the Bible story by his Nanya when he was 4½. The child is immeasurably distressed by the suffering of the son in the Passion, and his distress takes the standard form of a concern with the question of evil: how can a good and all-powerful god condone it? So the Wolf-child 'turned his critical dissatisfaction against God the Father', who was 'responsible himself for all wickedness and all torments'. He searches out 'the weak points of the sacred story'. Puzzled by the nature of the God/man, he asks Nanya 'whether Christ had a behind too'. The Wolf-child is represented as arriving at an ingenious answer: 'Since Christ had made wine out of nothing, he could also have made food into nothing and in this way have avoided defecating' (p. 252).

Freud relates these obsessions to Wolf-Man's continuing relation with the father: in his sadism towards animals 'he maintained his ancient identification with his father; but in his masochism he chose him as a sexual object' (p. 252). Freud details further complexities, then notes that the child's new-found knowledge of the Bible allowed him to sublimate the masochistic response to the father. 'He became Christ – which was made especially easy for him on account of their having the same birthday' (p. 253) – a detail that to the least attentive of readers has cried out for interpretation and at last, strategically, receives it. It is immediately referred to the issue of Christ's behind, at which Freud takes a bold exegetical leap: 'these ruminations can have had no other meaning but the question whether he himself could be used by his father like a woman – like his mother in the primal scene' (p. 253). The question, then, is one of passive homosexuality, and in the next paragraph Freud casually uses 'passive' to characterise Christ's relation to 'ill-treatment by his Father'. Wolf-Man begins to fear the God that would sacrifice his own son, 'and had ordered Abraham to do the same' (p. 254). And the next identification, predictable to the point of being over-determined, is quickly made: 'If he was Christ, then his father was God'. But there is a displacement here, and a resistance. 'He resisted God in order to be able to cling to his father, and in doing this he was really upholding the old father against the new' (p. 254).

The double image of the father/s here is a crucial element in the Freudian system. Freud proposes that the Wolf-Man is acting out a strong conflict of love and hate towards his own father, and that 'this struggle produced . . . the blasphemous ideas' (p. 255). As a means of atoning for his blasphemous feelings, he developed ritual breathing. Freud pauses here to make a long point. 'In his native language [still unidentified], "breath" is the same word as "spirit", so that here the Holy Ghost came in' (p. 255). Inhalation is a means of breathing in the Holy Ghost; exhalation is a means of driving out evil spirits, but – when the father is visited in the sanatorium, looking like 'the prototype of all the cripples, beggars and poor people in whose presence he was obliged to breathe out' (p. 256) – turns out to be another aspect of father identification. Freud's exegesis gleefully and imaginatively embellishes his patient's blasphemy: 'the heavy breathing was an imitation of the noise which he had heard coming from his father during the coitus' (footnote: 'Assuming the reality of the primal scene', as indeed, in order to make quite this point, one must: rutting dogs do not indulge in the right kind of heavy breathing). The next sentence concedes that it may also have had something to do with a childhood attack of malaria; but this is significant, it seems, only by virtue of coinciding with the primal scene. Therefore, in one of the boldest sentences of Freud's entire book: 'He had derived the Holy Ghost from this manifestation of male sensual excitement' (p. 256). This is desiring-production in its most literal form.

There is an unpleasant extension:

> When he heard that Christ had once cast out some evil spirits into a herd of swine which then rushed down a precipice, he thought of how his sister in the earliest years of her childhood, before he could remember, had rolled down onto the beach from the cliff-path above the harbour. She too was an evil spirit and a swine. It was a short road from here to 'God-swine'. (p. 256)

Women are to blame for everything, even including religion itself: 'Let us further bear in mind . . . that his piety originated under the influence of women (his mother and his nurse), while it was a masculine influence that set him free from it' (p. 311). Why is it only a short road from his sister to 'God-swine'? Freud adds at once: 'His father himself had shown that he was no less a slave to sensuality' (p. 256). The family romance rediscovers religious taboo.

Unable to purge his blasphemous thoughts in confession, the Wolf-child is finally cured of them at the age of 10 by his manly German tutor. This may have helped the Wolf-Man understand his earlier use of 'God-shit', because Freud's explanation of it, in terms of gift and child, works only in the German language, not Russian, as the English translation is forced to make clear:

> 'God-shit' was probably an abbreviation for an offering that one occasionally hears mentioned in its unabbreviated form. 'Shitting to God' ('*auf Gott scheissen*'), or 'shitting something to God' ('*Gott etwas scheissen*'), also means presenting him with a child or getting him to present one with a child. (p. 274)

What Freud does here is to construct from a phrase a scatological parody Incarnation, in which Wolf-Man is obliged 'to connect God with his faeces' (p. 274). He argues for the 'unity' of child, faeces and penis (p. 275), so that Wolf-Man's fear of his father is projected as a fear of God, who prescribes 'ritual circumcision of Christ and of the Jews in general' in the 'sacred story' (p. 277), and who therefore threatens his son with castration. We have already seen how castration is interpreted by Freud on behalf of Wolf-Man as the precondition of coitus with the father. The wolf is that which threatens castration: a father; Freud himself (p. 226); a frightening Latin teacher who causes a Freudian slip as Wolf-Man attempts to translate Latin *filius* ('son': Jesus) and gives it instead the French form ('son': Wolf-child); and, from the autobiography, not one but two dentists. The relation with the father is mediated by the wolf dream and by the religious reference throughout the case. Religion offers an ideal sublimation, concludes Freud in the final chapter. 'As Christ, he could love his father, who was now called God, with a fervour which had sought in vain to discharge itself so long as his father had been a mortal' (p. 309). It also offers Freud the unique bonding with which to cohere the numerous elements in the case. The religious reference is not merely one aspect of Wolf-Man's history. It is precisely the matrix of Freud's discourse, which ends as a meditation on religion in general, and on its shortcomings: 'religious doctrine is itself based upon a by no means unambiguous relation to God the Father' (p. 310).

Freud is by no means unconscious of his direction here. First, he explicitly compares the obsessional religious phase of Wolf-Man's career to his observations on the case of Dr Schreber. In this case Freud's work consists of a commentary on Dr Schreber's own *Memoirs of a Neurotic*.[11] Dr Schreber writes of God as the instigator of a plot against him, and who in a complicated way persecutes him '"in the matter of the call to sh__" (the need for evacuating the bowels)' (p. 122). This leads Schreber 'in self-defence to assume the part of a scoffer at God', but at the same time, in a counter-impulse, to identify with God, though Freud carefully points out that his is not 'the everyday form of Redeemer phantasy, in which the patient believes that he is a son of God': 'It is only at a very late stage . . . that his identification with Jesus Christ makes an undisguised appearance' (p. 125). (This is exactly the structural pattern that Freud emulates in the Wolf-Man history, holding back the identification for almost longer than is plausible.) Dr Schreber's new belief in God also wins him what Freud calls 'sexual enjoyment . . . of a most unusual character' (p. 129). He believes that he is God's wife; he speaks of his becoming woman, with an 'impression' of a bust and of 'female buttocks' (p. 130). Freud resolves the case, not as an analyst working with a patient but as an expert reader of Schreber's book, by arguing that Schreber has confused his psychiatrist, Dr Flechsig, with God, and that this confusion is really based on the fact that Schreber's own father was an eminent physician: in other words, Dr Schreber works out in his own body and in an esoteric religious system his love and hate for his own father – 'and in pointing this out', adds Freud, skittishly, 'I must disclaim all responsibility for the monotony of the solutions provided by psychoanalysis' (p. 154).

Secondly, Freud shows his sense of the larger implications of his study in his frequent references to wider religious and anthropological questions. The threat of the wolf to 'gobble up' a little child is staged as the ancient mythic contest between Jupiter and Saturn. At the outset of the case, Freud remarks that Wolf-Man's 'phantasies . . . corresponded exactly to the legends by means of which a nation that has become great and proud tries to conceal the insignificance and failure of its beginnings' (p. 203); at the end, he claims that the Oedipus complex and the response to the primal scene are 'precipitates from the history of human civilisation' and makes the bald summary of his interest in Wolf-Man's case: 'So it was that his mental life impressed one in much the same way as the religion of ancient Egypt' (p. 313). The key, deferred to the last minute, turns out to be Freud's own book *Totem and Taboo*, which exactly predicts Wolf-Man's progress from totemistic father-surrogate, the wolf, to the next form of father-surrogate, 'in which the father had regained his human form', the idea of God (p. 308). The Wolf-Man's case is therefore an addendum to Freud's theory of religion. I do not seek here necessarily to contradict readings of Wolf-Man's case based on transgression, by Stallybrass and White, or multilingualism, Abraham and Torok's *The Wolf-Man's Magic Word*, but I do wish to supplement them by insisting upon the failure of the case-history to liberate itself from Freud's own religious, or counter-religious, system. If one were a renegade Freudian, one might want to argue that Freud's theory is built on the ambivalent contest of love and hate in and for a Jewish father.

The system begins with *Totem and Taboo*, which coincides with Freud's work on Wolf-Man's case, but it reaches its culmination at the end of Freud's career with the third essay in the series *Moses and Monotheism*, which was finally published as one book in 1939, the last year of his life.[12] The best discussion of it is that by Michel de Certeau, who notes that Freud called its first part 'my novel', and sees it as a testament, in Rank's phrase, of the 'founding father' of psychoanalysis writing as 'a rebellious son who defends paternal authority'.[13] 'Two in the same place . . . the very question of the "I" . . . the son who must – but never truly can – dislodge the father' (pp. 322–3): for Freud, tradition 'reiterates what exists in the beginning – a murder'. At the site of the split subject is Freud himself, the Jew writing the Jew:

> The genesis of the historical figure of the Jew and the genesis of Freudian writing always intervene. The place from which Freud writes and the production of his writing enter into the text along with the object that he is taking up. (p. 312)

So *Moses and Monotheism*, like the case-study of the Wolf-Man, is full of the marks and traces of the writing process itself: three essays, the first two written in 1934 and published in *Imago* in 1937, the third with two prefatory notes, the first written in Vienna in 1938 forswearing publication because of the risk of ecclesiastical censorship that might take the form of 'our being prohibited from practising psychoanalysis', the second later in the year in London, recording that the German invasion of Austria proved Catholicism, 'to use the words of the Bible, "a broken reed"', and so enabled publication in 'lovely, free, magnanimous England'; all three characterised throughout by the regular play with the reader ('At this point I expect to be met by an objection to my hypothesis', p. 269) that marks the Wolf-Man study. Each of the first two parts, teasingly, claims to stop short of the most radical inference that might be drawn, and the work then continues, and shifts ground, again as in the Wolf-Man study. Freud again notes his inability to structure the work in a form that would supply the proof, and offers to his readers a bewildering and circular contract:

> Since I am addressing myself here to a wider audience, I can only beg the reader to grant a certain provisional credence to the abridged account [of neurotics' case-histories] I have given above; and this must be accompanied by an admission on my part that the implications to which I am now leading him need only be accepted if the theories on which they are based turn out to be correct. (p. 321)

It is a contract borrowed from exegesis: the sum and harmony of the parts is what determines the truth of the part. This is a fine exegetical parody:

since there is already 'distortion' in the text, only further 'distortion' has a chance of establishing the truth. It is Blake's road of excess, and leads to the palace of psychoanalytical wisdom. Its technique moves between brilliance and rapacious opportunism. The biblical text, and others' work, are used autocratically (Freud's own word) and selectively, as Freud candidly acknowledges in a note that demystifies all commentary:

> I am very well aware that in dealing so autocratically and arbitrarily with Biblical tradition – bringing it up to confirm my views when it suits me and unhesitatingly rejecting it when it contradicts me – I am exposing myself to serious methodological criticism and weakening the convincing force of my arguments. But this is the only way in which one can treat material of which one knows definitely that its trustworthiness has been severely impaired by the distorting influence of tendentious purposes. It is to be hoped that I shall find some degree of justification later on, when I come upon the track of these secret motives. Certainty is in any case unattainable and moreover it may be said that every other writer on the subject has adopted the same procedure.
>
> (p. 265, n. 4)

The book is billed as the fruit of psychoanalysis, but it is also its most daring and complete context.

Thus Freud introduces his thesis, that Moses was an Egyptian. As Certeau puts it: 'His lucidity assumes the form of a witticism that is both funny and blasphemous, the Egyptian Moses. . . . An oxymoron puts together two contradictory poles, the Jew and the Egyptian' (p. 314). The religion of the Jews was therefore founded by a foreigner, whose religion must have been that of Aten. Freud notes a possible relation between the words 'Aten' and 'Adonai' – should the Bible read: 'Hear O Israel, our god Aten is a sole god'? – but adds: 'Unfortunately I am totally incompetent to answer this question' (p. 263). Certainly, Freud continues, the religion of Aten is the first to be monotheistic, and it thus introduces religious intolerance into the world. Some of the characteristics of the biblical God are those of the Egyptian Moses, 'being of an irascible nature, flaring up easily' (p. 271), and they conflict with the characteristics of the volcano god Yahweh, who 'was an uncanny, bloodthirsty demon who went about by night and shunned the light of day' (p. 273). The characteristics of the biblical Moses also conflict: one moment he is a prince in Egypt, the next he is a humble Midian shepherd. How can this be? Freud does what Freud always does: he splits the subject. There were two Moses, not one, and the

> Moses of Kadesh and Midian, to whom tradition could actually attribute the erection of a brazen serpent as a god of healing (*Numbers* xxi, 9), is someone quite other than the aristocratic Egyptian inferred by us, who presented the people with a religion in which all magic and spells were proscribed in the strongest terms. Our Egyptian Moses is no less different, perhaps, from

the Midianite Moses than is the universal god Aten from the demon Yahweh in his home on the Mount of God. (p. 275)

Moreover, 'the Egyptian Moses was never at Kadesh and had never heard the name of Yahweh, and . . . the Midianite Moses had never been in Egypt and knew nothing of Aten' (p. 281). Freud then reconstructs the history. The first Moses and his followers leave Egypt voluntarily, not as described in Exodus, in order to practise their monotheism. They take with them from Egypt a religious rite, circumcision, which is Egyptian, not Jewish. Then the first Moses is murdered by his followers, whose descendants unite with the Midianite followers of the religion of Yahweh, thus causing efforts 'to deny explicitly that Yahweh was a new god, alien to the Jews' (p. 284), a false father. The whole system is expressed in a chain of dualities:

> Jewish history is familiar to us for its dualities: *two* groups of people who came together to form the nation, *two* kingdoms into which this nation fell apart, *two* gods' names in the documentary sources of the Bible. To these we add two fresh ones: the foundation of *two* religions – the first repressed by the second but nevertheless later emerging victoriously behind it, and *two* religious founders, who are both called by the same name of Moses and whose personalities we have to distinguish from each other. All of these dualities are the necessary consequence of the first one: the fact that one portion of the people had an experience which must be regarded as traumatic and which the other portion escaped. (p. 293)

There are two Gods and two founders called Moses. Or to put it in terms of common belief, God is not God and Moses is not Moses. (Likewise, as a footnote reminds us, Shakespeare was not Shakespeare but Edward de Vere, Earl of Oxford.) The reality is repression, and Freud's is the relevant expertise. Judaism is reinvented: the name of God is taboo because the name of God is division.

If these revelations disempower Judaism, they also disempower Christianity; the scandal of the murder of Moses actually removes the basis of Christian exegesis, for the apparent prophecies registering 'Messianic expectations' (p. 276) are simply a function of a much later hope 'among Jewish people that the man who had been so shamefully murdered would return from the dead and would lead his remorseful people, and perhaps not them alone, into the kingdom of lasting bliss' (p. 276). Freud's next sentence – 'The obvious connection of this with the destiny of the founder of a later religion does not concern us here' – is hardly calculated to remove a sting, given its use of the word 'obvious'.

History is recast in the mode of psychoanalysis. Forgotten traumas engender neuroses (p. 315); and in the first preface to the third part, Freud's fear of Catholic retaliation is explicitly identified as deriving from the fact that his conclusion 'reduces religion to a neurosis of humanity'. In the third part, Freud adheres to his alternative history in *Totem and Taboo* that has primal sons dominated by primal patriarchal fathers so that they are killed or castrated if they resist, until they unite and murder the primal father, committing both parricide and literal cannibalism. This is Freud's historical version of the *Urszene*. Freud also adds an explanation of Christianity: the fact that the Son of God must be killed is nothing more than an expression of guilt at the murder of the original Moses. 'It had to be a son, since it had been the murder of a father' (pp. 330–1). Not only is Christianity a late and misremembered Oedipal readjustment; it is also, in the form founded by Paul (in, as it were, the role of second Moses?), a regression, with its three gods in one slipping away from pure monotheism, 'a fresh victory for the priests of Amun over Akhenaten's god' (p. 333). The essay ends by becoming what its third part may have set out to be, an original and coruscating defence against anti-Semitism. The Christian has no right to say to the Jew, 'You killed our God', for religious people are people who kill their Gods. It is only that Jews, for cultural reasons that clearly fascinate Freud even as he leaves them alone, deny doing so. What Christians mean, Freud suggests, is: '"They will not accept it as true that they murdered God, whereas we admit it and have been cleansed of that guilt"' (p. 386). If by his own account in his dealings with individual patients Freud sometimes sounds autocratic and bullying, here, as he delivers the fruit of analysis to two major world religions in whose division has unfolded catastrophe and doom, there is the note of self-conscious heroism against overwhelming odds that often marks the blasphemer.

Religion is a neurosis of humanity. Freud's conclusion is uncompromising, and leaves no scope for misunderstanding. It is not that the 'delusions of psychotics' misrepresent the nature of religion; it is rather that they allow us to understand it, though psychotics, like blasphemers, have to bear an additional burden, what Freud calls 'the curse of isolation'. However, my point is not only that Freud is blasphemous – no reader of *Moses and Monotheism* could overlook that; it is that the blasphemy published there suffuses his psychoanalytical work, and imbues it with an unacknowledged purpose. At the least, Freud is drawn to neurotics who blaspheme, like Dr Schreber or Wolf-Man, and he places their blasphemies at the core of their cases. It might even be said that he substitutes their blasphemies for their histories: the individual cases are interpreted according to the pattern of the repressed religious history of the West, as characterised in *Moses and Monotheism*. This new context heals his patients discursively, by removing from them their 'curse of isolation'. Here there is some explanation after all for the elisions of personal circumstances and context: even in the case of Dora the failure to mention that she and her family are Jewish, for the same reason that Wolf-Man is never identified in so many words as Orthodox rather than Catholic, or indeed (until the 1923 footnote) as Russian. Nothing is allowed to intervene that will diminish his patients' community in archaic religious repression. If, as Certeau says, Freud authors his subjects, he authors them as blasphemers, in his own riven, paradoxical and rebellious image. One can apply to some of his case-histories, especially to Wolf-Man's, Certeau's judgement that 'Freud's subject is the end of religious tradition: the home that today has been abandoned by a society that no longer lives in it, the home that is no longer there' (p. 345). If so, however, he writes not only about that end, but inside it. The Freudian subject is a pre-eminently religious construction.

When Freud was preparing his third part of *Moses and Monotheism*, and in the same city of Vienna, Wolf-Man confronted global and personal disaster as the victim, I think, of a very Freudian elision. To read Wolf-Man's own account of what he calls the worst crisis of his life, one he faced without Freud, is to have one more illumination than Freud had; and it is to begin to read Freud no longer as scientist and outsider but as a blind and doom-bearing insider interpolated into Wolf-Man's life as a character in a tragic novel. There is a crucial fact about the Wolf-Man's life that goes unrecorded by Freud, partly no doubt because Freud was not personally well-positioned to recognise it but also because it was a fact too material for psychoanalysis. Wolf-Man is aptly named: he is a man who preys on women and destroys them. At points this is a matter of conscious intent: a man with gonorrhoea who continues to screw whores and servant-girls is no lover of women but an agent of his own revenge, and Ruth Mack Brunswick records her uncomfortable sense of being subject to Wolf-Man's contempt. It is not quite clear from either Freud's account or Wolf-Man's whether Wolf-Man also infects his own wife. Certainly, she is his main victim; but there is no need, probably, to conjecture conscious will or malice on his part, and he is devastated by her death. Wolf-Man himself is a survivor: he survives Freud, a succession of family cataclysms including the suicide of his sister and the death of his father, World War I, the Russian Revolution, exile, bankruptcy, World War II, and even arrest after the war for straying into the Russian-occupied zone on the anniversary of his sister's death. He unassumingly carries on with a professional antidote, his new career as a life insurance salesman. But he is fatal to women: they perish where he passes. The autobiography is a rollcall of women's deaths, evenly split between premature natural death and suicide. His grandmother's, probably by suicide after the death of her daughter at age 8 or 9, is the first recorded. His sister is the next. Then there is his cousin's wife, Lola, who makes advances to Wolf-Man and dies of breast cancer at the age of 36. There is the death of Freud's own elder daughter in 1920, and the death of his wife's daughter Else in 1919, of tuberculosis. Ruth Mack Brunswick herself dies suddenly in 1945, shortly after completing her extensive notes on

Wolf-Man's case. It is the death of his wife Therese, however, that dominates the autobiography.

It is a direct consequence of world affairs, for all that Wolf-Man refers to these as if they are unfortunate interruptions to his treatment: 'Unfortunately, I completed my analysis with Professor Freud at the time of the assassination of the Austrian Crown Prince, and World War I which followed on this ruined all our plans' (p. 89). Wolf-Man notes that 'Freud was quite indifferent to political questions', but appears little more so himself: Ruth Mack Brunswick represents him in 1945 as speaking of 'personal crises resulting in only small measure from world events'. Yet as Wolf-Man tells the story Therese's death is a result of the *Anschluss*, Hitler's invasion of Austria. Wolf-Man at first writes of them having lived together happily and prudently in Vienna for many years until this event. After her suicide, however, he finds letters indicating long premeditation, and recalls a depressive illness that must have lasted for several years. The immediate focus is money. Hitler's occupation had the effect of depreciating Austrian schillings, so that their income and savings were much reduced. Wolf-Man says that Therese was greatly distressed by this; as, to judge from Freud's and Brunswick's accounts of his pathological meanness, he would himself have been. Wolf-Man continues:

> After the occupation of Austria by Hitler, anti-Semitic rioting and all kinds of persecution of the Jews were of course to be expected. For that reason the Jewish people of Vienna were overcome by panic, causing a wave of suicides. Once when Therese and I were speaking about this, she remarked that it was unjust to consider the Jews cowardly, as only the Jews committed suicide and the Christians on the contrary were too cowardly to do so. From this remark it was clear that Therese regarded suicide as a heroic deed. This attitude of Therese's did not surprise me, as she had always glorified suicide. On the other hand, a proposal she made to me a few days later seemed sinister.
>
> It was a Saturday, and I had returned home about noon. Therese was lying on the bed, and I walked up and down in the room. Suddenly she looked at me as though an especially good idea had occurred to her.
>
> 'Do you know what we're going to do?' she asked me.
>
> 'Well, what?'
>
> 'We'll turn on the gas'.
>
> 'What gives you such a crazy idea? We aren't Jews'.
>
> Therese lowered her eyes and began to speak of something else just as if she had never spoken the earlier words.

It is an uneasy and uncanny reminiscence of aborted communication: Wolf-Man's simple acceptance on the Jewish sabbath of the persecution of the Jews ('of course to be expected') contrasts with Therese's 'glorification' of suicide, and creates a fissure between them that opens on the words: 'We aren't Jews', at which Therese 'lowered her eyes'.

A few days later, Wolf-Man takes Therese to a cafe and in the middle of office small-talk casually mentions the need for them to get their identity papers in order 'which would prove their Aryan descent, or – as people mockingly said at that time – that they had no Jewish grandmother' (p. 120). Wolf-Man remarks that it will be hard for him to proffer extensive documentation, but all Therese will need to do is 'inquire at her place of birth, Würzburg. When I mentioned this city, Therese gave me such a strange look that I asked her what was the matter and why she looked at me in such a strange way.' She replies: 'It's nothing'; and on 31 March 1938, Wolf-Man comes home from his day at work to find that 'something happened which I had never believed possible: while I was at the office, Therese did actually turn on the gas'.

All is mystery in this bleak and desolate text, signs that are recounted without understanding or sustained interrogation.

> I kept asking myself over and over again what could have been the cause of Therese's terrible decision, and whether and in what way Hitler's invasion might have triggered it. But what use would the answer to all these questions have been, when the most terrible thing for me was the fact that I had lost Therese unexpectedly and forever, and that I could not undo what had been done. (pp. 123–4)

Even so, the sense of mystery continues to nag Wolf-Man, and in June 1939 he visits Therese's older and estranged brother in Munich, where he is given to understand that 'there had been another Therese, leading a mysterious and romantic life' (p. 130). Therese had always told Wolf-Man that she had a Spanish grandmother, and 'she herself was actually closest to a Spanish type, which many people must have remarked on'. When Wolf-Man asks her brother about this, he denies it, adding 'with a sly smile' only that their grandmother 'is said to have had an affair with an officer of the Bavarian nobility' (p. 129). Wolf-Man speculates about what this might mean, and he does so in the clumsy psychoanalytical way one might expect of one who had come to regard himself as Freud's co-worker (p. 140): all his questions are about Therese's mental processes, and why such fantasy should have been important for her, and why she had not wished to 'destroy the romantic story' by sending to Würzburg for proof 'of her Aryan descent', even though 'in the Hitler period it would have been even better to have a German grandmother than a Spanish one' (p. 130). He is almost unbelievably obtuse, except for one locked in a Freudian vault.

Yet the signs of his text are not obtuse; they are almost extravagantly intelligible. There is Therese's swarthy appearance, the fact that she has altered her origins, the fact that she proposes suicide when only Jews are committing it, and lowers her eyes when he produces the master objection: 'we aren't Jews'. Is she not? Doesn't Wolf-Man's text make its readers believe that she was?

If she was, one question is whether Freud knew that she was: Freud, who suppresses a patient's Jewish origins in the case-history of Dora; the warm advocate and financial supporter of Wolf-Man's marriage to Therese; the Jewish exegete for whom the *Anschluss* provided the opportunity to publish the third part of *Moses and Monotheism* in order to 'make the knowledge I had held back accessible to the world' (p. 350), and who writes of himself as one who is

> completely estranged from the religion of his fathers – as well as from every other religion – but who has yet never repudiated his people, who feels that he is in his essential nature a Jew and who has no desire to alter that nature.
>
> (p. 51)

Was Freud complicit with Therese in an act of tacit and politic repudiation?

To entertain such a suspicion is to re-read Freud's case-study of Wolf-Man and his other work, and Wolf-Man's autobiography, and the lives of Freud and Wolf-Man and Therese, in a new and collapsed form – a form in which Freud's ideas develop a dire and unpredictable agency, and intractable historical realities 'invade their subjects' fantasies, an *Anschluss* of the self. If Dr Schreber's neurosis manifests itself as becoming Woman, Wolf-Man's in the 1920s takes the form of becoming Jew. Dr Brunswick notes of Wolf-Man's father dream: 'An association recalls an incident in which the patient's father was termed a "sale juif" – which of course he was not!' (p. 286). Wolf-Man dreams that Freud is his father, his father with a long nose, and he speaks of the sore on his own nose, as on his wife's nose. His relief at the lancing of his nose by the dermatologist/Freud can be read not as a form of orgasm but as a symbolic circumcision. We have seen Sander Gilman's reading of the Dora case, in which he translates a pun across two languages, German and Yiddish, to show that the woman's genitals hide the man's penis, that in Freudian analysis the feminine displaces and conceals the Jew, the circumcised Jew, and in Dora's case the syphilitic Jew, for Dora is the Jewish daughter of a syphilitic father. Therese's suicide notes all assert that she is in any case dying of a disease. Wolf-Man, who consistently denies all the signs he reads, is our sole authority for rejecting the idea, even as he recounts Therese's conviction over years that she is growing prematurely old and ill and ugly. When writing about Wolf-Man's nose phobia, Ruth Mack Brunswick associates two types of catarrh, nasal and gonorrhoeal (p. 269), and goes straight on to mention Wolf-Man's many 'Jewish contacts'. These signifiers crowd madly into narrow social and psychic spaces with promiscuous disregard for the boundaries between one text and another, texts and lives, fictions and facts, between the death wish and a gas oven. But what if being Jewish and having gonorrhoea are cognate and gendered secrets, Therese's Jewishness and Wolf-Man's disease; and what if the marriage between them consummates a deadly and unseen exchange?

Wolf-Man does not understand. He is a former patient of Freud's, and he believes that what is important lies within, in our psyche's coding of long-past events. He is a mainstay of Freud's system, a system that uses every ingenious blasphemy at its disposal to perpetuate a religious view of the self, a self with an essence:

> If the question were put to him: 'Since you have abandoned all these common characteristics of your countrymen, what is there left to you that is Jewish?' he would reply: 'A very great deal, and probably its very essence.' He could not now express that essence clearly in words; but some day, no doubt, it will become accessible to the scientific mind.[14]

Both rationalists and romantics, Freud and Wolf-Man together put forward one kind of truth to the twentieth century, and exemplify another – of which, with Therese, they are victims. Perhaps they are willing victims. Surely they are archetypal ones, writing the martyr's script of modernism in their bodies and in twentieth-century Europe. Theirs is a dream of lucidity: what happens in childhood is what counts, not Hitler, not gonorrhoea, not gas. We repress our position in history because history fails to recognise us as it drives by or over us. Therese's body is a literary monument of such repression. Freud needs to be told what a Jewish woman can tell him, a Jewish survivor of the Holocaust:

> In this century history stopped paying attention to the old psychological orientation of reality. I mean, these days, character isn't destiny any more. Economics is destiny. Ideology is destiny. Bombs are destiny. What does a famine, a gas chamber, a grenade care how you lived your life? Crisis comes, death comes, and your pathetic individual self doesn't have a thing to do with it, only to suffer the effects.[15]

But Wolf-Man, uncomprehending of nearly everything, yet knows what is really happening. He works in the twentieth century's own blasphemy business, life insurance: Viennese life insurance at that, guaranteed to work against the twentieth century as well as Harry Lime's antibiotics in *The Third Man*. Wolf-Man works in the same city and the same game as another rebellious Jewish son, Franz Kafka, who plays for the twentieth century the second and more brutal Moses to Freud's Egyptian aristocrat. Kafka moves like Wolf-Man through a maze of puns and multilingual fragments, through texts and intertexts, in a world without religion, a world of political apathy and overt gender confusion and distrust, of exile and rootlessness and other people's language. Theirs is a world where identity papers, not childhood memories, are currency, and epic fights for the soul are somehow bypassed in the demolition of 'essence'. Wolf-Man survived – longer than most. (Sergei Pankejeff died in 1979, at the age of 92.) As a prototype, Wolf-Man lives. Leaving his dead women behind him, he howls his way down a century or more of becoming Wolf.

Chapter 6

RUSHDIE AND THE WORLD OF WRESTLING

RUSHDIE AND BLASPHEMY

This prodigious blaspheming chaos deserves no mercy.
THE JUDGES OF GENEVA ON MICHAEL SERVETUS, 1553

The story of Freud and the Wolf-Man is one of displaced persons haunted by their lost homes. When he is more than 60 years old, Wolf-Man imperils his chances of staying in Vienna by wandering into the Russian sector. The occasion is his long-dead sister's birthday, and his ostensible purpose to draw a house that has caught his eye. Freud undertakes a personal exodus in the last year of his life, to Hampstead, and publishes the final form of the book that most poignantly speaks of belonging elsewhere, with Jews whose central beliefs he repudiates. In each case, there is the desire to assert an ancestral identity with the place and community that is shattered, out of bounds, or otherwise irretrievable. Both men act out a quixotic ritual of recovery – an impossible recovery, a failed resurrection; they do so repetitively and compulsively, and not without alarm recognise in each other their common cause. I have argued that it is Freud's project, blasphemy: it is through blasphemy that he and Wolf-Man can claim identity and abjure it, leave home and seek it, be at once enemies, strangers and friends. I have argued too that there is a cost: the textual product of the masculine collaboration between Freud and Wolf-Man is dead women. The continued failure to love women, to find a home, has different orders of consequence. Creatively, it causes signs to slip and recede in unending semiosis; destructively, it bears, or bears the mark of, an oblique and fatal agency.

In *The Satanic Verses* (1988), the main plot is of masculine collaboration – collaboration in love and hate, in good and evil – between Gibreel Farishta and Saladin Chamcha. They fall from a plane together; they betray one another; they bond as men bond. Gibreel, who represents Good and turns out to be Evil, saves Saladin from the fire at the Shaandaar cafe; Saladin, who represents Evil and turns out to be Good, or merely human, repays Gibreel by destroying him. The air of claustrophobic masculine bonding in this plot, supported by an ending in which Saladin comes to terms with his dying father, mirrors the portrait of religion in the book's other plot, and is parodically underscored by the murders of women on the streets of London. The controversy aroused by the book itself retains a character of claustrophobic masculinism, in which cultural paternalism meets religious fundamentalism. But the book is wiser than that. It has its roll-call of dead and doomed women: of Rekha Merchant, the terrorist in the aeroplane, Pamela Chamcha, Alleleuia Cone, and the many casualties of the Ayesha sequence. When men fall from the sky, they survive; when women fall, they die. Indeed, if the book is begun by the fall of men, it is framed, at the beginning and end, by a falling woman (Rekha Merchant and Alleleuia Cone). The women who die through Gibreel's agency are false choices – staying in India, becoming absolutely English – false homes. The central male figures are displayed as Muslims in India, then as migrants in Britain; their quest is for unavailable homes, and the salvation of the survivor Saladin lies in returning home, accepting home as his inheritance, and resolving to demolish it.

The most important point of all is made by Homi Bhabha. It is the transformation of home, not the transformation of Gibreel, that initiates the destabilising semiosis of the book. For Saladin's first home-coming of the novel is drastically unsuccessful. His mother is dead, having choked to death on a fish-bone; yet, on entering the house, Saladin believes that he catches sight of her. This is the novel's first reference to blasphemy: 'Oh God!' he exclaims, and is rebuked by the old servant Vallabh: 'Excuse, baba, but you should not blaspheme' (p. 66). It turns out that the 'ghost' is Vallabh's wife, wearing one of her mistress's saris, and lounging on an old sofa 'as sensually as any movie starlet, even though she was a woman well advanced in years' (p. 67). Her name is Kasturba – the name of the wife of Mahatma Gandhi, 'the mother of the independent Indian nation': Bhabha relates her naming to 'the empty promises of nationalist renaming where the untouchables were renamed Harijans – the people of God – by Gandhi'.[1] Thus 'it is the death of the mother that makes possible the process of renaming in the book' and 'enables the act of secular narration' (p. 61): the split sign of the mother opens up the cultural difference that allows transculturing and re-inscription. The same name attaches to more than one sign (in Gibreel's dream of Jahilia compared to the rest of the novel), and at the same time voices and languages multiply and their force becomes increasingly uncertain. Gibreel hears the clamour of voices in his head, and Saladin discovers the versatility of voice that makes him rich and dangerous. The field of Wolf-Man's life is likewise intersected by complex multilingual-ism and, on the other hand, the increasingly absurd repetition of the word and the name Wolf: one tutor and two dentists.

I have drawn attention to parallels and strange echoes between *The Satanic*

Verses and Wolf-Man's history in order to propose others, a correspondence between Rushdie and Freud – both of whom write the discourse of their mad subjects as blasphemy, and for whom that blasphemy arouses the most troubling questions of racial, religious and cultural belonging. Rushdie does to Muhammad what Freud does to Moses. It is plausible, I think, that *The Satanic Verses* functions as blasphemy in the Freudian mode, blasphemy as the ostensible structure of the narrative answering to blasphemy as the writer's own coding of identity. It is not historically true to claim: 'where there is no belief, there is no blasphemy',[2] but it is true of this discourse. Freud can only express his sense of identity as a Jew by blaspheming, by a stoic and subversive religion of the fathers. Home, if it is attainable at all, is already a displacement: for an Egyptian Moses the Promised Land is a migration, not a return. The conflict is a splitting of the subject that speaks through the splitting of the sign: one belongs where one cannot be, and one is where one does not belong. Such displacement, in religious terms, is transgression: to write of home is to write transgression, writing in two places, and to write of belonging is to blaspheme. Writes Bhabha: 'Blasphemy is the migrant's shame at returning home' (p. 61). The writer's community is foregrounded as a transaction between representation and bereavement, the living and the dead mother – Kasturba: 'The world, somebody wrote, is the place we prove real by dying in it.'[3]

This sounds very like Georges Bataille's concern for community, as I have described it in Chapter 4. Bataille's attempt to recuperate an already irrecoverable community is a manifestation of the Death of God: it plays out, through a quasi-religious ritual, the belatedness of the shared systems of belief that sustained it. Its only available modern form, therefore, is the paradoxical Nietzschean form, the absence of God, decreed by a present subject who is God: the schizoid form of religious mania that so fascinated Freud. Rushdie's comic version of this is his appearance as the God of his novel, balding and bespectacled, with dandruff on his collar. 'This God who quickens us beneath his clouds is mad. I know: I am he.' Bataille here restates Nietzsche's reflections on the death of God in *The Gay Science*, where Nietzsche supposes a 'demon' who taunts the reader with a fate of eternal repetition:

> 'This life as you have lived it and now live it, you will have to live once more and innumerable times more. . . . The eternal hourglass of existence is turned upside down again and again, and you with it, speck of dust!' Would you not throw yourself down and gnash your teeth and curse the demon who spoke thus? Or have you experienced a tremendous moment when you could reply to him: 'You are a *god*, and never have I heard anything more divine.'

As Simon During notes, 'The passage asks a version of Locke's old question: how to tell the difference between a god and a devil . . . now that neither

God nor Satan manifest themselves in the world, we find that their absence is also their "interlacement".[4] The term is Foucault's, from the essay on Bataille's friend Klossowski, in which Foucault goes on to discuss Klossowski's notion that our civilisation has long been one based not on signs but on simulacra. The term is a difficult one, but the present context allows an example that makes it accessible and lucid: if Saladin's mother is the sign, the servant Kasturba pretending to be Saladin's mother is the simulacrum. Another example from the subject matter of this present book supports Foucault's claim that the order of simulacra has a long historical tradition in Western culture: if Jesus Christ is the sign, James Nayler – self-consciously – is the simulacrum. The sign is gone, irreparably; yet its absence can be staged, or re-presented in the simulacrum, which transvalues the sign and records its belatedness. The simulacrum is at best an approximation of the sign and at worst either a deliberate or involuntary distortion of it. Freudian analysis works through simulacra – wolves, houses, warts – to refigure the historically past signs of childhood: coitus or incest, the mother or the father or the sister or the dog. And for Foucault, Klossowski's project is to recover the history of culture as an order of simulacra rather than signs by projecting analysis as a sequence of multiple, indistinct and unstably differentiated voices that can never reveal an undivided origin, and that serves to collapse notional distinctions between analysis and fiction, the real and the imaginary.

The inability to distinguish good and evil, the protean complicity of demons and gods, are staged in *The Satanic Verses*: they are staged in a multiple sequence of voices that play out an order of simulacra and never give stable access to signs or sources. Nietzsche's challenge is part of the plan of Rushdie's book, in something like Foucault's context, in which representation itself is rewritten according to the laws of simulacra and polyglot, multivocal schizophrenia. It seems to me that at least one line of attack on Rushdie's book is ineligible: the proposition that it is a rabid, nihilistic personal vendetta, without preconception or philosophical point. On the contrary, the evidence so far supports a view of it as written from an intellectual position that is philosophically important in the modern world and has been so since at least the seventeenth century. Objectors may not like the position, but they are wrong to hold it unaccountable or unprecedented. However, it is equally misconceived to present it as a statement of 'a dominant secular liberal culture',[5] whatever that may be (and would that any two of those terms went easily together). The position I have outlined is by no means intellectual common currency, and is far from the reason why certain British newspapers, for example, have given Rushdie grudging succour: 'We are not supporting Rushdie's boring book . . . but we defend his right to write.'[6] Rushdie's more articulate supporters have often failed to understand its implications (and may have misread Rushdie on 'the room of fiction'). You cannot proclaim an order of simulacra and at the same time claim for fiction a privileged and separate reality. You cannot therefore simply excuse blasphemy by saying 'This is happening in a madman's head', though the point does not lose its relevance. Nor can you have parts of *The Satanic Verses* and leave others. Gibreel's madness, Saladin's voices, the Qu'ranic blasphemy and the book's concerns with social and transcultural identity are consequences of one another. For Rushdie, as I have argued for Freud and for Bataille, the issues of community and blasphemy are simultaneous.

If my comparison between Rushdie and Freud has any merit, it requires a modification that is much to Rushdie's credit. In the matter of simulacra, the book is intensely self-conscious: the plot is only possible because its two protagonists are actors, and bring to their roles the familiarity of advertising in Saladin's case and, in Gibreel's, the theological sanction of the Indian film industry (Bombay talkies). It is in the world of such movies that we have prior knowledge of narratives allowing heroes to survive falls from exploding aircraft and metamorphosis of form into animals or giants or demons. The 'magic realism' of the Ayesha pilgrimage sequence has a distinctive sub-continental signature: Ayesha hears Gibreel's words in the form of Hindi popular songs, for that is the sort of plot in which here she has a starring role. Equally, I think, in the matter of gender Rushdie's book is on the whole clear-sighted. I have suggested that Freud and Wolf-Man are blind to the fact that their story and system are built on dead women's bodies, whereas Rushdie takes as his starting-point what he sees as a religious and cultural refusal – a violent, masculine refusal – to license the feminine.

As his starting-point: for that is what the so-called 'Satanic verses' mark, the reputed deletion from the Qu'ran of two verses that uniquely admitted the powers of three female divinities. That is why the Imam and the first Ayesha, the Empress – name-sake of the favourite wife of the Prophet and the butterfly girl – are introduced as implacable opposites; and predictably, in Gibreel's first dream-contact with the Imam, Ayesha metamorphoses into the leading female divinity, Al-Lat. The Imam orders Gibreel: 'Kill her' – and he does, after an epic wrestling match of giants.[7] As the Imam defines his religion, there is no room for women – as, indeed, there is no room for Time. It is not that women are denied a role in history; they are denied a history at all. Their only place is enclosure; and the book's true heroine is the Londoner Mishal, who breaks away from traditional repressions without compromising her cultural identity. Perhaps women goddesses would have proved as arbitrary and assertive as the male God, there being only a phoneme of difference between Allah and Al-Lat: thus the Ayesha of the pilgrimage sequence, who leads her followers to certain death and possible paradise, has an illegitimate baby stoned to death (cultural difference receiving the biblical punishment for blasphemy). She is like the woman hijacker, whose body is covered with bombs, not butterflies. They are both Imam-like in their preparedness to exercise power violently against difference. And they are thus constructions of the system that the Imam embodies – a religious system that I have not simply characterised as 'Islamic'.

For the Imam, as Rushdie depicts him, is wicked. For all the theatrical interchanges of Gibreel and Saladin, the Imam is by far the most genuinely evil presence in the novel. It is clear, since Gibreel's dreams bring him under the Imam's command, that the blasphemous madness of those dreams represents not only Gibreel's mental torment but also the religion of the Imam. That religion is not Islam but a travesty of Islam: its prophet is therefore not Muhammad but Mahound, and in it Qu'ranic revelation is perverted. The most sensitive of all that perversion is the rendering of the Qu'ranic signs, the prophet's wives and the veil, the *Hijab*, as simulacra, the whores of a brothel named the *Hijab*. The issue is again the religious status of women. Objection to this substitution of simulacra for signs comes from those who accept the Imam's religion as a representation of Islam; the novel, however, suggests that the blasphemy works in the reverse direction. The *fatwa* on Rushdie was pronounced by an Imam who proved not insensitive to the rather powerful portrait in the book. Ironically, it was pronounced in the name of Islam.

I have already listed two of the major blasphemies of the book. First, there is what is taken to be an attack on the *Hijab* and the wives of the Prophet, so that we are told by the book's opponents that Rushdie is calling all faithful Muslim women whores: whereas what I take him to be doing is tabling, in the most provocative manner, passionate questions about freedom. Whores are the slaves of men's pleasures; is it possible that religious law enslaves women, albeit in an entirely different fashion? Secondly, there is the fatal blasphemy: an unflattering and compelling portrait of the Imam, as a murderous modern tyrant masquerading in a guise of religious rectitude. Ferocious as it is, this is less vehement than Nawal el Saadawi's *The Fall of the Imam*.[8] Rushdie's attack reminds one of the terms of Achmed Kasravi's attacks on Shi'ism in 1944, arguing that it was 'a perversion whose origin lay neither in ethics nor in theological issues, but in a sordid struggle for power'.[9] In retaliation, a young Ayatollah Khomeini pronounced an early *fatwa*: 'The law of Islam declares that your blood can be shed with impunity', and Kasravi was assassinated by members of the Muslim brotherhood in 1946, on the day that Khomeini's associate, Ayatollah Khalkhali, hailed as 'the most beautiful day of my life'. Thirdly, there is the use of the 'Satanic verses' themselves, known in medieval Islamic tradition as the *Gharaniq* incident. The frequent assertion that this motif is alien to Islamic tradition and is an Orientalist's lie is a complex mistake. Patrick Bannerman writes –

in true Orientalist style – of 'populist' Islam that 'its adherents are generally ill-informed about Muslim beliefs and practices'.[10] Certainly, Rushdie, a Cambridge graduate in Islamic studies, knows more of unorthodox Muslim traditions than most. In fact, however, the charge of Orientalism has some justice – for the verses in question are not known anywhere in Islamic scholarship as 'the Satanic verses'. Rushdie took this too tempting title from the work of Western Oriental scholars such as Montgomery Watt, without realising that reference in this form to the *Gharaniq* incident would mean nothing to Muslims. Worse still, when the title is translated into Arabic it reads as 'the Satanic Qu'ran', or 'The Qu'ran is Satan's work'. There is therefore a very strong possibility that the book would have escaped such serious trouble under any other title. Of course, the implication of the title once read this way is borne out by the sequences describing the scribe Salman's inventions and additions to the text as dictated by Mahound – and leads to Anthony Johns's judgement that Rushdie's novel 'strikes at the heart of Islamic revelation'.[11] This is true only if Mahound is taken to be an especially insulting Western name for Muhammad. I have argued the contrary case, that it is used as simulacrum, not as sign, to build a case against the Imam's representation of Islam. Mahound is to Muhammad as Gibreel Farishta is to the angel Gabriel, and as the Imam is to – an Imam. According to the novel, it is the Imam's travesty of Islam that turns Muhammad into Mahound, and perverts religious law into a madman's dictation imperfectly transcribed.

Anthony Johns continues with the claim that such an impugning of revelation is immeasurably worse than any blasphemy against Christianity. I see no basis for this judgement, unless it is simply a statement about the actual virulence of its reception. A useful comparison is Apollinaire's story 'The Heresiarch', first published in 1910, which is just as blasphemous against Christianity as Rushdie's novel is against Islam – and in the same way, since Apollinaire's blasphemy is specifically presented as the work of a fictive blasphemer. The doctrine of the Trinity has been the site of the most rigorous contests about blasphemy in Christian history, and Apollinaire invents a new and witty transgression. His heresiarch, Benedetto Orfei, 'was a theologian and gastronome, at once pious and greedy', his devotional practice of mystic eroticism expressing itself in 'smutty language'.[12] Nevertheless, only his heresy prevented him from becoming a cardinal or even pope. Apollinaire concentrates a whole history of Christianity into his characterisation:

> Like all heresiarchs, he rejected the dogma of Papal infallibility and swore that God had ordained that he was to reform His church. I should imagine that if Benedetto Orfei had become Pope, he would have used the dogma of Infallibility to compel Catholics to believe in his doctrine, which none could then have denied without becoming a heretic. (p. 32)

Orfei's great vision comes to him in 'the form of a popular refrain':

> They were three men on Golgotha,
> Just as in Heaven
> They are the Trinity. (p. 33)

The good thief beside Jesus was God the Father, the bad thief was the Holy Ghost, whose 'infamous sexuality' had brought disgrace upon him. ('He was the true criminal, and suffered justly', p. 37). There is a second vision of 'the Most Blessed Virgin, standing between two women and saying to them: "You also are the small mothers of God, but men are not aware of your maternity"' (p. 35). Unable to exorcise him, the Pope excommunicates Orfei, announcing that his vision is the work of a demon; Orfei responds with a self-righteous letter, in the tone of the Calvin–Servetus correspondence. He lives out his life attempting to promulgate the true religion, in gourmandising and extreme asceticism. Apollinaire's story, like Rushdie's novel, is a study in extremes, in which sensuality contrasts with asceticism, beauty with obscenity. With the death of the heresiarch, it offers its 'truth': 'The truth is that the heresiarch was like all men, for all of us are at the same time sinners and saints, when we are not criminals and martyrs' (p. 40). It could serve as an obituary for Gibreel Farishta, and serve to highlight another aspect of Rushdie's extraordinary novel: it is a study in the temperament of religious leaders, and a sustained portrait of a blasphemer. But there is no easy separation of blasphemer and author, just as in the Apollinaire story the generalisation that 'Catholicity is indifferent to reformers and prophets, being no longer concerned with the substance of its faith' (p. 31) works as the prelude to a sustained effort to challenge its unconcern. Blasphemy infects both the subject of writing and the writing subject.

It is better, I think, to acknowledge the primacy of blasphemy in Rushdie's novel than to defend it out of existence, or find oneself defending Rushdie against a charge of having 'gone too far'. Whenever was there such a thing as tactful blasphemy? The argument has to be that at times blasphemy is both creative and necessary, and that it is not only integral but fundamental to the novel's culture, identity and community.

Here is another mistake in judgement: 'Rushdie, coming from a Muslim background, knows Muslim culture and its ethos. But having become acculturated in British Society, and protected by its institutions, he is holding up his abandoned culture to scorn.'[13] The judgement has become commonplace, and is part of the carnivalisation that comes with blasphemy. I use blasphemy here as, I think, a neutral description of Rushdie's project in the sense in which I have used it of Freud's, but with the realisation that it imperfectly describes the offence taken by some Muslims – whose closest legal category is probably that of *zandaqa*, the faith of the *zindiq* (atheists and free-thinkers; purveyors of seditious religious teaching).[14] The judgement I have quoted is one that works in terms of religious apostasy and/or political treason, and both are offered to justify a sentence of death for which there is in any case no Qu'ranic sanction. There is manifestly nothing in the book to support a view that Rushdie has 'become acculturated in British Society'. One of the themes of the book is the impossibility of such acculturation without freer movement between communities and the social commitment to transculturing. And it is for such acculturation that Saladin Chamcha is satirised in the early parts of the book. What is entirely concealed by allegations of apostasy is the community from which Rushdie derives and which he has far from 'abandoned': not a community under Muslim or any other religious law, but constitutionally secularist India. As Gayatri Spivak reminds us, it is in India too that the Rushdie affair began – before it was picked up by the Saudis and then the Iranians, or spread in the Pakistani community of Bradford. The greatest betrayal felt by Rushdie was the Indian government's decision to ban his book in the name of community relations: hence Rushdie's bitter open letter to Rajiv Gandhi, whom Rushdie might well have suspected of gaining revenge for the portrait of his mother in *Midnight's Children*.

Historically, the Muslim community of India had a secularist orientation: Jinnah's Muslim League, for example, was opposed by the mullahs. In the years since the foundation of the independent Indian state, however, religious interests have proved generally more adroit in identifying, articulating and exploiting community grievances – and have offered what appears an attractively idealist counter to often corrupt politicians. *The Satanic Verses* is another attempt to speak to the minority Indian community from which Rushdie comes and to come to terms with its shift in values since the time of his departure from it. There is not enough critical emphasis on Rushdie's identity as an Indian writer, writing in residence from another country, expressing a strong interest in migrant communities in that country, but never ceasing to address those who remained behind. Rushdie's residence in Britain does not unmake him as an Indian writer, any more than Sidney Nolan ceased to be an Australian artist when he moved to London, or indeed than Robert Graves ceased to be an English poet by virtue of living in Majorca. Indeed, if the Australian experience is anything to go by, expatriate writers often play a particularly significant role in consolidation of a national culture, all the more so when their experience of living in two countries is shared by many of their compatriots. It is grotesque to claim that Rushdie promotes 'deculturation': his key concern is with cross-cultural transactions, their difficulties and their consequences.

From Rushdie's viewpoint, his project resembles that of 'minor literature', as characterised by Deleuze and Guattari (1986). Minor literature, as exemplified for them in the works of Kafka, is 'minor' as in 'minority', as in a sense of being a literary stranger in the language that the writer writes, even if it is the same language that the writer speaks. In Kafka's case, he decides to write German, the bureaucratic language of the Austro-Hungarian empire, rather than Czech (or Yiddish, which at that time Kafka did not know). To realise how marked that choice was, one needs to refer to another story by Apollinaire (1991), 'The wandering Jew', in which the French narrator arrives in Prague from Dresden and asks in German for direction from passers-by. The first five 'did not understand a word of German only Czech'. The sixth smiles and answers in French, advising the speaker to speak French, 'for we hate the Germans much more even than the French do. We detest a race that forces its language on us, profits from our industries and our fertile soil which produces everything. . . . In Prague we speak only French' (pp. 1–2). To use German therefore raises the suspicion of siding with the exploiters, the colonisers – a suspicion allayed by Kafka's satiric portrait of German-speaking bureaucracy itself into which his narrator in *The Castle* is unable to fit himself and of which in *The Trial* he is a victim. Deleuze and Guattari's model foregrounds such ambivalent multilingualism, and the heteroglossic and experimental nature of minor literature itself. Major literature is that in which the theme exists before it is written – it is par excellence the literature of Word and Scripture. A minor literature, by contrast, 'begins by speaking . . . it only sees or conceives afterwards', as it improvises its way towards meaning.[15] Minor literature is a mode of defamiliarisation, and it is also overtly political: it tries where politics fails to construct a national tradition; in Kafka's case, the impossibly split tradition of Czech writing speaking German. Instead of appeasing the colonisers, such use of their language operates like mass migration: it takes becoming Czech into the German heartland.

We might compare Bhabha's formulation: 'Salman Rushdie's *The Satanic Verses* attempts to redefine the boundaries of the western nation, so that "foreignness of languages" becomes the inescapable cultural condition for the enunciation of the mother-tongue.'[16] The often repeated slur that Rushdie has 'sold out' to British culture fails to see that his use of English moves towards a minor literature: he writes many new and foreign voices into what might have seemed like British national discourses. Rushdie works by interpolation, just as Gibreel Farishta interpolates himself into the epic national dreams of the dying Rosa Diamond and transcultures them by appropriating the role of her husband Henry. When the literary tradition of the English and American novel meets Bombay talkies, the result is an alienation of both cultures – English and Indian – from a single point of origin. Rushdie writes the programme for a literary rescue, as well as an acting out, of what might seem to be the drastic social consequences of the enforced multiculturalism that results from mass migration – a multiculturalism of such sudden violence that it is imaged as a series of murders, or an asylum for freaks, or an exploding plane.

Rushdie's use of English is like Kafka's of German, and also represents a classic Indian dilemma. 'To give millions a knowledge of English,' said Gandhi (in English), 'is to enslave them.'[17] Yet the bureaucratic continuity of independent modern India depended on it, and still largely does so many years after the original timetable has expired for the transfer of its main functions into Hindi. Given separatist racial and religious movements it may be that the modern Indian nation – and so too the secularist ideals in which it is founded – exists only in English. And, as we know from *Midnight's Children*, the foundation of modern India is the foundation of Salman Rushdie. For Rushdie to write its national literature is at once to rewrite the cultural discourse of his own origins and community and to enter the English heartland as an invading force: Rosa Diamond dreams the Norman Conquest and meets Gibreel Farishta. Since English is, as Bhabha says, the mother tongue, and the mother of the novel is Kasturba, the Mother of the Nation, the use of English is the key with which to unlock a paradoxical national identity that is always already a transcultured exchange. Identity in *The Satanic Verses* explodes into identities: hence the novel's most puzzling and persistent formal feature, the use of a single name for multiple persons. While the multiplicity may become madness, as for Gibreel, the book nowhere envisages that it can be integrated or assimilated into anything culturally homogeneous. When Saladin Chamcha's phony upper-class English accent and his English wife betray him, he weeps into his pillow: 'Damn all Indians.'

The many-voiced heterogeneity is the result of the hidden history of the Western world, colonisation; and colonisation, as we have seen, rests on the sanction given by the discourse of blasphemy to the thoughtless annihilation of cultural difference. It is in understanding that history that any hope lies, not in the adamantine denial of it that is the creed of the Imam:

> After the revolution there will be no clocks; we'll smash the lot. The word *clock* will be expunged from our dictionaries. After the revolution there will be no birthdays. We shall all be born again, all of us the same unchanging age in the eye of Almighty God. (p. 214)

The enemy of history, and so of understanding, is fundamentalism, offering itself as religious but really political. Fundamentalism offers a false identity, a spurious recoding of the many as one. Because the book must fight fundamentalism in order for its inquiry to exist, one of its major resources is – has to be – blasphemy. And so arises the tragedy of *The Satanic Verses*. Its quest for community in cultural difference constructs another community altogether, one of Muslim fundamentalism.

What matters most now is that we do not accept a portrayal, either by fundamentalists or by Orientalists, of Islamic culture as a joyless and repressive monolith. We must not allow fundamentalists to speak as the sole voice of their religion, because to do so is to obscure prolific networks of plural cultural identity and difference. In the West, fundamentalism works in the name of a text, the Bible, only to deface the history of that text more comprehensively than ever Rushdie offends against the Qu'ran. A complex, rich and polymorphous biblical literature is simply colonised, and pressed into service as a puerile litany of fearful forecasts. As the cultural products of two Christian millennia we cannot cede the political control of Christian discourse that fundamentalists seek. Rushdie, and many other writers who are the cultural products of diverse Islamic societies, oppose Muslim fundamentalism, contesting it not in the cause of 'secularism' but on grounds of community, culture and identity. Several have died: Turkish feminists, Egyptian libertarians such as Farag Foda. It would be a poor tribute to their courage if one were to yield a monopoly over Islam to their killers. The controversy about *The Satanic Verses* has increased awareness in the West of the many facets of cultures that embrace forms of Islam. What we need now is the opposite of death sentences, dialogue, the dialogue we should be holding with Muslim scholars who have written very interestingly against Rushdie's book from what clearly are different cultural perspectives from mine, perspectives that I should like to understand better.[18]

There is, for example, a fear of hegemonic secularism: many such writers see themselves as defending Islam and the very grounds of cultural identity and difference that I believe motivate Rushdie too. If so, this is another example of the classic ruptured community of blasphemy with which this book opened – a frustrated communication where the rupture occurs at a point of common value. That is why it is so important to reclaim religion as culture from fundamentalism. In Rushdie's terms, all fundamentalists pervert their Scriptures, and turn holy books into Satanic verses. Writes one Muslim scholar, not unjustly: 'Some of those who vehemently criticise fundamentalism are becoming dangerously fundamentalist themselves.'[19] Quite so. But how else can one argue that fundamentalism is the biggest blasphemy around? And blasphemy, as the next part of this chapter will show, multiplies itself beyond its own knowledge and control.

The World of Wrestling

We're gonna kick some ass.

GEORGE BUSH, 1990

God, the flag, the family – I believe in that stuff.

HULK HOGAN, WWF wrestler, 1991

France

The famous essay on wrestling by Roland Barthes was first published as the opening piece of the volume *Mythologies* in 1957. Though, surprisingly, neither book nor essay was translated into English until 1972, they quickly became classic, largely avoiding the grudging irritability with which French theory is traditionally received in Britain and parts of North America. Deservedly so: the volume as a whole is sophisticated yet plain-speaking, coolly elegant without much jargon to frighten the British. Its semiotic approach to a world of signs other than those of printed books gave access to signifying systems in our culture that more aesthetic approaches to the texts of 'high' culture neither could nor wanted to provide. Thus it validated and established what at first won Barthes fewer British readers by being called semiology; and it legitimated study of popular culture, while bridging the gap between it and the arts. 'The world of wrestling' gave many of its readers the pleasant shock of taking seriously a taste they shared but had thought undignified to acknowledge.

Wrestling, according to Barthes, is not a sport at all: only a fool would bet on the outcome of a wrestling match. In wrestling, the 'fair fight' is the exception, and it is as generically over-determined and artificial as everything else. For wrestling is a form of street theatre: it belongs not to sport but to spectacle, presenting in fact 'a spectacle of excess' by means of a repertoire of 'excessive gestures exploited to the limit of their meaning'. A wrestler's defeat, notes Barthes, is not played down or accepted matter-of-factly, as in judo: it is emphasised in gestures held 'like a pause in music'. Barthes sees in all this a rhetoric of performance, 'a function of grandiloquence', which is corroborated by the bodies of the wrestlers themselves. These fall into a set of stock types that Barthes categorises, and mark them just as if they were characters in the *commedia dell'arte*: 'As soon as the adversaries are in the ring, the public is overwhelmed with the obviousness of the roles.' Subtlety is the opposite of what is sought, as 'light without shadow generates an emotion without reserve'. The public expects 'an orgy of evil which alone makes good wrestling', and looks for a catharsis (though Barthes avoids the term) like that of Greek theatre. Defeat is display as of the Cross and the pillory, even, Barthes claims to have heard spectators say, as in the death of Jesus. 'What is thus displayed for the public is the great spectacle of Suffering, Defeat and Justice.'

Yet 'only the image is involved in the game, and the spectator does not wish for the actual suffering of the contestant; he only enjoys the perfection of an iconography'. 'What the public wants is the image of passion, not passion itself' (passion here means suffering, as in crucifixion, as well as desire). Thus the world of wrestling is one in which every sign is saturated with its own clarity, and the play-space of the wrestling hall is a semiotic utopia: the grandiloquence of wrestling 'is nothing but the popular and age-old image of the perfect intelligibility of reality'. Thus, 'it is not true that wrestling is a sadistic spectacle: it is only an intelligible spectacle'. And it is in this sense that wrestling takes its place alongside other 'mythologies': not because it is true but because it is true to itself in avoiding the question of truth: 'there is no more a problem of truth in wrestling than in the theatre'.[20]

One major and obvious appeal of Barthes's essay, then, is that it works wrestling as a material allegory of fiction-making. The Professor of French Philip Thody, commenting on the essay, compares Barthes's view of wrestling with Greek myths or the Book of Genesis, in that all offer clear frameworks, explanations, aetiologies: 'fulfilling one of the paradoxes of art by appearing to tell, if not exactly lies, at least exceedingly tall stories'.[21] It sounds like a blueprint for certain types of fiction, fiction like that written by Salman Rushdie, who

> grew up in a literary tradition – one can mention the *Arabian Nights*, for instance, in which it was clearly understood that stories were untrue – where horses flew and so did carpets. And in spite of that blatant untruth, they reached for a deeper truth. So I grew up in a world in which it was understood that fiction was a lie – and the paradox was that the lie told the truth.[22]

Barthes's essay supplies a space for such paradoxical truth told by lies, or at least 'exceedingly tall stories'.

Brilliant as Barthes's reading of wrestling is, it suppresses certain features. First, it suppresses what I imagine is part of many men's response to the exaggerated gesture-play of dominance and submission, the homoerotic. It is as if, in his anxiety to speak for and as 'the public' of wrestling, Barthes distrusted and so suppressed his own sexuality. Yet many men, especially straight fatherly men like George Bush and Saddam Hussein, sublimate homoerotic impulses in personal violence. And violence is the second thing Barthes suppresses. Honourably, he writes as one with distaste for and no personal experience of fighting. His father was killed fighting in World War I before Barthes was one year old, he was ruled unfit for military service in 1937 (increasing, he wrote, his sense of exclusion and marginality), and he spent most of the war years in a sanatorium for the tubercular. May this contribute to the fact that, unblooded and unbloodied, he writes about wrestling in an impossibly sanitising manner, as if limbs were never broken nor blood regularly spilt, as if choreography never gave way to murderous temper?

Barthes's reading is, after all, aesthetic – most of all in his third suppression, of any political dimension in wrestling as a social practice. He sidesteps the political overtly. Whereas, he writes, in France the focus of wrestling encounters is ethical, so that the contest is read as a kind of morality drama, in America it is political: 'in America wrestling represents a sort of mythological fight between Good and Evil (of a quasi-political nature, the "bad" wrestler always being supposed to be a Red)' (p. 23). The distinction occurs late in the argument, and damages it, partly by being half-hearted ('*quasi*-political': even here Barthes cannot bring himself to admit the political seriously), and partly because the mythological aspect has been claimed as common to all wrestling. One is therefore tempted to ask whether American wrestling is distinctive in being political, or merely distinctive in the forms that being political takes. There is good reason not to follow Barthes here; but it is not enough to dismiss his distinction, as Thody does, as a symptom of the instinctive anti-Americanism of the French left.

The more political nature of wrestling in America is expressed in, and necessitates, a far more prodigal use of language by wrestlers than in the grunt-and-tumble dumbshow of British or European wrestling. Wrestlers' speech-acts out of the ring extend and sometimes explain their behaviour in it. A more political Barthes writing in the 1950s might have looked at their speech-acts and found that they belonged, by no means parodically, to the genre of a McCarthyite hearing, and that for the public before whom both were enacted the point was the same. Any such conclusion might then have raised many new questions about the nature of the truth that is not an issue in the wrestling ring, about the relation of play-space and play-time to social control, and about the status of fiction as a social practice. The question is: does Barthes's hermetic system leak?

America

The conduct and fortunes of the World Wrestling Federation, like those of the Gulf War, were transformed by cable television. The WWF's marketing people realised very quickly that cable offered an exponential increase in income: successful television programmes could guarantee not only astronomically full houses for major wrestling events (Wrestlemania vii in 1991 had an attendance of 117,000 in Los Angeles, with a ticket price averaging $70) but also phenomenal cable subscription (over three million homes for the same event, paying $39.95 for the showing). The formula required some updating, and the best new market was confidently identified: kids, from walking age upwards. The result was seen in Wrestlemania i in 1986, with its consummate video production values and an array of support stars like Cyndi Lauper. At first it was even called Rock and Roll Wrestling, but the title was dropped after it was seen to be inadvertently geriatric. The new image was so lucrative that WWF enterprises was soon sustaining nightly events in major centres through the USA, concurrent international tours to lucky countries like Australia, and three weekly television programmes. Where the kids flocked, it seemed that the parents were only too happy to follow. The chain store Toys R Us markets a huge and spectacularly unsalubrious range of WWF wrestler dolls, and reports that the line is consistently a best seller.

Many of the wrestlers were far from new to the circuit, although some were to find the demands of glamour wrestling beyond them – and their replacements were not slow in coming forward. Some of them were always intended to be short-term attractions, like the relatively young and relatively pretty woman (supposedly managed by Cyndi Lauper, who was present at ringside) chosen to be women's champion instead of the ancient, mottled and rotund professional Moolah. But it was important, no doubt, to find one wrestler who could be a figurehead for the new WWF, representing at once its old wrestling professionalism and its sweeping renovation. The major title in any fighting organisation is that of men's world heavyweight champion, and it was logical that its holder should fill this key promotional role. The holder was Hulk Hogan.

Hogan was ideal: experienced, not impossibly 'good' but only prepared to play dirty in a just cause, and unusually articulate within the favoured genre of 7-second muscle-tensing exhalations. He was ideal, that is, to capture the taste of Reagan's America. Like the President, he looked at least as good in the part as any of his rivals, for all that tabloid magazines at the store checkout hinted at chemical prophylaxis ('Aide admits: I dyed President's hair'; 'Steroids: you too can have a body like Hulk Hogan'). And like the President at least in this respect, he was by far the best deliverer of his pre-scripted lines. Hogan's major problem, however, as words like 'elation' and 'spiritual renewal' tripped gamely off his tongue, was disguising his intelligence; but as his fans came to know him better, this too became a sign of supermanhood, and he was able to make suavely urbane and upmarket ads for French male toiletries. Like the President, he was slow to anger but fiercely patriotic, irrepressible when riled, and an unembarrassed crowd-pleaser.

No more than his counterpart was Hogan in the first flush of youth. In Hogan's case, the problem was hair. His was in full retreat, and no man is in any position to hide this effectively by artful coiffure while sweating copiously and being thrown around a ring. Hogan took to wearing his hair longer at the back and sides, where it grew, but this only accentuated the absence on top. Out of the ring, he took to wearing gypsy-style kerchiefs knotted round his brows, a style drawn from American youth gangs, and his example did much to popularise the style with young people generally. Even then, as the months wore on, the area that his kerchiefs had to cover increased formidably: these days, Hogan struggles into sight from under what looks like a borrowed red tablecloth. Sadly, it remains true that a lot of media conditioning will have to be undone if we are ever again to see, for instance, a bald candidate for President of the United States; and WWF promoters must have been wondering how long they could sustain a balding champion. When RR retired, it looked like the end for HH. Certainly, he must have been by this stage an immensely wealthy man: one of my colleagues insists that he saw an article on Hogan as a respected Swiss magnate in a Swiss magazine. Time for a much younger and exciting man, if not in the White House then at least in the WWF: where Hogan eventually lost his championship in 1989 to a painted bodybuilder fresh from a comic, the Ultimate Warrior.

Perhaps there would have been a problem with the Ultimate Warrior in the long term, as the trusty tabloids at the checkout intimated ('AIDS widow charges: Ultimate Warrior had gay sex with my hubby'). But what brought Hogan back into the championship scenario was the invasion of Kuwait, and the need for a resurgence of good old cherry-pie patriotism in the face of evil.

Evil was quickly personified in the form of one Sergeant Slaughter, who dethroned the Ultimate Warrior in the summer of 1990 and had his character entirely rewritten in a way made familiar by soap opera, where different writing teams regularly show brutal disregard for each other's plots. Sergeant Slaughter was originally a disaffected Rambo figure, an ex-Marine of mysterious antecedents. But as the Iraqi threat blossomed, he turned out instead to be an Iraqi sympathiser, wearing Iraqi uniform and medals, carrying the Iraqi flag into the ring, and suddenly gaining an Iraqi manager by the name of General Adnan who just happened to be a Saddam Hussein lookalike. Having hitherto shown little wrestling ability in his defeat of the Ultimate Warrior, Slaughter was now built up as a monstrous and dirty opponent, who took particular delight in defeating by foul means flag-waving but pitifully naïve American opponents. Late in 1990, as war in the Gulf looked more and more likely, it was announced that his opponent in the Los Angeles Wrestlemania was to be Hulk Hogan. After the fighting started in the Gulf, Hogan came into his birthright.

By this stage, sport and war had in any event become, as we used to say in my trade, inextricably intertwined. This was partly a deliberate effect of Bush's rhetoric: before the war even began, remarks of his like 'We're gonna kick some ass' and 'What we say, goes' were drawn self-consciously from the rhetoric of sports coaching rather than international statesmanship, and helped build his image as one who drew lines in sand rather than having it kicked in his face. The cult of yellow ribbons that swept America in the early days of the war owed its curious origins to a World War I song and a John Wayne movie, but the sight of ubiquitous yellow ribbons – worn by the staff of department stores by order, on every palm tree in Southern California, from car aerials and in gardens – brought to mind the iconography of football rather than war. The neon signs by the freeway that devoted one side to advertising and the other to civic solidarity replaced benedictions on our troops for the usual support for local teams. Before the sports event of the year, Superbowl xxv, commentators and some players took a good half-hour of prime time explaining that sport was not war and war was not sport, even though teams talked of killing their opponents and of fighting to win. It is doubtful whether this late induction into metaphoric language altogether undid the impact of several weeks' calculated confusion. Sport was aligned with other social rituals of American solidarity.

This was the atmosphere in which Hulk Hogan appeared on television to warn the world against Sergeant Slaughter, who was, he said, thoroughly unscrupulous and would stop at nothing. He expressed the fear that Slaughter would 'waste a million gallons of oil' and would 'send Scud missiles against my little Hulkomaniacs'. Hogan uses 'Hulkomaniacs' or 'Hulksters', always prefaced by 'my little . . .', to refer to his child supporters; and the group of children he specifically targeted at this time were the children of men and women serving in the Gulf. Hogan toured major bases ('I've been to Fort Bragg, I've been to Fort Worth, I've been to Fort Knox') actually meeting such children whose parents were several thousand miles away, as he put it, 'fighting for our freedom in the Gulf'. And he was able to vouch: 'My little Hulkomaniacs, they know why we're there, they know why their mommas and poppas are there, they understand.' Hogan even managed a pun – Sergeant Slaughter would 'meet a plethora of Patriots'; he and his little Hulksters would defeat him by 'our prayers, our vitamins and our Harley Davidsons'. (I have been unable to establish whether Hogan's reference to Harley Davidsons was sponsored and paid for or whether in some strange way Hogan conceived of motor bikes as co-bulwarks with God of the American way of life. Certainly, the reference to vitamins was commercial and self-serving: WWF-sponsored Hulk Hogan vitamins are on sale at Kids R Us stores as the Hulkster's 'Children's Chewies'.)

The peroration was magnificent. 'I swear by my little Hulksters, little Hulkomaniacs . . . I swear . . . by God: I will be the next heavyweight champion of the WWF.' The interview took place in the ring at a major WWF function, and the audience, claimed to be 50,000 strong, applauded wildly. It was then that Hogan called upon them to stand and join him in pledging their allegiance to the flag. (As he had already announced, somewhat over-excitedly, 'God, the flag, the family – I believe in that stuff'.) So the entire audience and Hogan together recited the well-worn ritual of the oath of allegiance.

There was no discernible border here between play and reality: otherwise the audience would have felt that they were being called on to travesty the oath of allegiance, and this surely was neither the intent nor the perception. For the observer, it was a disturbing experience. Sergeant Slaughter with his Iraqi flag had become a visible representative of Saddam Hussein, and as the ceremony made clear he stood to be condemned as a criminal because, in Hogan's words, he 'has desecrated our flag'. It was Slaughter's desecration that prompted the ritual of allegiance. Sergeant Slaughter signalled by sacrilege his greater blasphemy against the American way, a way he had formerly claimed to espouse and from which he was therefore apostate. At the bottom of the Hogan/Slaughter confrontation, then, was precisely the combination of offences that characterised the Rushdie affair: most notably, blasphemy and apostasy. And in one attack on Sergeant Slaughter, at a time when the Pentagon was defending a policy of disinformation, Hogan flung to the winds his loyalty to a constitution that incorporates a First Amendment and managed to sound like a contributor to either side of the Rushdie affair: 'There's one thing I don't understand about Sergeant Slaughter. I don't understand why he's protected here to be a traitor to our flag.'

Even if it is not possible to cordon off here the areas of fiction or play, it may be objected that I am placing undue emphasis on what was 'only sport'. But my point is that the war was sold as sport, even to the debating tricks that enabled Fitzwater, the White House spokesman, to reach a point where language defeats all purpose any user but a cynic might seek for it. I mean the shocking moment when, defending a massive allied strike on an underground installation in Baghdad that killed hundreds of civilian women and children sheltering there, Fitzwater claimed, like any adversarial heavyweight contender, that the incident showed 'Saddam Hussein has a much lower regard for the sanctity of human life than we do.' Because this was a television war, the consonance between Hulk Hogan and Marlin Fitzwater, as unabashed enthusiasts of war, outweighed contextual differences.

I know that if I had been the actor playing Sergeant Slaughter I might have asked for police protection after Hogan's appearances, but more because mad Americans have insanely free access to guns than because I would have feared a breakdown in the audience's perceptual frame: it was the entire production that fed the war effort, and the blasphemer Slaughter, with his allegorical type-name, was the privileged mainspring of the plot. I do not know how the WWF's patriotic pantomime went down in middle America, but I know of only one protest against such clowning on the grounds that it was offensive to real war combatants and casualties – and that ironically came from a television commentator, Howard Rosenberg, whose promotion to front-page war commentator in the *Los Angeles Times* tacitly accepted the war/sport/television nexus that also licensed the WWF. Does the coarse style of wrestling enable it to offend with vulgar truth? At about the same time as the first body bags were being brought back from the Gulf, the WWF introduced a new character called 'The Undertaker', who would literally bag his vanquished opponents, no doubt to the edification of bereaved little Hulkomaniacs.

On one level, it is pleasant to report that the WWF miscalculated. Early estimates for the duration of the war varied, but it was generally agreed that it would take some months. Just as the peace movement was left behind by the speed of the American victory, so was the WWF left in the air. When Wrestlemania vii was first advertised for Sunday, 24 March, the date would have looked excellent for the topical Hogan/Slaughter match, occurring one week after the beginning of Ramadan, when, according to most experts, allied troops would have had to suspend or scale down operations for the benefit of fasting Saudis. As it was, the wrestling championship bout took place more than four weeks after the end of the war had been announced by President Bush. Long enough, indeed, for the euphoria of victory to dissipate into suspicion, suspicion that America had stopped too early, that Saddam Hussein was going to retain power and live to fight another day, that, by inciting his subjects to rebel and then standing self-righteously by while the Iraqi army slaughtered Saddam's enemies, America may even have strengthened Saddam's position.

Hulk Hogan won back his championship, of course; that was a foregone conclusion. But WWF registered the growing reservations of its public by having him ambushed on the way back to the dressing room and beaten up humiliatingly in view of the cameras by an unrepentant Slaughter and an enlarged band of henchmen. Like the aftermath of the war, the whole episode was suddenly unsure of its tone and somewhat fearful of the future. In Hogan's comic vulnerability, hindsight might claim one of the first signs that Bush was on his way to losing the presidency.

But that was all still to come when Hulk Hogan gave the interview from which I have quoted here, an interview in the week beginning 27 January untroubled by doubts about justice or worries about performance. His was a piece with Bush's speech the day he ordered a start to the war, proud and excited; Bush's expression at times, caught by the camera, seemed to be a curious half-smirk. That night, 16/17 January, Bush spent in prayer in the White House with Billy Graham. (He was unable to call on his regular pastor, who was outside the White House taking part in an anti-war demonstration.) And the weekend of 1 to 3 February was proclaimed by Bush to be a national weekend of prayer for victory.

Is it blasphemous to wonder whether, that weekend, millions of pious Americans prayed for Hulk Hogan to become heavyweight champion of the WWF?

The Gulf

Barthes's account of wrestling by no means prepares its reader for the use of wrestling as a medium of war propaganda. The essay remains authoritative in its analysis of grandiloquence and its perceptions of the theatrical. It simply goes nowhere near far enough in imagining perversions of what it describes. This is not a matter for blame. No more than Bernard Shaw can be blamed for failing in his criticism of Wagnerian opera to anticipate subsequent Nazi use of it, does it make sense to reprove Barthes for failure to see what had not yet occurred. Yet with hindsight Barthes's essay does appear curiously resistant to the potential for propaganda in the medium, though he fleetingly recognised that potential in American wrestling. The shortfall points to the quite radical lack of context in the essay. Barthes describes wrestling as if it is always going to be, in essence, the same; his language is that of timeless archetypes, Good and Evil, Suffering and Defeat, rather than that of particular circumstance. So his essay broke new ground by giving one side of a picture. The other side is always a theoretical unknown, subject to ceaseless variation: time, place, detail, local knowledge. The complicity between audience and performers always embraces such local knowledge.

The WWF case is particularly clever because it did away with the distinction between reality and play, not of course absolutely but selectively. That is, audience and performers know that they are engaged in a symbolic representation of war, not the war itself: nobody shoots Sergeant Slaughter because sane people realise he is not Saddam Hussein but stands for him in a linked narrative context. So audience and performers agree in a typology: Hogan/Bush/America meets Slaughter/Saddam/Iraq. But as soon as this is agreed, wrestling itself becomes the figure of international relations. The agreement does away with the possibility of peace, for both play and reality are seen to be grounded in the necessity of fighting. To understand this satiric complicity between audience and performers we need more explanation than Barthes gives. One possible place to look for it would be in the work of Mikhail Bakhtin, and particularly in Bakhtin's treatment of carnival and the carnivalesque.

Bakhtin's work was done in Stalin's Russia, though it was not translated into English until 1968, and often takes the form of a veiled political allegory of resistance, so that it is not always easy to gauge the degree of literalism with which his judgements are offered. His work on carnival constitutes a study of Rabelais, and puts forward the idea of carnival as festive comedy, an amoral and often cruel humour that arises from the folk and finds its own measure, as Bakhtin puts it, 'in the public square'. Such humour gives rise to the idea of the grotesque – except, as Bakhtin insists, the grotesque is not an idea at all, nothing remotely conceptual, and is based not on the individual but in the social collective. Rabelais's work, after all, deals with giants: Gargantua is born when his mother has a massive bout of diarrhoea, he drowns hundreds of people every time he urinates, and when pilgrims accidentally stray into his mouth they speak of his teeth as mountains and of their cavities as potholes. Bakhtin sees this as a dynamic reworking of medieval traditions of folk humour, giving rise to the grotesque Body: a collective Body made up of thousands of people being born, dying and being reborn in comedy, a Body to be measured by the waste it produces. Bakhtin's use of the term carnival is of course drawn from pre-Lenten carnival festivity, and from other occasions, such as the Feast of Fools in the medieval Church, on which ordinary everyday values were allowed to be turned upside-down: a boy would be crowned bishop for the day, or an ass set upon the bishop's throne, and satirically topsy-turvy decrees would be enacted. Bakhtin was aware of the main objection to his use of carnival as subversive, that such days were officially licensed and therefore that their inversion of reality dissipated rebellious feelings and reinforced everyday hierarchies, of power and of values, at all other times of year. Hence his expansion beyond the occasions of carnival to accommodate the carnivalesque, which is an omnium gatherum of forms and genres derived from carnival, and of types of playful or non-official language such as Billingsgate. These various features, found in Rabelais, resist the power of official utterance, dethrone official pretentiousness, bring the high low and thwart absolute order by laughter. They construct a discourse that inverts power, for within it 'Truth is irrelevant'.[23]

Bakhtin's formulation has been influential for so long because it brings together and places on the same side, the side of liberal and agnostic angels, popular culture and postmodern discourse. In a more powerful and wide-ranging way than Barthes, it would help us see, for instance, why it might be progressive to study wrestling. Like Barthes's essay, then, it fails to predict what went wrong with the WWF. But its failure is complex and interesting. Bakhtin's writing is a fine analysis of certain types of satiric representation that may, after Bakhtin, be called carnivalesque. The popular pillorying of Saddam Hussein through media such as the WWF was carnivalesque, as was the construction of a demonically gargantuan, Muslim-killing, playboy Rushdie in the Pakistani movie *International Guerillas*. Bakhtin also supplies a series of finely tuned tools for describing postmodern writing, like Rushdie's, in which 'any vertically integrated understanding of reality' is systematically disrupted, even if we now choose to reinterpret Bakhtin as in the following revision: 'Not carnivalism but communalism, conviviality and subterfuge: Rabelais [Rushdie?] depicts the varied and sometimes hostile, sometimes masked encounter of heterogeneous communities and heterogeneous ideologies, not their amalgamation in a universally valid synthesis, low or high, popular or elite.'[24] Where Bakhtin fails, and his failure is subject to increasing analysis, is in reclaiming an actual social practice of carnival for his idealist view of the carnivalesque. The fact is that licensed social occasions for popular festivity, carnival, almost invariably serve the interests of the dominant and are neither an escape from nor any form of opposition to social power. The presentation of the Gulf War in the WWF, however extreme, is far from being a lonely exception. And in correcting Bakhtin's account of carnival to admit this, we may find too that truth is relevant after all; that in such carnivalesque travesty, as Kinser argues of 'Rabelais' fantasy', references to reality are intensified rather than confused. That intensification is what made Hulk Hogan a potent evangelist of war.

The success of the WWF ploy depended on television for its speed and access to a mass public. This does not mean, however, that the effect is somehow inherent in the nature of television and our exposure to it, as is implied in Jean Baudrillard's postmodern declaration of the death of reality. Baudrillard's response to the Gulf War, which failed to stop short of self-parody, has been subjected to extended and angry scrutiny by Christopher Norris.[25] For Baudrillard, we live in hyperreality, in which our perceptions, formed by the constantly moving images of television and advertising, are compounds of truth and falsehood.[26] In a notorious and misunderstood passage, Baudrillard discusses the Holocaust as hyperreality, as a series of images generating television mini-series rather than as a historical actuality – an uncomfortable example, because Baudrillard seems to be flirting with the views of right-wing revisionist and anti-Semitic pseudo-historians. In fact, Baudrillard does not maintain that the Holocaust never took place but that its sole existence now is as hyperreal imagery. This is both perceptive and wrong. Perceptive because it addresses the other main effect of confusing war with sport, which is to sanitise images of war brought by the same television that brings us Hulk Hogan and the Superbowl. Such sanitising suits governments, who would minimise casualties and tell lies about the brutality of war. Wrong in that hyperreality is not inherent in the medium or natural in the viewer or a necessary aspect of postmodern existence: those who care about the Holocaust or war deaths or Muslim deaths in protests against *The Satanic Verses* will have their feelings intensified, not confused or diminished, by television images of them.

The sense of hyperreality is something that power seeks to induce, and Baudrillard is in danger of treating it without conscience, metaphysically, in the manner of Barthes on wrestling. Baudrillard's work naturalises power rather than emancipating its subjects. It is theory for admen: don't worry about truth, buy.

Like Barthes, Baudrillard seems overwhelmed by what he calls the banality of America, a banality he seems to view absurdly as all of a piece, Las Vegas neither more nor less real or hyperreal than the desert in which it rises. Television in Baudrillard's work often seems like a primal force rather than an industrial site of material and ideological production. Another way of saying this is that Baudrillard treats television like Barthes treats wrestling and Bakhtin treats carnival, as susceptible to generalisation without further reference to particularity of context or material contingency.

They are very different writers: Baudrillard at his best hypnotic and impersonal; Barthes ever humane but enveloped in the structure of a system that is at bottom aesthetically and hermetically conceived; Bakhtin staking out the most important ground and expressing the best idealisms of a pluralist Marxist intellectual. But Bakhtin's view of popular festivity is over-idealised, and he treats it as if it were unmediated; his view of the rapprochement between the learned and the popular in the carnivalesque is hopelessly over-optimistic, as it had to be if his own writing were a valid socialist project. For all their differences, the three writers' accounts seem united in their political naïvety when set against the manipulation of play or carnival in the example I have given: the use of television wrestling to increase public support for government policy and State power.

There is work going on in my profession that prevents a thoroughly sombre conclusion about our capacity to visualise real material circumstances and respond to them politically. Feminist studies, and now many lesbian and gay studies, are committed to the rehabilitation of material conditions, and show an acute consciousness of what it is to be on the receiving end of carnivalesque mockery. It remains to be seen whether the profession's institutional paradoxes will in the long term mute their impact, cause punches to be pulled or crucial political connections to go unmade – as is the case with the writers I have discussed. I did not select them rhetorically, to criticise them, but because theirs would be widely accepted as among the best work we have which is relevant to the issues raised here.

There is one more immediate problem arising directly from my critique of Barthes and Bakhtin, and implicit in my rejection of hyperreality as an essential modern condition. In modifying these views in order to provide a satisfactory account of WWF wrestling as war propaganda, I have destroyed their justification for fiction. All three offer a privileged area, though not exactly the same area, in which questions of truth are either irrelevant or inappropriate. None has survived in my analysis. It follows that the easiest defence of Rushdie ('you can't respond to fiction as if it were true') is unavailable, for the entire performance in the World Wrestling Federation is premised upon its opposite.

It is in various scenarios of fiction and truth, of popular and learned, of public and power, that I have grounded here connections between the Gulf War and the Rushdie affair. The central connection is anything but oblique: blasphemy. Sergeant Slaughter, the carnivalised Saddam Hussein, is accused of blasphemy against the American way as represented by the oath of allegiance and emblematised by the flag; the carnivalised Rushdie is accused of blasphemy against the prophet and the Qu'ran. And blasphemy, which is a function of carnival and so of power, operates with insidious economy, for it conflates positive and negative, one's reasons for dying and one's reasons for killing, into one symbol. To think of the Qu'ran is at once to love God and hate Rushdie; the undoing of Saddam Hussein is imprinted on Old Glory. It is awesomely simple, circular and closed. It is a genuinely clever discovery.

The last link in this discursive chain linking the Rushdie *fatwa* with the selling of the Gulf War is therefore material and historical. I suggest that in circumstantial actuality one was a rehearsal for the other: the outcry against Rushdie taught American propagandists the uses of blasphemy.

The notion would horrify most participants in the Rushdie affair, on either side of it, but probably would not overly disconcert the Iranians, for whom the Gulf War brought revenge on Saddam Hussein, or our allies the Saudis, who were paymasters of initial Muslim activity against Rushdie in Britain. The vast rage against Rushdie taught America a lesson it had forgotten – the amount of energy that is released when positive and negative forces are conjoined in the one symbolic drive of blasphemy.

And America watched, as Britain agonised over community relations, human rights and the status of an archaic law: while argument continued over book-burning and the desirability of a paperback, America bought nearly one million hardbacks and quietly conceptualised a forgotten type of hatred. The shock that the violence of Muslim anger caused, and what was certainly seen to be a fanatical upholding of an enemy's *fatwa*, allowed the re-emergence in America of crude racist and Orientalist stereotypes, and made it incalculably easier for the administration one year later to present itself as paying back Arabs in kind. I do not know how these claims might be verified – though they arise from my memory of seeing Lebanese students harassed on a University of California campus before the outbreak of fighting – but I cannot see that there is anything implausible or even surprising about them. Texts and events have their mutual influences – one way or another.

CONCLUSION

In this book I have sought to characterise blasphemy from the standpoint of orthodoxy. For the discourse of blasphemy is one devised and practised by orthodoxy. Blasphemy is an orthodoxy's way of demonising difference in order to perpetrate violence against it. That is what it does, and all that it is for, assuring orthodoxy of its own identity. It can be resisted by those who would respect difference or celebrate it, or effect a yet Utopian ideal of living without violence or fear in communities held together by their enjoyment of difference. One option for resistance is to blaspheme. But blasphemers are particularly vulnerable. They seek to reverse a discourse that is already made, and to use a weapon framed by their enemy.

Blasphemy is therefore a discourse that includes those who purport to be offended by it. Literature, representation and reading is potentially blasphemous. That is why blasphemy is so complex, and why it is so vital to understand its history. This study has aimed to be true to that complexity, and to call for a dialogue both sides will find difficult. I should like my closing comments to set out a negotiating position.

I have yet to find a single legal case of blasphemy that was worth bringing. All the cases known to me are either vexatious, or tyrannical, or they punish people who should have been helped. All three types are therefore oppressive. Current suggestions, that blasphemy laws in Britain, Australia and elsewhere be replaced by a law based on public order, fail to understand the historical role of provocation: organised breaches of public order have commonly been used to force prosecution, to suppress difference and displace people. Blasphemy, however defined, does not murder or cause physical wounds, and if it does not incite them it should go unpunished. The very ruptures of community that the issue of blasphemy reveals are also ruptures in its law. We have only one real choice, to rebuild communities or commit institutionalised violence. 'What we want is intellectual hospitality. Let the world talk.'

What has been frightening is to have realised the extent to which a violent (and, one might have thought, discredited) discourse of blasphemy still functions in our world. Blasphemy seems to be an old and faded thread: once pulled, it unravels much of our culture. In this book, I found it in the Bible and have taken it all the way to the wrestling ring and the theatre of war. These are not altogether surprising destinations. They are where I should like to leave blasphemy; they are where it has always belonged.

NOTES

CHAPTER 1

1. Levy (1981): 337–8.
2. Reynolds (1887): 12.
3. Coleman (1974): 100. The words are those of Anne Lennon in Sydney in 1932. She was fined £10.
4. Wright (1817): 26.
5. *Ibid.*: 26–7.
6. Holyoake (1851): v.
7. Levy (1981): 6.
8. Post (1988): 313.
9. Ingersoll (1888): 63, 22.
10. Scarman, quoted in Green (1990): 10.
11. Levy (1981): 222; see generally Noonan (1987).
12. Holyoake (1851): 62.
13. Blanc and Lopez (1974); Lefranc (1974).
14. *A Christian memento* (1814).
15. *A Help to a National Reformation* (1706): 27–8.
16. See below pp. 23–36.
17. Doolittle (1614): 61.
18. Marlorat (1570?): 264.
19. *The Strange Case . . . Anthony Paneter* (1614): B2.
20. *The Blasphemers Punishment* (1797).
21. Downame (1609): 10.
22. *A Discourse* (1698): 67–8.
23. Doolittle (1614): 4.
24. Hooton (1709): A1.
25. Citations are from the *Middle English Dictionary*.
26. Fowles (1698).
27. Moore (1985): 69–70.
28. Ginzburg (1990): 150.
29. *The Romish mass-book* (1683). See Chapter 4 below.
30. Stallybrass and White (1986): 25.
31. Foucault (1978): 84.
32. Laurence (1990): 347; see also Mack (1987).
33. Bynum (1991): 195.
34. Tanner (1977).
35. Hill (1987): 398.
36. *A Discourse against Profane Swearing* (1698): 34.
37. Ginzburg (1967): 16, 187.

38. Quoted in Schroeder (1919a): 169.
39. Cohn (1976). See Chapters 2 and 3 below.
40. à Wood (1820): 732.
41. Pepys (1663): IV, 209–10.
42. Quoted in Craig (1963): 22–5.
43. Friedman (1987): 84.
44. Hill (1987): 401.
45. Friedman (1987): 99, 112, 117–18; Smith (1983): 161–86; Smith (1989).
46. Levy (1981): 313–14.
47. Field (1815): 29.
48. *A Full and True Account* (1678): title page.
49. Blanc and Lopez (1974): 21, 54–60.
50. Wilson (1988): 200.
51. Friedman (1987): 89.
52. Smith (1983): 19.
53. Sade (1965): 142.
54. Friedman (1987): 104, 117.
55. Smith (1983): 14.
56. Bataille (1962): 127–8.
57. Cohn (1976): 105.
58. Smith (1989): 8, summarising Davis (1986).
59. Smith (1989): 9.
60. Ginzburg (1982): 4.
61. On Mandeville, see Greenblatt (1991).
62. Eco (1983): 78, 79–80.
63. Camille (1992): 10.
64. Campbell (1988): 18.
65. Defoe (1726): 143–4.
66. Glendinnen (1987).
67. Alexander (1976): 89.
68. Ignatieff (1984), quoted in Scarry (1990): 890; see also Delumeau (1986).

Chapter 2

1. [Castellio] (1935): 242.
2. Gellner (1992).
3. Scarry (1986).
4. Levy (1981); Kelly (1972); Chadwick (1960a) and (1967); Daniélou (1964).
5. Levy (1981): 93–4.
6. Toon and Spiceland (1980): 50, citing Wiles (1967); Lonergan (1976).
7. Layton (1987): 47.
8. Bainton (1953): 3.
9. *Ibid.*: 49.
10. Willis (1877): 307.
11. *Table Talk*, 3 January 1834, quoted in Wilbur (1945): 185.
12. Willis (1877): 237.

13. Bainton (1953): 236–7.
14. Vico (1968).
15. C[rane], R[ichard] (1660): title page.
16. Ashby (1699): A2. Other references as in Bibliography.
17. Cheyney (1676): 2.
18. Faldo (1673): title page.
19. Bugg (1700): xii–xiii.
20. Levy (1981): 263.
21. *Reliquiae Baxterianae* (London, 1696), quoted in Brailsford (1927).
22. Davis (1986): 90.
23. *State Trials* (1656): 815. Trial details from this volume unless otherwise stated.
24. Many of Nayler's tracts have no pagination. Quotation from the final page of *Love to the Lost* (1656a). For other references, see Bibliography.
25. Bittle (1986): 106.
26. Levy (1981): 195, 269.
27. Brailsford (1927): 127.
28. Bittle (1986): 103.
29. Reproduced as Frontispiece to Fogelklau (1931); Bittle (1986): 109–10.
30. Levy (1981): 275.
31. Moore (1985): 86.
32. *Ibid.*: 64.
33. Brailsford (1927): 139, 135.
34. Levy (1981): 282; Brailsford (1927): 134. Quoted from Carlyle's *Cromwell*.
35. *State Trials* (1656): 818.
36. Brailsford (1927): 154.
37. Quoted in Brailsford (1927): 154–5.
38. *Memoirs of the Life* (1719): 5.
39. Brailsford (1927): 154.
40. Levy (1980): 43.
41. Breed (1948): 56, 59–60.
42. Levy (1981): 61; see also Miller (1990).
43. Cohn (1967): xv.
44. *Ibid.*: xi–xii.
45. Dollimore (1991): 24.
46. Harvey (1976): 127.
47. Blinzler (1959): 4.
48. Winter (1974): xi.
49. Smallwood (1976): 338.
50. Lewis (1988): 190–1, 193.

CHAPTER 3

1. Craun (1983). Levy does not argue that heresy and blasphemy were interchangeable for the medieval Church; see also Casagrande (1987).
2. Gray (1985): 11.
3. *Ibid.*

  4. Gilman (1991): 18–19.
  5. Gurevich (1988): 64–70.
  6. Moore (1985): 183.
  7. Gurevich (1988): 50.
  8. Roth (1978): 77.
  9. Obolensky (1948): 266.
 10. *Ibid.*
 11. Wakefield (1974): 195–8.
 12. *Ibid.*
 13. Roth (1978): 8.
 14. Cohen (1982): 227–9.
 15. Tanner (1977).
 16. Levy (1981): 90, 134; Wilbur (1945).
 17. Levy (1981): 129.
 18. Cohen (1982).
 19. Dundes (1991).
 20. Cohen (1982): 28.
 21. Shachar (1974): 13, 25.
 22. Stallybrass and White (1986): 27–79.
 23. Paris, 27–8.
 24. Blanc and Lopez (1974); Lefranc (1974).
 25. Keen (1986): 14.
 26. Leff (1986): 118.
 27. Heyworth (1968).
 28. Wycliff (1966); Kenny (1986).
 29. Hudson (1978): 29.
 30. Roth (1978): 41; Cohen (1982); Richards (1991): 95.
 31. Davis (1970).
 32. Deleuze and Guattari (1983) and (1987); Stallybrass and White (1986).
 33. Deleuze and Guattari (1983): 144, 153.
 34. See above, pp. 51–6; Marin (1989): 3–28.
 35. Rossi-Landi (1975).
 36. Lawton (1985): 17–35.
 37. Goux (1990): 24, 118–19, 129, 211.
 38. Patterson (1991): 367–421. Rushdie reference: *Sydney Morning Herald*,
     29 December 1990.
 39. Camille (1989): 90.
 40. Russell (1971): 43–51; Wakefield (1974): 43–7.
 41. Russell (1971): 43.
 42. Benjamin (1973): 244.
 43. Lawton (1992): 111–12; Lochrie (1991): 203–35.
 44. Wycliff (1966): 1.
 45. On this issue see Lawton (1992): 95.
 46. Kempe (1985): 126–7.
 47. Bynum (1990): 151–79; Lawton (1992): 112.
 48. Irigaray (1985): 191–2.
 49. Obelkevich, Roper and Samuel (1987): 189.

50. Nancy (1991): x.
51. Le Roy Ladurie (1978).
52. Justice (forthcoming).

CHAPTER 4

1. *A Special Report* (1856): 16. Attorney-General's submission, supposedly based on Chief Justice Prisot. But see below, p. 127.
2. Calder-Marshall (1972): 5.
3. See above, Chapter 1, pp. 8–9.
4. Manuel and Manuel (1979): 222–42; Bruno (1964). For Menocchio, see Chapter 1, pp. 36–42.
5. Crashaw (1641): A2.
6. Dering (1641): 54.
7. *The Romish mass-book* (1683): 43, 48.
8. Burke and Caldwell (1968): 253.
9. Dawes (1694): 26.
10. Assheton (1694): A1.
11. Atterbury (1706): 1.
12. Howe (1694): 81–2.
13. Brown (1797): 12.
14. Levy (1981): 199–205; Wilbur (1945): 191–208.
15. Levy (1981): 205–7, 213–23; Wilbur (1945): 191.
16. Schroeder (1919a): 308–11.
17. Levy (1981): 322; Wilbur (1945): 229.
18. Frend (1793): xviii.
19. *Ibid.*: liii.
20. [Frend] (1788): 7.
21. Wilbur (1945): 313.
22. Levy (1981): 308–12.
23. Levy (1973): 127; Schroeder (1919a): 446–7.
24. Levy (1973): 95.
25. Schroeder (1919a): 435.
26. Wolkovich (1973): 81.
27. Porter (1813): 78.
28. Cradlebaugh (1877): 13
29. Calder-Marshall (1972): 13.
30. Emlyn (1719): xx.
31. Perceval [attrib.] (1840).
32. Wilbur (1945): 246, from Benjamin Hoadly, *Works* (London, 1773), 1, 357.
33. Bonner (1912, 1913, 1934).
34. Calder-Marshall (1972): 5.
35. Holyoake (1851): 60.
36. Levy (1973): 189.
37. Hetherington (1840): 16.
38. Coleman (1974): 27.

39. *Ibid.*: 88.
40. Reynolds (1887): 2.
41. Ingersoll (1888): 64.
42. Doctorow (1971): 75.
43. Jauss (1982): 327.
44. Nancy (1991): 135.
45. Quoted in *ibid.*: 144.
46. Schroeder (1919b): 11.
47. Sangharakshita (1978): 24.
48. Weitzmann (1983): 8.
49. Saadawi (1990): viii.

CHAPTER 5

1. Dollimore (1991): 18.
2. Deleuze and Guattari (1983): 109.
3. On Freud's system of reading, see Møller (1991); Certeau (1986): 7–29.
4. Wolf-Man (1971): 335; Sprengnetter (1990).
5. Wolf-Man (1971): 340.
6. Abraham and Torok (1986).
7. Deleuze and Guattari (1987): 28.
8. Gilman (1991): 87.
9. Wolf-Man (1971): 268.
10. Gilman (1991): 82.
11. Freud (1911).
12. Quotations are from Freud (1985).
13. Certeau (1988): 327.
14. Freud (1985): 51.
15. Rushdie (1988): 432.

CHAPTER 6

1. Bhabha (1992): 61. Cf. Spivak (1989).
2. Rushdie (1988): 380.
3. *Ibid.*: 533.
4. During (1992): 84, quoting from Nietzsche (as in Klossowski [1988]: xxiv) and from Foucault (1964): 448; see also Klossowski (1988): xxvi.
5. Green (1990): 12.
6. Editorial from *Star* newspaper, January 1989.
7. Rushdie (1988): 214–15.
8. See Chapter 4, pp. 140–1.
9. Pipes (1990): 102.
10. Bannerman (1988): 14.
11. Johns (1989): 8.
12. Apollinaire (1991): 33.

13. Kazi (1989): 2.
14. Lewis (1973): 228.
15. Deleuze and Guattari (1986): 23.
16. Bhabha (1990): 317.
17. Bailey (1991): 144.
18. See especially Sardar (1990); Sardar and Wyn Davies (1990).
19. Kazi (1989): 1.
20. Barthes (1973): 1, 5, 14.
21. Thody (1977): 5.
22. Rushdie: interview.
23. Bakhtin (1968).
24. Kinser (1990): 255.
25. Norris (1992).
26. Baudrillard (1983) and (1990).

BIBLIOGRAPHY

Abraham, Nicolas and Maria Torok (1986). *Wolf-Man's Magic Word: A cryptonymy*. Trans. Nicholas Rand. Minneapolis: University of Minnesota Press.

Alexander, Michael (ed.) (1976). *Discovering the New World*. New York: Harper & Row; London: London Editions.

The Anatomy of Dr. Gauden's idolized nonsence and blasphemy, in his pretended Analysis, or setting forth the true sense of the covenant, that is to say, of that sacred covenant taken by the Parliament . . . (1660). London.

Anderson, Benedict (1991). *Imagined Communities: Reflections on the origin and spread of nationalism*. Rev. edn. London and New York: Verso.

Anderson, George K. (1965). *The Legend of the Wandering Jew*. Hanover, NH: Brown University Press.

Anees, Munawar A. (comp.) (1989). *The Kiss of Judas: Affairs of a brown sahib*. Kuala Lumpur: Quill Publishers.

Apollinaire, Guillaume (1991). *The Heresiarch and Co.* Cambridge, MA: Exact Change.

Ashby, Richard (1699). *The True Light Owned and Vindicated, and the Believers in It Defended: and Blasphemy and Blasphemers justly detected*. London: T. Sowle.

Assheton, William (1694). *A discourse against blasphemy: being a conference with M. S. concerning 1. the rudeness of atheistical discourse, 2. the certainty and eternity of hell-torments, 3. the truth and authority of the Holy Scriptures: . . .* London: T. B. and Richard Simpson.

Atterbury, Francis (1706). *The Axe laid to the Root of Christianity: or, A specimen of the prophaneness and blasphemy that abounds in some late writings*. London: J. Morphew.

à Wood, Anthony (1820). *Athenæ Oxonienses: An exact history of all the writers and bishops who have had their education in the University of Oxford*. London: Reprints; New York: Burt Franklin, 1967.

Bailey, Richard W. (1991). *Images of English: A cultural history of the language*. Ann Arbor: University of Michigan Press.

Bainton, Roland H. (1953). *Hunted Heretic: The life and death of Michael Servetus 1511–1553*. Boston: Beacon Press.

Bakhtin, Mikhail Mikhailovich (1968). *Rabelais and His World*. Trans. Helene Iswolsky. Cambridge, MA: MIT Press.

Bammel, Ernst (ed.) (1970). *The Trial of Jesus: Cambridge studies in honour of C. F. D. Moule*. Naperville, IL: A. R. Allenson.

Bannerman, Patrick (1988). *Islam in Perspective: A guide to Islamic society, politics and law*. London: Routledge/Royal Institute of International Affairs.

Barbour, Hugh (1964). *The Quakers in Puritan England*. New Haven and London: Yale University Press.

Barron, Anne (1989). 'Legal discourse and the colonisation of the self in the modern state'. In Carty (1989): 107–25.

Barthes, Roland (1973). *Mythologies*. Trans. Annette Lavers. St Albans: Paladin.

Bataille, Georges (1962). *Erotism: Death & sensuality*. Trans. Mary Dalwood. New York: Walker. Reprinted 1990 San Francisco: City Lights Books.

Bataille, Georges (1973). *Literature and Evil*. Trans. Alastair Hamilton. London: Calder & Boyars (Signature Series). Reprint, New York: Marion Boyars, 1985.

Bataille, Georges (1989). *Theory of Religion*. Trans. Robert Hurley. New York: Zone. Originally published 1973.

Baudrillard, Jean (1983). *Simulations*. Trans. Paul Foss, Paul Patton and Philip Beitchman. New York: Semiotext(e).

Baudrillard, Jean (1990). *Revenge of the Crystal: A Baudrillard reader*. London: Pluto Press.

Benjamin, Walter (1973). 'The work of art in the age of mechanical reproduction'. In *Illuminations*. Ed. Hannah Arendt. London: Fontana: 219–53.

Beverley, John (1793). *The trial of William Frend, M.A. and fellow of Jesus College, Cambridge: In the vice-chancellor's court. For writing and publishing a pamphlet entitled Peace and union, recommended to the associated bodies . . .* Cambridge: F. Hodson and J. Deighton.

Bhabha, Homi K. (1990). 'DissemiNation: Time, narrative and the margins of the modern nation'. In Homi K. Bhabha (ed.), *Nation and Narration*. New York and London: Routledge: 291–322.

Bhabha, Homi K. (1992). 'Postcolonial authority and postmodern guilt'. In Grossberg *et al.* (1992): 56–68.

Bittle, William G. (1988). *James Naylor, 1618–1660: The Quaker indicted by Parliament*. York, England: W. Sessions; Richmond, IN: Friends United Press.

Blanc, Nicole, and Marie-Claude Lopez (1974). 'Moeurs et religion en Espagne au XVIIIe siècle: L'affaire de Teruel.' Dissertation, Toulouse.

Blanchot, Maurice (1988). *The Unavowable Community*. New York: Station Hill.

The Blasphemers Punishment, or, the cries of the Son of God to the whole world. Being a true account of one Eliz. Dover (1791). London.

Les Blasphèmes de la Fausse Lettre de Chelles (1729). Paris: n.p.

Blinzler, Josef (1959). *The Trial of Jesus: The Jewish and Roman proceedings against Jesus Christ described and assessed from the oldest accounts*. Trans. from the 2nd revised and enlarged edn, Isabel and Florence McHugh. Westminster: Newman.

Bloch, Howard (1977). *Medieval French Literature and Law*. Berkeley and Los Angeles: University of California Press.

Blom-Cooper, Louis (1981). *Blasphemy: An ancient wrong or a modern right?* London: Essex Hall Bookshop.

Bonner, Hypatia (Bradlaugh) (ed.) (1912). *Penalties Upon Opinion: Or, some records of the laws of heresy and blasphemy*. London: Watts.

Bonner, Hypatia (Bradlaugh) (ed.) (1913). *Penalties Upon Opinion: Or, some records of the laws of heresy and blasphemy*. 2nd revised and enlarged edn. London: Watts.

Bonner, Hypatia (Bradlaugh) (ed.) (1934). *Penalties Upon Opinion; Or, some records of the laws of heresy and blasphemy*. 3rd edn, revised and enlarged by F. W. Read. London: Watts.

Bordoni, Francesco (1703). *Opus posthumum, de recenti primo in lucem proditur: quod consistit in duas appendices ad Manuale consultorum in causis Sancti Officii contra haereticam pravitatem occurrentibus . . . in prima diffusa ostenditur . . .* Parma: Paul Monti.

Bourdieu, Pierre (1990). *The Logic of Practice*. Trans. Richard Nile. Cambridge: Polity Press.

Brailsford, Mabel (1927). *A Quaker from Cromwell's Army*. London: Bell.

Brandon, S. G. F. (1968). *The Trial of Jesus of Nazareth*. New York: Stein and Day.

Breed, David K. (1948). *The Trial of Christ from a Legal and Scriptural Viewpoint: With a foreword by Clarence Edward Macartney*. St Louis: Thomas Law Book Co.

Brennan, Timothy (1989). *Salman Rushdie and the Third World: Myths of the nation*. London: Macmillan.

Brooke, Rosalind and Christopher (1984). *Popular Religion in the Middle Ages*. New York and London: Thames & Hudson.

Brooks, Peter (1985). *Reading for the Plot: Design and intention in narrative*. New York: Vintage Books.

Brown, Harold O. J. (1984). *Heresies*. New York: Doubleday.

Brown, John (1780). *The absurdity and perfidy of all authoritative toleration of gross heresy, blasphemy, idolatry, popery, in Britain, in two letters to a friend, in which the doctrine of the Westminster confession of . . .* Glasgow: John Bryce.

Brown, John (1797). *A Compend of the Letters of the Reverend Mr John Brown, late minister of the gospel in Hoddington, on the Authoritative toleration of gross heresy*. Preface by William Fletcher. Stirling [no publisher named].

Brown, Judith C. (1986). *Immodest Acts*. Oxford: Oxford University Press.

Brown, Peter (1988). *The Body and Society: Men, women and sexual renunciation in early Christianity*. New York: Columbia University Press.

Brown, Peter (1992). *Power and Persuasion in Late Antiquity: Towards a Christian Empire*. Madison: University of Wisconsin Press.

Bruno, Giordano (1964). *The Expulsion of the Triumphant Beast*. Trans. Arthur D. Imerti. Lincoln, NE, and London: University of Nebraska.

Bugg, Francis (1700). *A modest defence of my book entituled, Quakerism expos'd: as also of my broad sheet: with a scheme of the Quakers yearly synod, and other books presented anno 1699 to the Parliament*. London: R. Janeway, Jun. and J. Robinson.

Burke, Joseph, and C. Caldwell (1968). *Hogarth: The complete engravings*. London: Thames and Hudson.

Burke, Peter (1978). *Popular Culture in Early Modern Europe*. London: Temple Smith.

Bynum, Caroline Walker (1990). *Fragmentation and Redemption*. New York: Zone.

Cabell, James Branch (1919). *Jurgen*. London: Bodley Head.

Calder-Marshall, Arthur (1972). *Lewd, Blasphemous, and Obscene: Being the trials and tribulations of sundry founding fathers of today's alternative societies*. London: Hutchinson.

Camille, Michael (1989). *The Gothic Idol: Ideology and image-making in medieval art*. Cambridge: Cambridge University Press.

Camille, Michael (1992). *Images on the Edge: The margins of medieval art*. London: Reaktion Books.

Campbell, Mary B. (1988). *The Witness and the Other World: Exotic European travel writing 400–1600*. Ithaca and London: Cornell University Press.

Carty, Anthony (ed.) (1989). *Post-Modern Law: Enlightenment, revolution and the death of man*. Edinburgh: Edinburgh University Press.

Casagrande, Carla and Silvana Vecchio (1987). *I peccat; della limgua: disciplina ed etica della parola nella cultura medievale*. Rome: Instituto della Enciclopedia Italiana.

[Castellio, Sebastian] (1935). *Concerning Heresies*. Ed. Roland H. Bainton. Reprint, New York: Octagon Books.

Catchpole, David R. (1971). *The Trial of Jesus: A study in the Gospels and Jewish historiography from 1770 to the present day*. Leiden: E. J. Brill.

Cavalca, Domenico (1552). *Pugi lingua. Il libro molto vtile al fidele Christiano, intitolato Pungi lingua, nelquale trattansi tutti i peccati che procedono de olla, co alcuni estempli, iquali dimostrano il guiditio de dio sopra alcui huomini*. Venetia: M. Sesta.

Certeau, Michel de (1984). *The Practice of Everyday Life*. Trans. Steven Rendall. Berkeley and Los Angeles: University of California Press.

Certeau, Michel de (1986). *Heterologies: Discourse on the other*. Trans. Brian Massumi. Minneapolis: University of Minnesota Press.

Certeau, Michel de (1988). 'The fiction of history: The writing of *Moses and Monotheism*'. In *The Writing of History*. Trans. Tom Conley. New York: Columbia University Press: 308–54.

Chadwick, Henry (1960a). 'Faith and order at the Council of Nicaea'. *Harvard Theological Review* 53: 171–92.

Chadwick, Henry (1960b). *History and Thought of the Early Church*. London: Variorum Reprint, 1982.

Chadwick, Henry (1967). *The Early Church*. Penguin History of the Church I. Harmondsworth: Penguin.

Chakrabarty, Dipesh (1992). 'Postcoloniality and the artifice of history: Who speaks for "Indian" Pasts?' *Representations* 37: 1–26.

Charest, Gilles (1980). *Sacrés et blasphèmes québecois; illustré par Girard*. Montreal: Québec/Amerique.

Chaucer, Geoffrey (1987). *Works: The Riverside Chaucer*. Ed. Larry D. Benson. New York: Houghton Mifflin.

Cheyney, John (1676). *A Skirmish upon Quakerism*. London: R. Butler.

C[heyney], J[ohn] (1677). *Quakerism proved to be gross blasphemy and anti-Christian heresie*. London: Richard Butler.

Cheyney, John (1678). *A Vindication of Oaths and Swearing (against Quakers)*. London: R. Butler.

Choueiri, Youssef M. (1990). *Islamic Fundamentalism*. Boston: Twayne.

A Christian memento: to which are added observations on some of the prevalent amusements and vices of the present day (1816). Philadelphia: Benjamin & Thomas Kite.

Christine de Pisan (1983). *The Book of the City of Ladies*. Trans. Earl Jeffrey Richards. London: Pan Books.

'Christophilus' (pseud.) (1821). *Vindiciae Britannicae. Christianity interested in the dismissal of ministers. A vindication of the people from the charge of blasphemy, and a defence of the freedom of the press. In six letters, addressed to William Wilberforce*. London: W. Simpkin and R. Marshall.

Cohen, Jeremy (1982). *The Friars and the Jews: The evolution of medieval anti-Judaism*. Ithaca: Cornell University Press.

Cohn, Haim (1967). *The Trial and Death of Jesus*. New York and London: Harper & Row.

Cohn, Norman (1976). *Europe's Inner Demons*. St Albans: Granada.

Coleman, Peter (1974). *Obscenity, Blasphemy, Sedition: 100 years of Censorship in Australia*. Revised edn. Sydney: Angus & Robertson.

Consoli, Antonino (1957). *Il reato di vilipendio della religione cattolica*. Milan: A. Giuffre.

Cradlebaugh, John (1877). *Mormonism. A doctrine that embraces polygamy, adultery, incest, perjury, blasphemy, robbery, and murder. Speech of Judge Cradlebaugh in the House of Representatives in 1863*. Salt Lake City.

Craig, Alec (1963). *Suppressed Books: A history of the conception of literary obscenity*. New York and Cleveland: World Publishing.

C[rane], R[ichard] (1660). *Something spoken in Vindication and Clearing of the People of God called Quakers*. London: Richard Crane.

Crashaw, William (1641). *The bespotted leavite: whose gospell is full of blasphemy against the blood of Christ . . .* London: Bar. Alsop.

Craun, Edwin D. (1983). *'"Inordinata Locutio"*: Blasphemy in pastoral literature'. *Traditio* 39: 125–62.

Daniélou, Jean (1964). *The Development of Christian Doctrine before the Coucil of Nicaea* (3 vols). Trans. and ed. John A. Baker. London: Darton, Longman and Todd.

Darnton, Robert (1984). *The Great Cat Massacre and Other Episodes in French Cultural History*. Harmondsworth: Penguin.

Davis, J. C. (1986). *Fear, Myth and History: The Ranters and the historians*. Cambridge: Cambridge University Press.

Davis, Natalie Zelmon (1975). *Society and Culture in Early Modern France*. Stanford: Stanford University Press.

Davis, Norman (ed.) (1970). *Non-Cycle Plays and Fragments*. EETS ss 1. Oxford: Oxford University Press.

[Dawes, Sir William, Archbishop of York] (1694). *An Anatomy of Atheisme: A Poem*. London: Thomas Speed.

Deacon, John (1656). *The Grand Imposter Examined, or, The Life, Tryal and Examinations of James Nayler, The Seduced and Seducing Quaker, with the Manner of his Riding into Bristol*. London: Henry Brome.

Defoe, Daniel (1726). *The Political History of the Devil*. London: T. Warner.

Defoe, Daniel (1728). *A System of Magick: or, a History of the Black Art*. London: Andrew Miller.

Deleuze, Gilles, and Felix Guattari (1983). *Anti-Oedipus: Capitalism and schizophrenia*. Trans. Robert Hurley. Minneapolis: University of Minnesota Press.

Deleuze, Gilles, and Felix Guattari (1986). *Kafka: Toward a minor literature*. Trans. Dana Polan. Minneapolis: University of Minnesota Press.

Deleuze, Gilles, and Felix Guattari (1987). *A Thousand Plateaus*. Trans. Brian Massumi. Minneapolis: University of Minnesota Press.

Del Re, Michele C. (1982). *Culti emergenti e diritto penale*. [Naples]: Jovene.

Delumeau, Jean (1989). *Injures et blasphèmes*. Paris: Editions Imago.

Delumeau, Jean (1991). *Sin and Fear: The emergence of Western guilt culture, 13th–18th centuries*. New York: St Martin's Press.

Dering, Sir Edward (1641). *The fower cardinali-vertues of a Carmalite-fryar, fraud, folly, foul-language, blasphemy. Discovered by Sir Edward Dering . . . And by him sent backe againe to their author, Simon Stocke, alias Father Simons*. London: I. R. for R. Whitaker.

Derrett, J. Duncan M. (1968). *Religion, Law and the State in India*. London: Faber & Faber.

A Discourse against Profane Swearing and cursing: wherin I. Those vices are describ'd and reprov'd, II. Both magistrates and private persons are excited to their duty in order to the suppressing 'em by the execution (1698). Dublin: Matthew Gunn.

Doctorow, E. L. (1971). *The Book of Daniel*. London: Pan.

Dollimore, Jonathan (1991). *Sexual Dissidence: Augustine to Wilde: Freud to Foucault*. Oxford: Clarendon Press.

Donaldson, James (1698). *A pick-tooth for swearers, or, A looking glass for atheists and prophane persons: wherein the greatness of the party offended, the solemn giving of the law, together with the strickness and purity thereof*. Edinburgh: John Reid.

Doolittle, Thomas (1614). *The swearer silenced, or, The evil and danger of prophane swearing and perjury: demonstrated by many arguments and examples of Gods dreadful judgments upon sinful swearers*. London: J. Astwood for Jonathon Greenwood.

Downame, John (1609). *Foure Treatises, tending to Disswade all Christians from foure no lesse heinous then common sinnes*. London: Felix Kingston for William Welby.

Drexel, Jeremias (1631). *Hier. Drexelii Orbis Phaeton, hoc est, de universis vitiis linguae*. Cologne.

Dundes, Alan (ed.) (1991). *The Blood Libel Legend: A casebook in anti-Semitic folklore*. Madison: University of Wisconsin Press.

During, Simon (1989). 'What was the West? Some relations between modernity, colonisation and writing'. *Meanjin* 4: 759–76.

During, Simon (1992). *Foucault and Literature: Towards a genealogy of writing*. London and New York: Routledge.

Eco, Umberto (1983). *The Name of the Rose*. London: Secker & Warburg.

Eco, Umberto (1989). *Foucault's Pendulum*. London: Secker & Warburg.

Edmonds, George (1836). *Appeal to the labourers of England: an exposure of aristocrat spies, and the infernal machinery of the poor law murder bill*. London: S. Wilson.

Emlyn, Thomas (1719). *A true narrative of the proceedings of the dissenting ministers of Dublin against Mr. Thomas Emlyn; and of his prosecution (at some of the dissenters instigation) in the secular court, and his sufferings thereupon*. London: J. Darby.

England and Wales. An act against several atheistical, blasphemous and execrable opinions, derogatory to the honor of God, and destructive to humane society (1650). London: Edward Husband and John Field, for Parliament.

Faldo, John (1673). *A vindication of Quakerism no Christianity &c.: against the very vain attempts of William Pen in his pretended ansvver: with some remarkable passages out of the Quakers church registry wherein their near approach* . . . London: B. Griffin, J. Robinson and Rob. Boulter.

Farina, Antonio (1959). *Il processo di Frine*. Naples: Libraria scientifica editrice.

Ferguson, Frances (1991). 'Sade and the pornographic legacy'. *Representations* 36: 1–21.

Field, Barron (1815). *A Review of the late publications on libel of Messrs. George, Holt, Starkie & Jones: in which the authority of the case of Rex v. Taylor, upon which the late Attorney General rested the prosecution at common law of* . . . London: Reed and Hunter.

Fischer, Peter (1967). *Die Asebieklage des attischen Rechts*. Erlangen: J. Hogl.

Fogelklou, Emilia (1931). *James Nayler: The rebel saint 1618–1660*. London: Ernest Benn.

Forkmann, Göran (1972). *The Limits of the Religious Community: Expulsion from the religious community within the Qumran sect, within Rabbinic Judaism, and within primitive Christianity*. Lund: Gleerup.

Forrer, Dietrich (1973). *Der Einfluss von Naturrecht und Aufklärung auf die Bestrafung der Gotteslästerung*. Zurich: Juris.

Foucault, Michel (1964). 'La prose d'Acteon'. *La Nouvelle Revue Française* 135: 444–59.

Foucault, Michel (1978). *The History of Sexuality. Vol 1*. Trans. Robert Hurley. New York: Random House.

Fowles, Susannah (1698). *The trial of Susannah Fowles of Hammersmith: that was try'd at London for blaspheming Jesus Christ. And cursing the Lords Prayer . . .* [London].

[?Frend, William] (1788). *An address to the members of the Church of England and to Protestant Trinitarians in general, exhorting them to turn from the false worship of three persons to the worship of One True God*. Cambridge: [n.p.].

Frend, William (1793). *An Account of the Proceedings in the University of Cambridge against Wm Frend, MA, Fellow of Jesus College, Cambridge . . .* Cambridge: Wm Frend (Flower).

Freud, Sigmund (1911). *Psychoanalytical Notes Upon an Autobiographical Account of a Case of Paranoia*. In Freud (1963): 103–86.

Freud, Sigmund (1913). *Totem and Taboo*. In Freud (1985): 43–224.

Freud, Sigmund (1918). *From the History of an Infantile Neurosis*. In Freud (1963): 187–316.

Freud, Sigmund (1939). *Moses and Monotheism: Three Essays*. In Freud (1985): 237–386.

Freud, Sigmund (1963). *Three Case Histories*. Ed. Philip Rieff. Trans. James Strachey. New York: Macmillan.

Freud, Sigmund (1985). *The Origins of Religion*. Trans. and ed. James Strachey. Harmondsworth: Penguin.

Friedman, Jerome (1978). *Michael Servetus: A case study in total heresy*. Geneva: Droz.

Friedman, Jerome (1987). *Blasphemy, Immorality, and Anarchy: The Ranters and the English Revolution*. Athens, OH: Ohio University Press.

A Full and True Account of the Notorious Wicked Life of that Grand Imposter, John Taylor, one of the Sweet-Singers of Israel (1678). London: Benjamin Harris.

Garnsey, Peter (1984), 'Religious toleration in classical antiquity', *Studies in Church History* 21: 27.

Gataker, Thomas (1642). *An answer to Mr. George Walkers vindication, or rather, fresh accusation: wherin he chargeth Mr. Wotton, besides his former foul aspersions of heresie and blasphemy, with Arianism, Mr. Gataker with Socinianism, . . .* London: E. G. for F. Clifton.

Gaustad, Edwin Scott (1990). *A Religious History of America*. Revised edn. New York: HarperCollins.

Gay, Peter (1988). *Freud: A life for our time*. New York: Norton.

Gellner, Ernest (1992). *Postmodernism, Reason and Religion*. London: Routledge.

Gilman, Sander L. (1991). *The Jew's Body*. New York and London: Routledge.

Ginzburg, Carlo (1982). *The Cheese and the Worms: The cosmos of a sixteenth-century miller*. Trans. John and Anne Tedeschi, Harmondsworth: Penguin. Originally published in 1976.

Ginzburg, Carlo (1990). *Myths, Emblems, Clues*. Trans. John and Anne Tedeschi. London: Hutchinson.

Ginzburg, Carlo (1991). *Ecstasies: Deciphering the Witches' Sabbath*. Trans. Raymond Rosenthal. New York: Pantheon.

Ginzburg, Eugenia (1967). *Into the Whirlwind*. London: Collins Harvill.

Glassman, Bernard (1975). *Anti-Semitic Stereotypes without Jews: Images of the Jews in England 1290–1700*. Detroit: Wayne State University Press.

Glendinnen, Inga (1987). 'Franciscan missionaries in sixteenth-century Mexico'. In Obelkevich *et al.* (1987): 229–45.

Gods glory vindicated and blasphemy confuted: being a brief and plain answer to that blasphemous book intituled, Twelve arguments against the deity of the Holy Ghost, written by Tho. Bidle, Master of Arts, and . . . (1647). London: William Ley.

Goux, Jean-Joseph (1990). *Symbolic Economies: After Marx and Freud.* Ithaca: Cornell University Press; London: Methuen.

Gray, Douglas (ed.) (1985). *The Oxford Book of Late Medieval Verse and Prose.* Oxford: Clarendon Press.

Green, J. S. D. (1990). 'Beyond *The Satanic Verses*: Conservative religion and the liberal society'. *Encounter* (June 1990): 12–20.

Greenblatt, Stephen (1980). *Renaissance Self-Fashioning: From More to Shakespeare.* Chicago: Chicago University Press.

Greenblatt, Stephen (1991). *Marvellous Possessions.* Oxford: Clarendon Press.

Grigg, William (1658). *The Quakers Jesus: or, the unswadling of that Child James Nailer, which a wicked Toleration hath midwiv'd into the World.* London: M. Simmons.

Grossberg, Lawrence, Cary Nelson and Pamela A. Treichler (1992). *Cultural Studies.* New York and London: Routledge.

Gurevich, Aron (1988). *Medieval Popular Culture: Problems of belief and perception.* Cambridge: Cambridge University Press.

Haight, Anne Lyon (1955). *Banned Books.* 2nd edn. New York: Bowker.

Harvey, Anthony Ernest (1976). *Jesus on Trial: A study in the fourth gospel.* London: SPCK.

Haydock, Roger (1676). *The Skirmisher confounded: being a collection of several passages taken forth of some books of John Cheyney's, who stiles himself the author of the skirmish upon Quakerism: in which is the baseness . . .* [n.p.].

Haydock, Roger (1700). *A Collection of Christian Writings, Labours, Travels and Sufferings of that Faithful and Approved Minister of Jesus Christ, Roger Haydock, to which is added, An Account of His Death and Burial.* London: T. Sowle.

A Help to a National Reformation: Containing an abstract of the penal-laws against prophaneness and vice . . . : To which is added, An account of the progress of the reformation of manners in England . . . (1706). 5th edn with additions. London: Joseph Downing.

Hetherington, Henry (1840). *A full report of the trial of Henry Hetherington: on an indictment for blasphemy, before Lord Denman and a special jury, at the Court of Queen's Bench, Westminster, on Tuesday, December 8, 1840.* London: H. Hetherington.

Heyworth, P. L. (ed.) (1968). *Jack Upland, Friar Daw's Reply and Jack Upland's Rejoinder.* Oxford: Clarendon Press.

Hildegard of Bingen (1987). *Hildegard of Bingen's Book of Divine Works with Letters and Songs.* Trans. and ed. Matthew Fox. Santa Fe, New Mexico: Bear & Co.

Hill, Christopher (1987). 'God and the English Revolution'. In Obelkevich *et al.* (1987): 393–409.

Hiro, Dilip (1989). *Holy Wars: The rise of Islamic fundamentalism.* New York and London: Routledge.

Hodgson, Leonard (1943). *The Doctrine of the Trinity.* London: James Nesbit.

Hogan, Patrick Colin (1990). *The Politics of Interpretation: Ideology, professionalism and the study of literature.* Oxford and New York: Oxford University Press.

Holyoake, George Jacob (1851). *The History of the Last Trial by Jury for Atheism in England.* Reprint, New York: Arno Press, 1972.

Holzgraber, Rudolf (1921). *Die Gotteslästerung.* Greifswald: H. Adler.

Hooton, Henry (1709). *A bridle for the Tongue, or, Some Practical Discourses under these following Heads: viz. Of Prophane, or Atheistical Discourse* . . . London: W. Taylor.

Howe, John (1684). *The Redeemer's tears wept over lost souls; a treatise on Luke XIX, 41, 42. With an appendix, wherein somewhat is occasionally discoursed concerning the blasphemy against the Holy Ghost, and how God is said* . . . London: J. Astwood for Thomas Parkhurst.

Howe, John (1694). *A Calm and Sober Enquiry Concerning the Possibility of a Trinity in the Godhead: in a letter to a Person of Worth.* London: Thomas Pankhurst.

Hudson, Anne (ed.) (1978). *English Wycliffite Writings.* Cambridge: Cambridge University Press.

Hunter, Ian, David Saunders and Dugald Williamson (1993). *On Pornography: Literature, sexuality and obscenity law.* London: Macmillan.

Hutcheon, Linda (1989). *The Politics of Postmodernism.* London and New York Routledge.

Huttemann, Renate (1964). *Gotteslästerung und Beschimpfung im geltenden und kommenden Strafrecht.* Marburg: [s.n.] (Cologne: Gouder & Hansen).

Ignatieff, Michael (1984). *The Needs of Strangers.* London: Chatto & Windus.

Ingersoll, Robert Green (1888). *Trial of C. B. Reynolds for Blasphemy at Morristown, N. J., May 19th and 20th, 1887: Defence; stenographically reported by I. N. Baker and revised by the author.* New York City: C. P. Farrell.

Ireland, Lord Lieutenant (1665). *Whereas the sins of prophane swearing and cursing are offenses forbidden by the word of God, and do highly provoke his wrath, nor onely against the persons that are guilty thereof but also against the place where such crimes are permitted to pass unpunished.* Dublin: John Crooke and Samuel Dancer.

Irigaray, Luce (1985). *Speculum of the Other Woman.* Trans. Gillian C. Gill. Ithaca and London: Cornell University Press.

James Nailler's Recantation, penned and directed by Himself to all the People of the LORD, *Gathered and Scattered. And may most fitly serve as an Antidote against the infectious Poyson of Damnable Heretics, Although couched under the most spetious Vailes of Pretended Sanctity* (1659). London: Edw. Farnham.

Jauss, Hans Robert (1982). *Toward an Aesthetic of Reception.* Brighton: Harvester.

Johns, Anthony H. (1989). 'Notes on "Islamic" Elements in *Satanic Verses*'. *Australian Religious Studies* 2: 1 (April 1989): 5–8.

Justice, Steven (forthcoming). *Writing and Rebellion: England in 1381.* University of California Press.

Kazi, Abdul K. (1989) 'Forum on *The Satanic Verses*'. *Criticism, Heresy and Interpretation* 2: 1–4.

Keen, Maurice (1986). 'Wyclif, the Bible and transubstantiation'. In Kenny (1986): 1–16.

Kelly, J. N. D. (1972). 'Nicene Creed'. In *Early Christian Creeds*. 3rd edn. London: Longham: 205–62.

Kempe, Margery (1985). *The Book of Margery Kempe.* Trans. Barry Windeatt. Harmondsworth: Penguin.

Kenny, Anthony (ed.) (1986). *Wyclif in His Times.* Oxford and New York: Oxford University Press.

Kesel, Günther (1968). *Die Religionsdelikte und ihre Behandlung im künftigen Strafrecht.* Munich: F. Frank.

Kinser, Samuel (1990). *Rabelais' Carnival: Text, context, metatext*. Berkeley and Los Angeles: University of California Press.

Klossowski, Pierre (1988). *The Baphomet*. Trans. S. Hawkes and S. Sartarelli. Introduction by M. Foucault. New York: Eridanos Library.

Kneeland, Abner (1834a). *An introduction to the defence of Abner Kneeland, charged with blasphemy, before the Municipal Court, in Boston, Mass. at the January term, in 1834*. Boston: Abner Kneeland.

Kneeland, Abner (1834b). *Report of the arguments of the attorney of the commonwealth: at the trials of Abner Kneeland, for blasphemy, in the Municipal and Supreme Courts, in Boston, January and May, 1834*. [Boston]: Beals, Homer & Co.

Kramer, Jane (1991). 'Letter from Europe', *New Yorker*, 14 Jan.: 60–75.

Laurence, Anne (1990). 'A priesthood of she-believers: Women and congregations in mid-seventeenth century England'. In Sheils and Wood (1990): 345–64.

Lawton, David (1985). *Chaucer's Narrators*. Cambridge: D. S. Brewer.

Lawton, David (1992). 'Voice, Authority and Blasphemy in *The Book of Margery Kempe*'. In Sandra J. McEntire (ed.), *Margery Kempe: A book of essays*. New York: Garland: 93–115.

Layton, Bentley (ed. and trans.) (1987). *The Gnostic Scriptures*. New York: Doubleday.

Leff, Gordon (1986). 'Wyclif and Hus'. In Kenny (1986): 105–26.

Lefranc, Marie-Geneviève (1974). 'Mémoire sur les blasphèmes et les blasphémateurs dans le Royaume de Valence aux XVIe et XVIIe siècles'. Dissertation, Toulouse.

Le Roy Ladurie, E. (1978). *Montaillou*. London: Scolar Press.

Leutenbauer, Siegfried (1984). *Das Delikt der Gotteslästerung in der bayerischen Gesetzgebung*. Cologne: Bohlau.

Levy, Leonard Williams (1973). *Blasphemy in Massachusetts: Freedom of conscience and the Abner Kneeland case, a documentary record*. Ed., with an introduction by Leonard W. Levy. New York: Da Capo Press.

Levy, Leonard Williams (1981). *Treason against God: A history of the offense of blasphemy*. New York: Schocken Books.

Lewis, Bernard (1973). *Islam in History*. London: Alcove Press.

Lewis, Norman (1988). *The Missionaries: God against the Indians*. London: Arena.

Lewis, Suzanne (1986). 'Tractatus adversus Judaeos in the Gulbenkian Apocalypse'. *Art Bulletin* 68: 543–66.

Lochrie, Karma (1991). *Margery Kempe and Translations of the Flesh*. Philadelphia: University of Pennsylvania Press.

Lonergan, Bernard Joseph Francis (1976). *The Way to Nicea: The dialectical development of Trinitarian theology*. Trans. Conn O'Donovan. London: Darton, Longman and Todd.

Loveland, Samuel C. (1814). *The sin and blasphemy against the Holy Ghost carefully examined and faithfully illustrated in two discourses*. Windsor, VT: Jesse Cochran.

Loveland, Samuel C. (1818). *A discourse on the blasphemy against the Holy Ghost: delivered in Barre, the last Sunday in August, in Hancock, the first Sunday in September, and in Bethel, the first in October, 1818*. Woodstock, UT: David Watson.

McEntire, Sandra, M. (ed.) (1992). *Margery Kempe: A book of essays*. New York: Garland.

Mack, Phyllis (1987). 'Feminine symbolism and feminine behaviourism in radical religious movements: Franciscans, Quakers and the followers of Gandhi'. In Obelkevich *et al.* (1987): 115–30.

Mackey, James P. (1983). *The Christian Experience of God in Trinity*. London: SCM.

'Mandeville' (1983). *The Travels of Sir John Mandeville*. Ed. C. W. R. D. Moseley. Harmondsworth: Penguin.

Manuel, Frank E. and Fritzie P. Manuel (1979). *Utopian Thought in the Western World*. Cambridge, MA: Belknap Press.

Marin, Louis (1986). *La parole mangée et autres essais théologico-politiques*. Paris: Meridiens Klincksiek.

Marin, Louis (1989). *Food for Thought*. Trans. Mette Hjort. Baltimore and London: Johns Hopkins University Press.

Marlorat, Augustine (1570?). *A treatise of the sin against the Holy Ghost*. London: J. Allde for L. Harrison.

Maslowski, Peter (1930). *Gotteslästerung, Religion und Strafrecht: Zu den Religionsdelikten ([Paragraphen] 181–183) im Entwurf zum neuen Strafgesetzbuch*. Berlin: MOPR.

Mejsner, Ernst (1705). *Einhundertdrey-unddreyssig gotteslästerliche, gottlose, schändliche und schädliche . . . Spruch-Wörter . . . samt derselben Schrifft- und recht-massigen Wiederlegung . . . dargelegt durch Ernst Majsnern*. Eisenberg: J Bielcke. Reprint, Leipzig: Zentralantiquariat der Deutschen Demokratischen Republik, 1974.

Memoirs of the Life, Ministry, Tryal and Sufferings of that Very Eminent Person, James Nailer, The Quaker's Great Apostle (1719). London: J. Roberts.

Menzel, Adolf (1979). *Hellenika: Gesammelte kleine Schriften*. Darmstadt: Scientia.

Merriell, D. Juvenal (1990). *To the Image of the Trinity: A study in the development of Aquinas' teaching*. Toronto: Pontifical Institute of Mediaeval Studies.

Millar, Fergus (1990). 'Reflections on the trial of Jesus', *Journal for the study of the Old Testament*, Supplement Series 100: 355–81.

Møller, Lis (1991). *The Freudian Reading: Analytical and Fictional Constructions*. Philadelphia: University of Pennsylvania Press.

Montaigne, Michel de (1991). *The Essays of Michel de Montaigne*. Trans. and ed. M. A. Screech. London and New York: Allen Lane.

Moore, R. I. (1985). *The Origins of European Dissent*. Revised edn. Oxford: Blackwell.

Morton, Arthur Leslie (1970). *The World of the Ranters: Religious radicalism in the English Revolution*. London: Lawrence & Wishart.

Mourre, Michel (1953). *In Spite of Blasphemy*. Trans. A. W. Fielding. London: J. Lehmann.

Nancy, Jean-Luc (1991). *The Inoperative Community*. Trans. and eds Peter Connor *et al.* Minneapolis: University of Minnesota Press.

Nayler, James (1655a). *A Discovery of the Beast Got into the Seat of the False Prophet . . .* London: Giles Calvert.

Nayler, James (1655b). *Satans design discovered*. London: Giles Calvert.

Nayler, James (1656a). *Love to the Lost, and a Hand Held Forth to the Helpless. To Lead Out of the Dark*. London: Giles Calvert.

Nayler, James (1656b). *A Vindication of Truth, As held Forth in a Book, entituled, Love to the Lost. From the Lies Slanders and Deceits of T. Higgenson . . .* London: Giles Calvert.

Nayler, James (1656c). *A Foole answered according to his folly*. London: Giles Calvert.

Nayler, James (1659). *Having heard that some have wronged my words which I spoke before the Committee of the Parliament concerning Jesus Christ and concerning the old and New Testaments, some have printed Word which I spoke not: also some have printed a Paper and calls it James Nayler's Recantation: unknown to me.* London: Thomas Siddons.

Nichols, Anne E. (1988). 'The Croxton *Play of the Sacrament*: A re-reading'. *Comparative Drama* 22: 117–37.

Niles, Samuel (1752). *A vindication of divers important gospel-doctrines, and of the teachers and professors of them: against the injurious reflections & misrepresentations contained in a late printed discourse of the Rev.* . . . . Boston: S. Kneeland.

Nokes, G. D. (1926). *A History of the Crime of Blasphemy*. London: Sweet and Maxwell.

Noonan, John T., Jr. (1987). *The Believers and the Powers that Are : Cases, history, and other data bearing on the relation of religion and government.* New York: Macmillan, London: Collier Macmillan.

Norris, Christopher (1992). *Uncritical Theory: Postmodernism, intellectuals and the Gulf War.* London: Lawrence & Wishart.

Obelkevich, Jim, Lyndal Roper and Raphael Samuel (eds) (1987). *Disciplines of Faith: Studies in religion, politics, and patriarchy.* New York and London: Routledge.

Obholzer, Karin (1982). *The Wolf-Man Sixty Years Later: Conversations with Freud's controversial patient.* New York: Continuum.

Obolensky, Dimitri (1948). *The Bogomils: A study in Balkan neo-Manicheanism.* Twickenham: Anthony C. Hall.

Okoboi, Felix (1978). *The Final Blasphemy.* Nairobi: Kenya Literature Bureau.

An ordinance of the Lords & Commons assembled in Parliament, for the punishing of blasphemies and heresies. With the several penalties therein expressed . . . (1648). London: E. Husband.

Padman, John, Jr (1797). *A layman's protest against the profane blasphemy, false charges, and illiberal invective of Thomas Paine, author of a book, entitled The age of reason, part I, and II. Being an investigation . . .* London: John Padman, Jr.

Pahud de Mortanges, René (1987). *Die Archetypik der Gotteslästerung als Beispiel für das Wirken archetypischer Vorstellungen im Rechtsdenken.* Fribourg: Universitätsverlag.

Pandey, Gyanendra (1992). 'In defense of the fragment: Writing about Hindu–Muslim riots in India today'. *Representations* 37: 27–55.

Paris, Matthew (1852–4). *Matthew Paris's English History, from the year 1234 to 1273.* Trans. Rev. J. A. Giles. 3 vols. London: H. G. Bohn.

Patterson, Lee (1991). *Chaucer and the Subject of History.* Madison: University of Wisconsin Press.

The Penitent swearer's soliloquy and prayer (1811). New York: Protestant Episcopal Society of Young Men for the Distribution of Religious Tracts. (New York: T. and J. Swords).

Pepys, Samuel (1663). *The Diary of Samuel Pepys. Vol. III.* Ed. Robert Latham and Wm Matthews. Berkeley and Los Angeles: University of California Press.

Péquigney, Joseph (1991). 'Sodomy in Dante's *Inferno* and *Purgatorio*'. *Representations* 36: 22–42.

Perceval, Spencer [attrib.] (1840). *An inquiry into the state of the law in Ireland, respecting the denial of the Trinity/by a barrister.* Dublin: Hodges and Smith.

Peters, Edward (ed.) (1980). *Heresy and Authority in Medieval Europe.* London: Scolar Press.

Pfaff, William (1991). 'Islam and the West'. *New Yorker*, 28 Jan.: 83–8.

Pipes, Daniel (1990). *The Rushdie Affair: The novel, the Ayatollah and the West*. New York: Birch Lane Press.

Porter, Noah (1813). *Perjury prevalent: a sermon, delivered in Farmington, at the Freemen's meeting, September, 1813*. Hartford, CT: Peter B. Gleason & Co.

Post, Robert C. (1988). 'Cultural heterogeneity and law: Pornography, blasphemy, and the First Amendment'. *California Law Review*, 76: 297–335.

Post, Robert (ed.) (1991). *Law and the Order of Culture*. Berkeley and Los Angeles: University of California Press.

Pullan, Brian (1983). *The Jews of Europe and the Inquisition of Venice 1550–1670*. Oxford: Blackwell.

Quilligan, Maureen (1991). *The Allegory of Female Authority: Christine de Pizan's Cité des Dames*. Ithaca and London: Cornell University Press.

Rahner, Karl (1975). *The Trinity*. Trans. Joseph Donceel. London: Burns and Oates.

Reynolds, Charles B. n.d. [1887]. *Blasphemy and the Bible*. New York: The Truth Seeker Co.

Rich, Robert (1657). *Copies of some few of the papers given into the House of Parliament in the time of James Naylers tryal there, which began the fifth of December, 1656*. [London].

Richards, Jeffrey (1990). *Sex, Dissidence and Damnation: Minority groups in the Middle Ages*. London and New York: Routledge.

Robertson, Elizabeth (1990). *Early English Devotional Prose and the Female Anchorite*. Knoxville: University of Tennessee Press.

The Romish mass-book faithfully translated into English with notes and observations thereupon: plainly demonstrating the idolatry and blasphemy thereof . . . With unanswerable arguments proving it no service of God . . . (1683) London: G. Larkin for T. Malthus.

Rossi-Landi, Ferruccio (1975). *Linguistics and Economics*. The Hague: Mouton.

Roth, Cecil (1978). *A History of the Jews in England*. 3rd edn. Oxford: Clarendon Press.

Rushdie, Salman (1988). *The Satanic Verses*. London and New York: Viking.

Rushdie, Salman (1990a). *In Good Faith*. London: Granta.

Rushdie, Salman (1990b). 'Is Nothing Sacred?' *Granta* 31: 97–111.

Rushdie, Salman (1991). *Imaginary Homelands*. London: Granta.

Russell, Jeffrey B. (1965). *Dissent and Reform in the Early Middle Ages*. Berkeley and Los Angeles: University of California Press.

Russell, Jeffrey B. (ed.) (1971). *Religious Dissent in the Middle Ages*. New York and London: John Wiley & Sons.

Russell, Jeffrey B. (1988). *The Prince of Darkness*. Ithaca and London: Cornell University Press.

Saadawi, Nadal el (1990). *The Fall of the Imam*. Trans. Sherif Hetata. London: Methuen.

Sade, Marquis de (1965). *Justine, or the Misfortunes of Virtue*. Trans. Alan Hull Walton. London: Corgi Books.

Sangharakshita, Bhikahu (1978). *Buddhism and Blasphemy: Buddhist reflections on the 1977 blasphemy trial*. [London]: Windhorse Publications.

Sardar, Ziauddin (1990). 'The Rushdie malaise: Orthodoxy of doubt in the "Little Room" of postmodernist fiction'. *The Muslim World Book Review* 11: 3–15.

Sardar, Ziauddin and Meryl Wyn Davies (1990). *Distorted Imaginations: Lessons from the Rushdie affair*. London: Grey Seal Books; Kuala Lumpur: Berita.

Scarry, Elaine (1986). *The Body in Pain*. Oxford: Oxford University Press.

Scarry, Elaine (1990). 'Consent and the body'. *New Literary History* 21: 867–96.

Schick, Martin (1968). *Kunstwerkgarantie und Strafrecht: Dargestellt am Beispiel der Gotteslästerung und Religionsbeschimpfung.* Bamberg: R. Rodenbusch.

Schilling, Werner (1966). *Gotteslästerung strafbar?: Religionswissenschaftliche, theologische und juristische Studie zum Begriff der Gotteslästerung und zur Würdigung von Religionsschutznormen im Strafgesetz.* Munich: Claudius Verl.

Schrag, Carl Herbert (1936). *Gefühlszustände als Rechtsgüter im Straftrecht.* Berne: E. Fluck.

Schroeder, Theodore Albert (1918). *Blasphemy and Free Speech: Being sample portions of an argument which a Connecticut judge refused to read: printed to promote the repeal of blasphemy laws.* New York: Free Speech League.

Schroeder, Theodore Albert (1919a). *Constitutional Free Speech Defined and Defended in an Unfinished Argument in a Case of Blasphemy.* New York: Free Speech League.

Schroeder, Theodore Albert (1919b). *Law of Blasphemy; The modern view exhibited in model instructions to a jury, prepared by Theodore Schroeder . . .* New York: Free Speech League.

A Seasonable Word, or, A word in season: soberly proposed to the confederation of all such whose hearts are affected with those floods of reproach and blasphemy, which the cause of God in these nations . . . (1660). London.

Seward, Desmond (1974). *The Monks of War: The military religious orders.* St Albans: Paladin.

Shachar, Isaiah (1974). *The Judensau: A medieval anti-Jewish motif and its history.* London: Warburg Institute.

Sheils, W. J., and Diana Wood (eds) (1990). *Women in the Church. Studies in Church History* 27. Oxford: Blackwell.

Smallwood, E. Mary (1976) *The Jews under Roman Rule: From Pompey to Diocletian.* Leiden: E. J. Brill.

Smith, Don (1979). *Early Christianity and the Homosexual: A postscript to a trial.* London: Quantum Leap Publications.

Smith, Donald Eugene (1963). *India as a Secular State.* Princeton NJ: Princeton University Press.

Smith, Nigel (ed.) (1983). *A Collection of Ranter Writings from the Seventeenth Century.* London: Junction Books.

Smith, Nigel (1989). *Perfection Proclaimed: Language and literature in English radical religion 1640–1660.* Oxford: Clarendon Press.

A Special Report of the trial of the Rev. Vladimir Petcherine, (one of the Redemptorist fathers), in the court house, Green-street, Dublin, December, 1855: on an indictment charging him with burning the Protestant bible . . . (1856). Dublin: James Duffy.

Spivak, Gayatri Chakravorty (1987). *In Other Worlds: Essays in cultural Politics.* New York and London: Routledge.

Spivak, Gayatri Chakravorty (1989). 'Reading *The Satanic Verses*'. *Public Culture* 2: 79–99.

Sprengnetter, Madelon (1990). *The Spectral Mother: Freud, feminism and psychoanalysis.* Ithaca and London: Cornell University Press.

Stallybrass, Peter, and Allon White (1986). *The Politics and Poetics of Transgression.* Ithaca and London: Cornell University Press.

State Trials: A Complete Collection of State Trials and Proceedings for High Treason and

Other Crimes and Misdemeanours (1793). Compiled by T. B. Howell. Volume V, 2–13, Charles II, 1650–61. London: T. C. Hansard.

The Strange Punishment and Judgement of GOD, upon a Cursed blasphemer: Anthony Paneter, caryer (1615). London: John Trundle.

Taheri, Amir (1987). *Holy Terror: Inside the world of Islamic terrorism*. London: Hutchinson.

Tanner, Norman P. (ed.) (1977). *Heresy trials in the diocese of Norwich 1428–31*. London: Royal Historical Society.

A Testimony against John Pennyman's lyes, slanders, and false accusation of blasphemy, &c. (1671).

Thody, Philip (1977). *Roland Barthes: A conservative estimate*. London: Macmillan.

Tinkler, John F. (1987). 'Renaissance humanism and the *genera eloquentiae'*. *Rhetorica* 5: 279–309.

Toon, Peter, and James D. Spiceland (eds) (1980). *One God in Trinity*. London: Samuel Bagster.

Vico, Giambattista (1968). *The New Science of Giambattista Vico*. Revised trans. of 3rd edn (1774) by Thomas Goddard Bergin and Max Harold Frisch. Ithaca: Cornell University Press.

Villa, Anna Antoniazzi (1986). *Un processo contro gli Ebrei nella Milano del 1488: Crescita e declinodella comunita ebraica lombarda alla fine del Medioevo*. Bologna: Cappelli.

Vitali, Enrico G. (1964). *Vilipendio della religione dello Stato: contributo all'interpretazione dell'art. 204 del Codice penale*. Padova: CEDAM.

Wakefield, Walter L. (1974). *Heresy, Crusade and Inquisition in Southern France 1100– 1250*. Berkeley and Los Angeles: University of California Press.

Wakefield, Walter L., and Austin R. Evans (eds) (1969). *Heresies of the High Middle Ages*. New York and London: Columbia University Press.

Walter, Nicolas (1990). *Blasphemy: Ancient and modern*. London: Rationalist Press Association.

Webster, Richard (1990). *A Brief History of Blasphemy: Liberalism, censorship and 'The Satanic Verses'*. Southwold: Orwell Press.

Weitzman, Sarah Brown (1983). *Eve and Other Blasphemy*. New York: New York Contemporary Press.

Whitehead, George (1691). *Christ's Lambs defended from Satan's rage: in a Just Vindication of the People Called Quakers . . . from the Unjust Attempts of John Pennyman and Abettors in his Malicious Book styled The Quakers Unmasked*. London.

Wilbur, Earl Morse (1945). *A History of Unitarianism: Socinianism and its antecedents*. Boston: Beacon Press.

Wiles, Maurice (1967). *The Making of Christian Doctrine*. Cambridge: Cambridge University Press.

Wilkinson, Louis Umfreville (1969). *Blasphemy and Religion: A dialogue about John Cowper Powys' 'Wood and stone' and Theodore Powys' 'The soliloquy of a hermit'*. Hamilton, NY: Colgate University Press.

Willis, R. (1877). *Servetus and Calvin*. London: Henry S. King.

Wilson, Peter L. (1988). *Scandal: Essays in Islamic heresy*. Brooklyn, NY: Automedia.

Winter, Paul (1974). *On the Trial of Jesus*. 2nd edn, revised and ed. T. A. Burkill and Geza Vermes. Berlin: de Gruyter. (First published 1961).

Winterson, Jeanette (1985). *Oranges are Not the Only Fruit*. London: Vintage.

Wolf-Man [Sergei Pankejeff] (1971). *The Wolf-Man by the Wolf-Man*. Ed. Muriel Gardiner. New York: Hill and Wang.

Wolkovich, William L. (1973). *Bay State 'Blue' Laws and Bimba: A documentary study of the Anthony Bimba trial for blasphemy and sedition in Brockton, Massachusetts, 1926*. Brockton, MA: Forum Press.

Wright, F. B. (1817). *A narrative of proceedings in a late prosecution against John Wright, on a charge of blasphemy: said to be contained in a sermon delivered by him, on the evening of April 8, 1817, in the Long Room, Marble . . .* Liverpool: F. B. Wright.

Wright, John [Unitarian minister] (1817). *A sermon delivered at the Long Room, Marble Street, Liverpool: on Tuesday evening, April 8th, 1817: for which a prosecution is commenced on a charge of blasphemy*. Liverpool: F. B. Wright.

Wycliff, John (1966). *Tractatus de blasphemia. Now first edited from the Vienna ms. 4514. With critical and historical notes by Michael Henry Oziewicki*. Reprint, New York: Johnson.

INDEX